WORKING CAPITAL MANAGEMENT

WORKING CAPITAL MANAGEMENT

Khushboo Manoj

CENTRUM PRESS
NEW DELHI-110002 (INDIA)

CENTRUM PRESS

H.O.: 4360/4, Ansari Road, Daryaganj,
New Delhi-110002 (India)
Tel: 23278000, 23261597, 23255577, 23286875

B.O.: No. 1015, Ist Main Road, BSK IIIrd Stage,
IIIrd Phase, IIIrd Block, Bangalore-560085 (INDIA)
Tel: 080-41723429

Email: centrumpress@gmail.com
Visit us at: www.centrumpress.com

Working Capital Management

First Edition, 2011

ISBN 978-93-80921-04-4

PRINTED IN INDIA

Printed at Balaji Offset, Delhi.

Contents

Preface

Working capital is commonly understood as the fund needed to meet the day-to-day expenses of an enterprise. For a finance manager it is the fund locked up in current assets and, therefore, he/she looks for liquidity support in net working capital (NWC), which is equivalent to the excess of current assets over current liabilities.

A banker also looks at the size of NWC as the long-term stake of the business in funding the current assets. But for a production manager, liquidity is synonymous to uninterrupted supply of material inputs to the production lines. Similarly for a marketing manager, if there is no production, his/her marketing outlets dry up despite demand in the market. While the finance manager discourages overstocking of inventory, the production manager and the marketing manager dread of being out of stock. In this conflict the goal of the organization often takes a back seat.

This book aims at resolving these conflicts by adopting a techno-financial approach to working capital management. Hope, this book provides all the necessary information required to know while learning working capital management.

Author

1

Concept of Working Capital Management

AN OVERVIEW

Every business needs adequate liquid resources in order to maintain day-to-day cash flow. It needs enough cash to pay wages and salaries as they fall due and to pay creditors if it is to keep its workforce and ensure its supplies. Maintaining adequate working capital is not just important in the short-term. Sufficient liquidity must be maintained in order to ensure the survival of the business in the long-term as well. Even a profitable business may fail if it does not have adequate cash flow to meet its liabilities as they fall due.

- The net working capital of a business is its current assets less its current liabilities. Current Assets include:
  - Stocks of raw materials
  - Work-in-progress
  - Finished goods
  - Trade debtors
  - Prepayments
  - Cash balances
- Current Liabilities include:
  - Trade creditors
  - Accruals
  - Taxation payable
  - Dividends payable
  - Short-term loans

Therefore, when businesses make investment decisions they must not only consider the financial outlay involved with acquiring the new machine or the new building, etc, but must also take account of the additional current assets that are usually involved with any expansion of activity. Increased production tends to engender a need to hold additional stocks of raw materials and work in progress. Increased sales usually mean that the level of debtors will increase. A general increase in the firm's scale of operations tends to imply a need for greater levels of cash.

NEEDS OF A BUSINESS

Different industries have different optimum working capital profiles, reflecting their methods of doing business and what they are selling.

- Businesses with a lot of cash sales and few credit sales should have minimal trade debtors. Supermarkets are good examples of such businesses;
- Businesses that exist to trade in completed products will only have finished goods in stock. Compare this with manufacturers who will also have to maintain stocks of raw materials and work-in-progress.
- Some finished goods, notably foodstuffs, have to be sold within a limited period because of their perishable nature.

Larger companies may be able to use their bargaining strength as customers to obtain more favourable, extended credit terms from suppliers. By contrast, smaller companies, particularly those that have recently started trading may be required to pays their suppliers immediately.

Some businesses will receive their monies at certain times of the year, although they may incur expenses throughout the year at a fairly consistent level. This is often known as "seasonality" of cash flow.

For example, travel agents have peak sales in the weeks immediately following Christmas. Working Capital Needs Also Fluctuate during the Year The amount of funds tied up in working capital would not typically be a constant figure throughout the year. Only in the most unusual of businesses would there be a constant need for working capital funding. For most businesses there would be weekly fluctuations. Many businesses operate in industries that have seasonal changes in demand. This means that sales, stocks, debtors, etc. would be at higher levels at some predictable times of the year than at others.

In principle, the working capital need can be separated into two parts:

- A fixed part, and
- A fluctuating part

The fixed part is probably defined in amount as the minimum working capital requirement for the year.

Current Assets Minus Current Liabilities

Working capital measures how much in liquid assets a company has available to build its business. The number can be positive or negative, depending on how much debt the company is carrying.

In general, companies that have a lot of working capital will be more successful since they can expand and improve their operations. Companies with negative working capital may lack the funds necessary for growth also called net current assets or current capital. Working capital is a financial metric which represents the amount of day-by-day operating liquidity available to a business.

Along with fixed assets such as plant and equipment, working capital is considered a part of operating capital. It is calculated as current assets minus current liabilities. A company can be endowed with assets and profitability, but short of liquidity, if these assets cannot readily be converted into cash. Current assets and current liabilities include three accounts which are of special importance. These accounts represent the areas of the business where managers have the most direct impact:

- Accounts receivable
- Inventory, and
- Accounts payable

In a situation where a company carries more cash than the minimum amount needed to maintain operations, the excess portion is usually excluded from working capital. In addition, the current portion of debt is critical, because it represents a short-term claim to current assets. Common types of short-term debt are bank loans and lines of credit. An increase in working capital indicates that the business has either increased current assets or has decreased current liabilities, for example has paid off some short-term creditors. Implications on M&A.

The common commercial definition of working capital for the purpose of a working capital adjustment in an M&A transaction is equal to:

Current Assets: Current Liabilities excluding deferred tax assets/liabilities, excess cash, surplus assets and/or deposit balances.

Cash balance items often attract a one-for-one purchase price adjustment. Decisions relating to working capital and short term financing are referred to as *working capital management*. These involve managing the relationship between a firm's short-term assets and its short-term liabilities.

The goal of Working capital management is to ensure that the firm is able to continue its operations and that it has sufficient cash flow to satisfy both maturing short-term debt and upcoming operational expenses.

DECISION CRITERIA

By definition, Working capital management entails short term decisions - generally, relating to the next one year period which is "reversible". These decisions are therefore not taken on the same basis as Capital Investment Decisions rather they will be based on cash flows and/ or profitability.

One measure of cash flow is provided by the cash conversion cycle - the net number of days from the outlay of cash for raw material to receiving payment from the customer. As a management tool, this metric makes explicit the inter-relatedness of decisions relating to inventories, accounts receivable and payable, and cash. Because this number effectively corresponds to the time that the firm's cash is tied up in operations and unavailable for other activities, management generally aims at a low net count. In this context, the most useful measure of profitability is Return on capital. The result is shown as a percentage, determined by dividing relevant income for the 12 months by capital employed; Return on equity shows this result for the firm's shareholders.

Firm value is enhanced when, and if, the return on capital, which results from working capital management, exceeds the cost of capital, which results from capital investment decisions. ROC measures are therefore useful as a management tool, in that they link short-term policy with long-term decision making.

MANAGEMENT OF WORKING CAPITAL

Guided by the criteria, management will use a combination of policies and techniques for the management of working capital. These policies aim at managing the *current assets* and the short term financing, such that cash flows and returns are acceptable.

Cash Management

Identify the cash balance which allows for the business to meet day to day expenses, but reduces cash holding costs:

Inventory Management

Identify the level of inventory which allows for uninterrupted production but reduces the investment in raw materials - and minimizes reordering costs - and hence increases cash flow; Just In Time ; Economic order quantity ; Economic production quantity.

Debtors Management

Identify the appropriate credit policy, *i.e.* credit terms which will attract customers, such that any impact on cash flows and the cash conversion cycle will be offset by increased revenue and hence Return on Capital.

Short Term Financing

Identify the appropriate source of financing, given the

cash conversion cycle: the inventory is ideally financed by credit granted by the supplier; however, it may be necessary to utilize a bank loan, or to "convert debtors to cash" through "factoring".

FINANCIAL RISK MANAGEMENT

Risk management is the process of measuring risk and then developing and implementing strategies to manage that risk. Financial risk management focuses on risks that can be managed using traded financial instruments. Financial risk management will also play an important role in cash management.

This area is related to corporate finance in two ways. Firstly, firm exposure to business risk is a direct result of Investment and Financing decisions. Secondly, both disciplines share the goal of creating, or enhancing, firm value. All large corporations have risk management teams, and small firms practice informal, if not formal, risk management.

Derivatives are the instruments most commonly used in financial risk management. Because unique derivative contracts tend to be costly to create and monitor, the most cost-effective financial risk management methods usually involve derivatives that trade on well-established financial markets. These standard derivative instruments include options, futures contracts, forward contracts, and swaps.

RELATIONSHIP WITH OTHER AREAS IN FINANCE

Investment Banking

Use of the term "corporate finance" varies considerably across the world. In the United States it is used to describe activities, decisions and techniques that deal with many aspects of a company's finances and capital. In the United Kingdom and Commonwealth countries, the terms "corporate finance" and "corporate financier" tend to be associated with investment banking - *i.e.* with transactions in which capital is raised for the corporation.

Personal and Public Finance

Corporate finance utilizes tools from almost all areas of finance. Some of the tools developed by and for corporations have broad application to entities other than corporations, for example, to partnerships, sole proprietorships, not-for-profit organizations, governments, mutual funds, and personal wealth management.

But in other cases their application is very limited outside of the corporate finance arena. Because corporations deal in quantities of money much greater than individuals, the analysis has developed into a discipline of its own. It can be differentiated from personal finance and public finance.

Capital Structure

In finance, capital structure refers to the way a corporation finances its assets through some combination of equity, debt, or hybrid securities. A firm's capital structure is then the composition or 'structure' of its liabilities. For example, a firm that sells $20bn dollars in equity and $80bn in debt is said to be 20% equity financed and 80% debt financed. The firm's ratio of debt to total financing, 80% in this example, is referred to as the firm's leverage. The Modigliani-Miller theorem, proposed by Franco Modigliani and Merton Miller, forms the basis for modern thinking on capital structure, though it is generally viewed as a purely theoretical result since it assumes away many important factors in the capital structure decision. The theorem states that, in a perfect market, the value of a firm is unaffected by how that firm is financed.

This result provides the base with which to examine real world reasons why capital structure *is* relevant, that is, a company's value is affected by the capital structure it employs. These other reasons include bankruptcy costs, agency costs and asymmetric information. This analysis can then be extended to look at whether there is in fact an 'optimal' capital structure: the one which maximizes the value of the firm.

CAPITAL STRUCTURE IN A PERFECT MARKET

Assume a perfect capital market ; firms and individuals

can borrow at the same interest rate; no taxes; and investment decisions aren't affected by financing decisions. Modigliani and Miller made two findings under these conditions. Their first 'proposition' was that the value of a company is independent of its capital structure. That is, you cannot change the size of a cake by cutting it into different sized pieces.

Their second 'proposition' stated that the cost of equity for a leveraged firm is equal to the cost of equity for an unleveraged firm, plus an added premium for financial risk. That is, as leverage increases, while the burden of individual risks is shifted between different investor classes, total risk is conserved and hence no extra value created.

Their analysis was extended to include the effect of taxes and risky debt. Under a classical tax system, the tax deductibility of interest makes debt financing valuable; that is, the cost of capital decreases as the proportion of debt in the capital structure increases. The optimal structure then would be to have virtually no equity at all.

Capital Structure in the Real World

If capital structure is irrelevant in a perfect market, then imperfections which exist in the real world must be the cause of its relevance. The theories try to address some of these imperfections, by relaxing assumptions made in the M&M model.

Trade-off Theory

Trade-off theory allows bankruptcy costs to exist. It states that there is an advantage to financing with debt, the tax benefit of debt and there is a cost of financing with debt, the bankruptcy costs of debt.

The marginal benefit of further increases in debt declines as debt increases, while the marginal cost increases, so that a firm that is optimizing its overall value will focus on this trade-off when choosing how much debt and equity to use for financing. Empirically, this theory may explain differences in D/E ratios between industries, however it doesn't explain differences within the same industry.

Pecking Order Theory

Pecking Order theory tries to capture the costs of asymmetric information. It states that companies prioritize their sources of financing according to the law of least effort, or of least resistance, preferring to raise equity as a financing means "of last resort". Hence internal debt is used first, and when that is depleted debt is issued, and when it is not sensible to issue any more debt, equity is issued.

This theory maintains that businesses adhere to a hierarchy of financing sources and prefer internal financing when available, and debt is preferred over equity if external financing is required. Thus, the form of debt a firm chooses can performanceas a signal of its need for external finance.

The pecking order theory is popularized by Myers when he argues that equity is a less preferred means to raise capital because when managers issue new equity, investors believe that managers think that the firm is overvalued and managers are taking advantage of this over-valuation. As a result, investors will place a lower value to the new equity issuance.

Agency Costs

There are three types of agency costs which can help explain the relevance of capital structure.

- Asset substitution effect: As D/E increases, management has an increased incentive to undertake risky projects. This is because if the project is successful, share holders get all the upside, whereas if it is unsuccessful, debt holders get all the downside. If the projects are undertaken, there is a chance of firm value decreasing and a wealth transfer from debt holders to share holders.
- Underinvestment problem: If debt is risky, the gain from the project will accrue to debtholders rather than shareholders. Thus, management have an incentive to reject positive NPV projects, even though they have the potential to increase firm value.
- Free cash flow: unless free cash flow is given back to investors, management has an incentive to destroy

firm value through empire building and perks etc. Increasing leverage imposes financial discipline on management.

Other

- The neutral mutation hypothesis—firms fall into various habits of financing, which do not impact on value.
- Market timing hypothesis—capital structure is the outcome of the historical cumulative timing of the market by managers.

Arbitrage

Similar questions are also the concern of a variety of speculator known as a capital-structure arbitrageur. A capital-structure arbitrageur seeks opportunities created by differential pricing of various instruments issued by one corporation. Consider, for example, traditional bonds and convertible bonds. The latter are bonds that are, under contracted-for conditions, convertible into shares of equity.

The stock-option component of a convertible bond has a calculable value in itself. The value of the whole instrument *should* be the value of the traditional bonds *plus* the extra value of the option feature. If the spread, the difference between the convertible and the non-convertible bonds grows excessively, then the capital-structure arbitrageur will bet that it will converge.

Capital Budgeting

Capital budgeting is the planning process used to determine a firm's long term investments such as new machinery, replacement machinery, new plants, new products, and research and development projects.

Many formal methods are used in capital budgeting, including the techniques such as

- Net present value
- Profitability index
- Internal rate of return

- Modified Internal Rate of Return, and
- Equivalent annuity.

These methods use the incremental cash flows from each potential investment, or *project*. Techniques based on accounting earnings and accounting rules are sometimes used - though economists consider this to be improper - such as the *accounting rate of return*, and "return on investment." Simplified and hybrid methods are used as well, such as *payback period* and *discounted payback period*.

Net Present Value

Each potential project's value should be estimated using a discounted cash flow valuation, to find its net present value. This valuation requires estimating the size and timing of all of the incremental cash flows from the project. These future cash flows are then discounted to determine their *present value*. These present values are then summed, to get the NPV. The NPV decision rule is to accept all positive NPV projects in an unconstrained environment, or if projects are mutually exclusive, accept the one with the highest NPV.

The NPV is greatly affected by the discount rate, so selecting the proper rate - sometimes called the *hurdle rate* - is critical to making the right decision. The hurdle rate is the minimum acceptable return on an investment. It should reflect the riskiness of the investment, typically measured by the volatility of cash flows, and must take into account the financing mix. Managers may use models such as the CAPM or the APT to estimate a discount rate appropriate for each particular project, and use the weighted average cost of capital to reflect the financing mix selected. A common practice in choosing a discount rate for a project is to apply a WACC that applies to the entire firm, but a higher discount rate may be more appropriate when a project's risk is higher than the risk of the firm as a whole.

Internal Rate of Return

The internal rate of return is defined as the discount rate that gives a net present value of zero. It is a commonly used measure of investment efficiency. The IRR method will result in the same decision as the NPV method for independent projects in an unconstrained environment, in the usual cases where a negative cash flow occurs at the start of the project, followed by all positive cash flows. In most realistic cases, all independent projects that have an IRR higher than the hurdle rate should be accepted. Nevertheless, for mutually exclusive projects, the decision rule of taking the project with the highest IRR - which is often used - may select a project with a lower NPV. In some cases, several zero NPV discount rates may exist, so there is no unique IRR. The IRR exists and is unique if one or more years of net investment are followed by years of net revenues.

But if the signs of the cash flows change more than once, there may be several IRRs. The IRR equation generally cannot be solved analytically but only via iterations. One shortcoming of the IRR method is that it is commonly misunderstood to convey the actual annual profitability of an investment. However, this is not the case because intermediate cash flows are almost never reinvested at the project's IRR; and, therefore, the actual rate of return is almost certainly going to be lower. A measure called Modified Internal Rate of Return is often used.

Despite a strong academic preference for NPV, surveys indicate that executives prefer IRR over NPV, although they should be used in concert. In a budget-constrained environment, efficiency measures should be used to maximize the overall NPV of the firm. Some managers find it intuitively more appealing to evaluate investments in terms of percentage rates of return than dollars of NPV.

Equivalent Annuity Method

The *equivalent annuity* method expresses the NPV as an annualized cash flow by dividing it by the present value of the annuity factor. It is often used when assessing only the costs of specific projects that have the same cash inflows. In this form it is known as the *equivalent annual cost* method and is the cost per year of owning and operating an asset over its entire lifespan. It is often used when comparing investment projects of unequal lifespans. For example if project A has an expected lifetime of 7 years, and project B has an expected lifetime of 11 years it would be improper to simply compare the net present values of the two projects, unless the projects could not be repeated.

The use of the EAC method implies that the project will be replaced by an identical project. Alternatively the *chain method* can be used with the NPV method under the assumption that the projects will be replaced with the same cash flows each time. To compare projects of unequal length, say 3 years and 4 years, the projects are *chained together, i.e.* four repetitions of the 3 year project are comparing to three repetitions of the 4 year project. The chain method and the EAC method give mathematically equivalent answers. The assumption of the same cash flows for each link in the chain is essentially an assumption of zero inflation, so a real interest rate rather than a nominal interest rate is commonly used in the calculations.

Real Options

Real options analysis has become important since the 1970s as option pricing models have gotten more sophisticated. The discounted cash flow methods essentially value projects as if they were risky bonds, with the promised cash flows known.

But managers will have many choices of how to increase future cash inflows, or to increase future cash outflows. In other words, managers get to manage the projects - not simply accept or reject them. Real options analysis tries to value the choices - the option value - that the managers will have in the future and adds these values to the NPV.

Ranked Projects

The real value of capital budgeting is to rank projects. Most organizations have many projects that could potentially be financially rewarding. Once it has been determined that a particular project has exceeded its hurdle, then it should be ranked against peer projects. The highest ranking projects should be implemented until the budgeted capital has been expended.

The Dividend Decision

The Dividend Decision, in Corporate finance, is a decision made by the directors of a company. It relates to the amount and timing of any cash payments made to the company's stockholders. The decision is an important one for the firm as it may influence its capital structure and stock price. In addition, the decision may determine the amount of taxation that stockholders pay.

There are three main factors that may influence a firm's dividend decision:

- Free-cash flow
- Dividend clienteles
- Information signalling

The Free Cash Flow Theory of Dividends

Under this theory, the dividend decision is very simple. The firm simply pays out, as dividends, any cash that is surplus after it invests in all available positive net present value projects. A key criticism of this theory is that it does not explain the observed dividend policies of real-world companies. Most companies pay relatively consistent dividends from one year to the next and managers tend to prefer to pay a steadily increasing dividend rather than paying a dividend that fluctuates dramatically from one year to the next. These criticisms have led to the development of other models that seek to explain the dividend decision.

Dividend Clienteles

A particular pattern of dividend payments may suit one type of stock holder more than another. A retiree may prefer to invest in a firm that provides a consistently high dividend yield, whereas a person with a high income from employment may prefer to avoid dividends due to their high marginal tax rate on income. If clienteles exist for particular patterns of dividend payments, a firm may be able to maximise its stock price and minimise its cost of capital by catering to a particular clientele. This model may help to explain the relatively consistent dividend policies followed by most listed companies. A key criticism of the idea of dividend clienteles is that investors do not need to rely upon the firm to provide the pattern of cash flows that they desire. An investor who would like to receive some cash from their investment always has the option of selling a portion of their holding. This argument is even more cogent in recent times, with the advent of very low-cost discount stockbrokers. It remains possible that there are taxation-based clienteles for certain types of dividend policies.

Information Signaling

A model developed by Merton Miller and Kevin Rock in 1985 suggests that dividend announcements convey information to investors regarding the firm's future prospects. Many earlier studies had shown that stock prices tend to increase when an increase in dividends is announced and tend to decrease when a decrease or omission is announced. Miller and Rock pointed out that this is likely due to the information content of dividends.

When investors have incomplete information about the firm they will look for other information that may provide a clue as to the firm's future prospects. Managers have more information than investors about the firm, and such information may inform their dividend decisions.

When managers lack confidence in the firm's ability to generate cash flows in the future they may keep dividends constant, or possibly even reduce the amount of dividends paid out. Conversely, managers that have access to information that indicates very good future prospects for the firm are more likely to increase dividends.

Investors can use this knowledge about managers' behaviour to inform their decision to buy or sell the firm's stock, bidding the price up in the case of a positive dividend surprise, or selling it down when dividends do not meet expectations. This, in turn, may influence the dividend decision as managers know that stock holders closely watch dividend announcements looking for good or bad news. As managers tend to avoid sending a negative signal to the market about the future prospects of their firm, this also tends to lead to a dividend policy of a steady, gradually increasing payment.

In a fully informed, efficient market with no taxes and no transaction costs, the free cash flow model of the dividend decision would prevail and firms would simply pay as a dividend any excess cash available.

The observed behaviour of firms differs markedly from such a pattern. Most firms pay a dividend that is relatively constant over time. This pattern of behaviour is likely explained by the existence of clienteles for certain dividend policies and the information effects of announcements of changes to dividends.

The dividend decision is usually taken by considering at least the three questions of: how much excess cash is available? What do our investors prefer? and What will be the effect on our stock price of announcing the amount of the dividend? The result for most firms tends to be a payment that steadily increases over time, as opposed to varying wildly with year-to-year changes in free cash flow.

ANALYSING YOUR FINANCIAL RATIOS

Any successful business owner is constantly evaluating the performance of his or her company, comparing it with the company's historical figures, with its industry competitors, and even with successful businesses from other industries. To complete a thorough examination of your company's effectiveness, however, you need to look at more than just easily attainable numbers like sales, profits, and total assets. You must be able to read between the lines of your financial statements and make the seemingly inconsequential numbers accessible and comprehensible.

This massive data overload could seem staggering. Luckily, there are many well-tested ratios out there that make the task a bit less daunting. Comparative ratio analysis helps you identify and quantify your company's strengths and weaknesses, evaluate its financial position, and understand the risks you may be taking. As with any other form of analysis, comparative ratio techniques aren't definitive and their results shouldn't be viewed as gospel.

Many off-the-balance-sheet factors can play a role in the success or failure of a company. But, when used in concert with various other business evaluation processes, comparative ratios are invaluable. This discussion contains descriptions and examples of the eight major types of ratios used in financial analysis: Income, Profitability, Liquidity, Working Capital, Bankruptcy, Long-Term Analysis, Coverage, and Leverage.

PURPOSES AND CONSIDERATIONS OF RATIOS AND RATIO ANALYSIS

Ratios are highly important profit tools in financial analysis that help financial analysts implement plans that improve profitability, liquidity, financial structure, reordering, leverage, and interest coverage. Although ratios report mostly on past performances, they can be predictive too, and provide lead indications of potential problem areas.

Ratio analysis is primarily used to compare a company's financial figures over a period of time, a method sometimes called trend analysis. Through trend analysis, you can identify trends, good and bad, and adjust your business practices accordingly. You can also see how your ratios stack up against other businesses, both in and out of your industry.

There are several considerations you must be aware of when comparing ratios from one financial period to another or when comparing the financial ratios of two or more companies.

- If you are making a comparative analysis of a company's financial statements over a certain period of time, make an appropriate allowance for any changes in accounting policies that occurred during the same time span.
- When comparing your business with others in your industry, allow for any material differences in

accounting policies between your company and industry norms.

- When comparing ratios from various fiscal periods or companies, inquire about the types of accounting policies used. Different accounting methods can result in a wide variety of reported figures.
- Determine whether ratios were calculated before or after adjustments were made to the balance sheet or income statement, such as non-recurring items and inventory or pro forma adjustments. In many cases, these adjustments can significantly affect the ratios.
- Carefully examine any departures from industry norms.

TYPES OF RATIOS

- Income
- Profitability
- Liquidity
- Working Capital
- Bankruptcy
- Long-Term Analysis
- Coverage
- Leverage

Income Ratios

Turnover of Total Operating Assets = Turnover of Total Operating Assets Ratio Obviously, an increase in sales will necessitate more operating assets at some point; conversely, an inadequate sales volume may call for reduced investment. Turnover of Total Operating Assets or sales to investment in total operating assets tracks over-investment in operating assets. Total operating assets = total assets. This ratio does not measure profitability. Remember, over-investment may result in a lack of adequate profits.

Net Sales to Tangible Net Worth

Net Sales/ Tangible Net Worth= Net Sales to Tangible Net Worth Ratio This ratio indicates whether your investment in the business is adequately proportionate to your sales volume. It may also uncover potential credit or management problems, usually called "overtrading" and "undertrading."

Overtrading, or excessive sales volume transacted on a thin margin of investment, presents a potential problem with creditors. Overtrading can come from considerable management skill, but outside creditors must furnish more funds to carry on daily operations. Undertrading is usually caused by management's poor use of investment money and their general lack of ingenuity, skill or aggressiveness. Tangible Net Worth = owner's equity - intangible assets

Gross Margin on Net Sales

Gross Margin/ Net Sales= Gross Margin on Net Sales Ratio You can identify whether it is necessary to examine company policies relating to credit extension, markups, purchasing, or general merchandising.

*Gross Margin = net sales - cost of goods sold

Note: An increase in gross margin may result from higher sales, lower cost of goods sold, an increase in the proportionate volume of higher margin products, or any combination of these variables.

Operating Income to Net Sales Ratio

Operating Income/ Net Sales= Operating Income to Net Sales Ratio This ratio reveals the profitability of sales resulting from regular business as well as buying, selling, and manufacturing operations. Operating income derives from ordinary business operations and excludes other revenue, extraordinary items, interest on long-term obligations, and income taxes.

Acceptance Index

Applications Accepted/Applications Submitted= Acceptance Index Obviously, a high sales volume that comes from just two or three major accounts is much riskier than the same volume coming from a large number of customers. Losing one out of three major accounts is disastrous, while losing one out of 150 is routine. A growing firm should try to spread this risk of dependency through active sales, promotion, and credit departments. Although the quality of customers stems from your general management policy, the quantity of newly opened accounts is a direct reflection on your sales and credit efforts. This index of effectiveness does not apply to every type of business.

Profitability Ratios

Closely linked with income ratios are profitability ratios, which shed light upon the overall effectiveness of management regarding the returns generated on sales and investment.

Gross Profit on Net Sales

$$\frac{\text{Net Sales-Cost of Goods Sold}}{\text{Net Sales}} = \text{Gross Profit on Net Sales Ratio}$$

Does your average markup on goods normally cover your expenses, and therefore result in a profit? This ratio will tell you. If your gross profit rate is continually lower than your average margin, something is wrong! Be on the lookout for downward trends in your gross profit rate. This is a sign of future problems for your bottom line.

This percentage rate can and will vary greatly from business to business, even those within the same industry. Sales, location, size of operations, and intensity of competition are all factors that can affect the gross profit rate.

NET OPERATING PROFIT RATIOS

Net Profit on Net Sales

$$\frac{\text{EAT*}}{\text{Net Sales}} = \text{Net Profit on Net Sales Ratio}$$

This ratio provides a primary appraisal of net profits related to investment. Once your basic expenses are covered, profits will rise disproportionately greater than sales above the break-even point of operations.

*EAT= earnings after taxes

Sales expenses may be substituted out of profits for other costs to generate even more sales and profits.

Net Profit to Tangible Net Worth

$$\frac{\text{EAT}}{\text{Tangible Net Worth}} = \text{Net Profit on Tangible Net Worth Ratio}$$

This ratio acts as a complementary appraisal of net profits related to investment. This ratio sizes up the ability of management to earn a return.

Net Operating Profit Rate of Return

$$\frac{\text{EBIT}}{\text{Tangible Net worth}} = \text{Net Operating Profit Rate of Return Ratio}$$

Your Net Operating Profit Rate of Return ratio is influenced by the methods of financing you utilize. Notice that this ratio employs earnings before interest and taxes, not earnings after taxes.

Profits are taken after interest is paid to creditors. A fallacy of omission occurs when creditors support total assets. If financial charges are great, compute a net operating profit rate of return instead of return on assets ratio. This can provide an important means of comparison.

Management Rate of Return

$$\frac{\text{Operating Income}}{\text{Fixed Assets + Net Working Capital}}$$

$$= \text{Management Rate of Return Ratio}$$

Fixed Assets + Net Working Capital

This profitability ratio compares operating income to operating assets, which are defined as the sum of tangible fixed assets and net working capital. This rate, which you may calculate for your entire company or for each of its divisions or operations, determines whether you have made efficient use of your assets. The percentage should be compared with a target rate of return that you have set for the business.

Earning Power

$$\frac{\text{Net Sales}}{\text{Tangible Net Worth}} \times \frac{\text{EAT}}{\text{Net Sales}} = \text{Earning Power Ratio}$$

The Earning Power Ratio combines asset turnover with the net profit rate. That is, Net Sales to Tangible Net Worth multiplied by Net Profit on Net Sales. Earning power can be increased by heavier trading on assets, by decreasing costs, by lowering the break-even point, or by increasing sales faster than the accompanying rise in costs.

Liquidity Ratios

While liquidity ratios are most helpful for short-term creditors/suppliers and bankers, they are also important to financial managers who must meet obligations to suppliers of credit and various government agencies. A complete liquidity ratio analysis can help uncover weaknesses in the financial position of your business.

Current Ratio

$$\frac{\text{Current Assets}}{\text{Current Liebilities}} = \text{Current Ratio}$$

Popular since the turn of the century, this test of solvency balances your current assets against your current liabilities. The current ratio will disclose balance sheet changes that net working capital will not.

Current Assets = net of contingent liabilities on notes receivable. Current Liabilities = all debt due within one year of statement data

The current ratio reveals your business's ability to meet its current obligations.

Quick Ratio

$$\frac{\text{Case + Marketable Securities + Accounts Receivable (net)}}{\text{Current Liabilites}}$$

$$= \text{Quick Ratio}$$

Also known as the "acid test," this ratio specifies whether your current assets that could be quickly converted into cash are sufficient to cover current liabilities. Until recently, a Current Ratio of 2:1 was considered standard. A firm that had additional sufficient quick assets available to creditors was believed to be in sound financial condition. The Quick Ratio assumes that all assets are of equal liquidity. Receivables are one step closer to liquidity than inventory. However, sales are not complete until the money is in hand.

Absolute Liquidity Ratio

$$\frac{\text{Case + Marketable Securities}}{\text{Current Liablities}} = \text{Absolute Liquidity Ratio}$$

A subsequent innovation in ratio analysis, the Absolute Liquidity Ratio eliminates any unknowns surrounding receivables. The Absolute Liquidity Ratio only tests short-term liquidity in terms of cash and marketable securities.

Basic Defence Interval

$$\frac{\text{(Case + Receivable + Marketable Security)}}{\text{(Operating Expenses + Interest + Income Taxes)/365}}$$

$$= \text{Basic Defense Interval}$$

If for some reason all of your revenues were to suddenly cease, the Basic Defence Interval would help determine the number of days your company can cover its cash expenses without the aid of additional financing.

Receivables Turnover

$$\frac{\text{Total Credit Sales}}{\text{Average Receivable Owing}} = \text{Receivables Turnover Radio}$$

Another indicator of liquidity, Receivables Turnover Ratio can also indicate management's efficiency in employing those funds invested in receivables. Net credit sales, while preferable, may be replaced in the formula with net total sales for an industry-wide comparison. Closely monitoring this ratio on a monthly or quarterly basis can quickly underscore any change in collections.

Average Collection Period

$$\frac{\text{(Accounting + Notes Receivable)}}{\text{(Annual Net Credit Sales)/ 365}} = \text{Average Collection Period}$$

The Average Collection Period is another litmus test for the quality of your receivables business, giving you the average length of the collection period. As a rule, outstanding receivables should not exceed credit terms by 10-15 days.

If you allow various types of credit transactions, such as a retail outlet selling both on open credit and installment, then the ACP must be calculated separately for each category. Discounted notes which create contingent liabilities must be added back into receivables.

Inventory Turnover

$$\frac{\text{Cost of Goods Sold}}{\text{Average Inventory}} = \text{Inventory Turnover Ratio}$$

Rule of Thumb: Multiply your inventory turnover by your gross margin percentage. If the result is 100 per cent or greater, your average inventory is not too high.

WORKING CAPITAL RATIOS

Many believe increased sales can solve any business problem. Often, they are correct. However,, sales must be built upon sound policies concerning other current assets and should be supported by sufficient working capital. There are two types of working capital: gross working capital, which is all current assets, and net working capital, which are current assets less current liabilities. Moody's Investors Service has listed net working capital since 1922. If you find that you have inadequate working capital, you can correct it by lowering sales or by increasing current assets through either internal savings or external savings. Following are ratios you can use to evaluate your business's net working capital.

Working Capital Ratio

Use "Current Ratio" in the part on "Liquidity Ratios."

This ratio is particularly valuable in determining your business's ability to meet current liabilities.

Working Capital Turnover

$$\frac{\text{Net Sales}}{\text{Net Working Capital}} = \text{Working Capital Turnover Ratio}$$

This ratio helps you ascertain whether your business is top-heavy in fixed or slow assets, and complements Net Sales to Tangible Net Worth. A high ratio could signal overtrading. A high ratio may also indicate that your business requires additional funds to support its financial structure, top-heavy with fixed investments.

Current Debt to Net Worth

$$\frac{\text{Current Liabilities}}{\text{Tangible Net worth}} = \text{Current Debt to Net Worth Ratio}$$

Your business should not have debt that exceeds your invested capital. This ratio measures the proportion of funds that current creditors contribute to your operations. For small businesses a ratio of 60 per cent or above usually spells trouble. Larger firms should start to worry at about 75 per cent.

Funded Debt to Net Working Capital

$$\frac{\text{Long-Tern Debt}}{\text{Net Working Capital}} = \text{Funded Deft to Net Working Capital Ratio}$$

Funded debt (long-term liabilities) = all obligations due more than one year from the balance sheet date. Long-term liabilities should not exceed net working capital.

Bankruptcy Ratios

Many business owners who have filed for bankruptcy say they wish they had seen some warning signs earlier on in their company's downward spiral. Ratios can help predict bankruptcy before it's too late for a business to take corrective action and for creditors to reduce potential losses. With careful planning, predicted futures can be avoided before they become reality. The first five bankruptcy ratios in this part can detect potential financial problems up to three years prior to bankruptcy. The sixth ratio, Cash Flow to Debt, is known as the best single predictor of failure.

Working Capital to Total Assets

$$\frac{\text{Net Working Capital}}{\text{Total Assets}} = \text{Working Capital to Total Assets Ratio}$$

This liquidity ratio, which records net liquid assets relative to total capitalization, is the most valuable indicator of a looming business disaster. Consistent operating losses will cause current assets to shrink relative to total assets. A negative ratio, resulting from negative net working capital, presages serious problems.

Retained Earn ings to Total Assets

$$\frac{\text{Retained Earnings}}{\text{Total Assets}} = \text{Retained Earnings to Total Assets Ratio}$$

New firms will likely have low figures for this ratio, which designates cumulative profitability. Indeed, businesses less than three years old fail most frequently. A negative ratio portends cloudy skies. However, results can be distorted by manipulated retained earnings data.

EBIT to Total Assets

$$\frac{\text{EBIT}}{\text{Total Assets}} = \text{EBIT to Total Assets Ratio}$$

How productive are your business's assets? Asset values come from earning power. Therefore, whether or not liabilities exceed the true value of assets depends upon earnings generated. Maximizing rate of return on assets does not mean the same as maximizing return on equity. Different degrees of leverage affect these separate ceases.

Sales to Total Assets

$$\frac{\text{Toral Sales}}{\text{Total Assets}} = \text{Sales to Total Assets Ratio}$$

This ratio, which uncovers management's ability to

function in competitive situations while not excluding intangible assets, is inconclusive if studied by itself. But when viewed alongside Working Capital to Total Assets, Retained Earnings to Total Assets, and EBIT to Total Assets, it can confirm whether your business is in imminent danger. A result of 200 per cent is more reassuring than one of 100 per cent.

Equity to Debt

$$\frac{\text{Market Value of Common + Perferred Stock}}{\text{Total Current + Long=Term Debt}}$$

= Equity to Debt Ratio

This ratio shows you by how much your business's assets can decline in value before it becomes insolvent. Those businesses with ratios above 200 per cent are safest.

Cash Flow to Debt

$$\frac{\text{Case Flow*}}{\text{Total Debt}} = \text{Case Flow to Debt Ratio}$$

Also, refer to "Debt Cash Flow Coverage Ratio" in the part on "Coverage Ratios." Since debt does not materialize as a liquidity problem until its due date, the closer to maturity, the greater liquidity should be. Other ratios useful in predicting insolvency include Total Debt to Total Assets and Current Ratio.

*Cash flow = Net Income + Depreciation

Because there are various accounting techniques of determining depreciation, use this ratio for evaluating your own company and not to compare it to other companies.

LONG-TERM ANALYSIS

Current Assets to Total Debt

$$\frac{\text{Current Assets}}{\text{Current+Long-Term Debt}} = \text{Current Assets to Total Deft Ratio}$$

This ratio determines the degree of protection linked to short- and long-term debt. More net working capitalprotects short-term creditors. A high ratio shows that if liquidation losses on current assets are not excessive, long-range debtors can be paid in full out of working capital.

Stockholders' Equity Ratio

$$\frac{\text{Stockholders' Equity}}{\text{Total Assets}} = \text{Stockholders' Equity Ratio}$$

Relative financial strength and long-run liquidity are approximated with this calculation. A low ratio points to trouble, while a high ratio suggests you will have less difficulty meeting fixed interest charges and maturing debt obligations.

Total Debt to Net Worth

$$\frac{\text{Current+Deferred Debt}}{\text{Tangible Net Worth}} = \text{Total Debt to Net Worth Ratio}$$

Rarely should your business's total liabilities exceed its tangible net worth. If it does, creditors assume more risk than stockholders. A business handicapped with heavy interest charges will likely lose out to its better financed competitors.

COVERAGE RATIOS

Times Interest Earned

$$\frac{\text{EBIT}}{\text{I}} = \text{Times Interest Earned Ratio}$$

EBIT = earnings before interest and taxes

I = dollar amount of interest payable on debt

The Times Interest Earned Ratio shows how many times earnings will cover fixed-interest payments on long-term debt.

Total Coverage Ratios

$$\frac{\text{EBIT}}{\text{I}} + \frac{\text{s}}{\text{l-h}} = \text{Total coverage Ratio}$$

I = interest payments

s = payment on principal figured on income after taxes. This ratio goes one step further than Times Interest Earned, because debt obliges the borrower to not only pay interest but make payments on the principal as well.

Leverage Ratios

This group of ratios calculates the proportionate contributions of owners and creditors to a business, sometimes a point of contention between the two parties. Creditors like owners to participate to secure their margin of safety, while management enjoys the greater opportunities for risk shifting and multiplying return on equity that debt offers. Although leverage can magnify earnings, it exaggerates losses.

Equity Ratio

$$\frac{\text{Comman Shareholders' Equity}}{\text{Total Capital Employed}} = \text{Equity Ratio}$$

The ratio of common stockholders' equity to total capital of the business shows how much of the total capitalization actually comes from the owners. Residual owners of the business supply slightly more than one half of the total capitalization.

Debt to Equity Ratio

$$\frac{\text{Debt+Preferred Long-Term}}{\text{Command Stockholders' Equity}} = \text{Debt to Equity Ratio}$$

A high ratio here means less protection for creditors. A low ratio, on the other hand, indicates a wider safety cushion.

Total Debt to Tangible Net Worth

If your business is growing, track this ratio for insight into the distributive source of funds used to finance expansion.

Debt Ratio

$$\frac{\text{Current + Long-Term Debt}}{\text{Total Assets}} = \text{Debt Ratio}$$

What percentage of total funds is provided by creditors? Although creditors tend to prefer a lower ratio, management may prefer to lever operations, producing a higher ratio.

TIMES INTEREST EARNED

Common-Size Statement

When performing a ratio analysis of financial statements,

it is often helpful to adjust the figures to common-size numbers. To do this, change each line item on a statement to a percentage of the total.

This technique is quite useful when you are comparing your business to other businesses or to averages from an entire industry, because differences in size are neutralized by reducing all figures to common-size ratios. Industry statistics are frequently published in common-size form.

When comparing your company with industry figures, make sure that the financial data for each company reflect comparable price levels, and that it was developed using comparable accounting methods, classification procedures, and valuation bases. Such comparisons should be limited to companies engaged in similar business activities. When the financial policies of two companies differ, these differences should be recognized in the evaluation of comparative reports.

For example, one company leases its properties while the other purchases such items; one company finances its operations using long-term borrowing while the other relies primarily on funds supplied by stockholders and by earnings. Financial statements for two companies under these circumstances are not wholly comparable.

2

Working Capital Policies

WORKING CAPITAL RESEARCH

No evidence was found of an empirical examination that directly addresses the question of aggressive/conservative working capital policy. The predictive power of financial ratios has been a recurring subject of analysis, and researchers have also focused on grouping ratios into useful classifications. Another area of research has focused on the issue of using regression analysis versus traditional financial ratios for analysis and prediction, for example Frecka and Lee.

His dealt with the strategic determinants of working capital on a product line basis. He used factor analysis to test 166 variables against the working capital policies of over 1700 businesses, or product lines, from 1971 to 1978. His final 12 *Journal of Financial and Strategic Decisions* multiple regression model contained 19 variables pertaining to production, sales, accounting, competitive position, and industry factors. His model was used to explain why working capital levels differ between firms both within and across industries.

Some earlier work by Gupta and Gupta and Huefner examined the differences in financial ratio averages between industries. The cease of both studies was that differences do exist in ratio means amongst industry groups. Pinches, Mingo and Caruthers used factor analysis to develop seven classifications of ratios, and found that the classifications were stable over the 1951-1969 time period. Johnson extended this work by finding cross-sectional stability of ratio groupings for both retailers and primary manufacturers.

Similarly, Gombola and Ketz examined the stability of financial ratio patterns between manufacturing and retail firms and found them to be very stable over time, although the structure of the ratio patterns varied.

Much of recent working capital literature focuses on special subsets of business. Ferconio and Lane, Kincaid, and Chu, Zollinger, Kelly, and Saywell looked at the healthcare industry. Belt and Smith examined Australian companies; Kim, Rowland, and Kim investigated Japanese manufacturers in the United States; and Burns and Walker studied small businesses. However, these studies did not address the issue of differences in aggressive/conservative working capital policies.

METHODOLOGY

Aggressive asset management results in capital being minimized in current assets versus long-term investments. This has the expectation of higher profitability but greater liquidity risk. As an alternative, a more conservative policy places a greater proportion of capital in liquid assets, but at the sacrifice of some profitability.

To measure the degree of aggressiveness the current asset to total asset ratio is used, with a lower ratio meaning a relatively more aggressive policy. Aggressive financing policies utilize higher levels of normally lower cost short-term debt and less long-term capital. Although lowering capital costs, this increases the risk of a short-term liquidity problem.

A more conservative policy uses higher cost capital but postpones the principal repayment of debt, or avoids it entirely by using equity. The total current liability to total asset ratio is used to measure the degree of aggressive financing policy, with a high ratio being relatively more aggressive. The data set includes quarterly levels of current liabilities, current assets, and total assets for companies in ten different industries between 1984 and 1993.

The ten industries, identified by SIC number, cover durable and nondurable goods, and include a variety of manufacturing, service, and retail. The number of companies ranged from 15 to 33 in each industry, with a total of 216 in the final sample. All data was obtained using *Compustat.* To arrive at the final sample, a company was eliminated if there were three or more years of data missing during the ten year total period. For better inter-industry comparability, calendar rather than fiscal year data was compiled.

This eliminates the distorting impact of different reporting periods and seasonality patterns. To remove the effects of seasonality, quarterly data for all firms in each industry was added and averaged together. Therefore, a sequence of ten yearly figures for each ratio per industry was generated. To maintain the integrity of the yearly figures, if a given company had one or more quarters of data missing the entire year was deleted. A ten year industry mean was also computed for each ratio by averaging the individual yearly means.

Differences in Policies

One objective was to determine if a significant difference exists in the aggressive/conservative working capital policies between industries. Industry investment policy is the first examined. To determine if significant differences exist in the current asset to total asset ratio means, a one-way ANOVA was applied to the set of 10 ten year average ratio means. As indicated by the F-ratio of 495.89 the differences in the means is highly significant. To further examine the strength of differences between industry values, Tukey's HSD test was also performed, comparing the industry means on a paired sample basis.

Both The ANOVA and Tukey's HSD tests clearly show a distinctive difference in the asset management policies between industries. Differences in the relative degree of aggressive/conservative liability management were tested by performing a one way ANOVA on the total current liability to total asset means. Tukey's HSD was also applied to this data and 26 of the 45 comparisons showed a significant difference at the one per cent level, and one more at 5 per cent. This left 18 pairs of industries with ratios whose differences were not statistically significant. It is apparent that significant industry differences do exist in the relative degree of aggressive/

conservative working capital policies for both asset and liability management. However, both the ANOVA and Tukey's HSD tests show these differences are generally broader and more significant when examining asset management. One is motor vehicles, apparel, computers, retail stores, and food; the other is petroleum, publishing, steel, transportation, and chemicals.

The differences between industries within the two groups were not significant, but industry differences between the two groups were significant. At least with respect to this data set, the industries with a somewhat heavier consumer orientation appear to have more aggressive financing policies, but a deeper investigation into the nature of the industries' asset and liability composition would be required to draw a more definitive cease.

Stability Between Policies

Having established that the ten year ratio means were significantly different between industries, next examined was the stability of these relative differences over time. Rank order correlations were used as a test of relative stability. For each of the ten years the current asset/total asset ratio was computed for each industry and then ranked from the highest to lowest ratio. The base year rankings were then sequentially compared to the rankings of each succeeding year.

Each industry maintained its relative level of aggressiveness with respect to working capital investment over time. The only exception is the relationship between the food and steel industries, which had very close ratios during the last five years and changed places in 1990 and back again in 1992.

Not surprisingly, Tukey's HSD shows the mean differences between the steel and food industries is one of the two comparisons that is not significant. The industries were also ranked each year on the basis of current liabilities to total assets and these rank order correlations.

The relationship between these ratios was less stable than the current asset/total asset ratios, but still significant at either the 1% or 5% level for the first nine years. The abrupt change in the publication industry ratio from the second lowest to the highest value in 1993 caused a drop in the level of significance to 10%.

ASSET AND FINANCING POLICIES

Another relationship examined was how aggressive asset management corresponded to aggressive financial management. This relationship was tested on a year by year basis. For the first year, the industries were ranked from low CA/TA ratios to high ratios, corresponding to ascending order of relatively aggressive policies. Rankings were also ordered, for the first year, from high to low TCL/TA ratios, again corresponding to an ascending order of aggressiveness. Rank order correlations between the two policies were then computed for year one. Without exception the correlations between the two policies were highly negative each year, and they are significant at the 1 or 5 per cent level except for 1993 which is at 10 per cent. It is evident that industries which pursued relatively aggressive asset policies simultaneously followed relatively conservative financing policies.

Changes in Policies

To the extent that industry policies change over time, the question arises whether they change in the same direction and at the same time, indicating a possible macroeconomic influence. Regression analysis was used to examine the relationship in the changes between industries. The ten current asset to total asset ratios for each industry were regressed against the ratios for each other industry. All of the relationships are positive, and 29 of the 45 regressions have significant results at the 1% or 5% level. Steel and petroleum are the only two industries that do not tend to change their working capital investment policies with the other industries.

The policies of both motor vehicles and transportation were highly correlated with those of the other industries in the study. The high correlation between the working capital investment policies of these industries appears to suggest a possible relationship between the policies and some external macroeconomic factor such as the business cycle.

EFFECTIVE POLICIES AND PROCEDURES

FINAL IN CASH TO CASH CYCLE SERIES

In the past four weeks, we've brought to light four key areas in which you can save $250,000 each — for a total of $1,000,000. Point by point, we've shown you just how cash flows through these areas, making up the Cash to Cash Cycle.

And as we've seen, the cash cycle is undoubtedly the single most important process to optimize for any business – from when you spend money to when you get money. So now let's put it all together.

Cash to Cash Cycle Definition

By definition, the cash to cash cycle is a financial ratio that shows the length time for which a company must finance its own inventory. It measures the number of days between the initial cash outflow to the subsequent cash inflow.

Cash Conversion Cycle and Cash Flows

One way to express this is the length of time between the purchase of Inventory and the collection of accounts Receivable created from the sale of your product — also called the cash conversion cycle. Why is this most important? Because this is your cash flow.

OPERATIONS ASSESSMENT AND WORKING CAPITAL

Businesses live and die by the cash generated from operations. If your operations don't create cash, then they consume it. A cash-consuming operation means that you have negative cash flow and you are living on financing.

But the Cash to Cash Cycle also shows you the amount of working capital you have committed to your organization. Just add the number of days of inventory to the number of days of receivables outstanding, and then subtract the number of days of payables outstanding. The result is the number of days of working capital your organization has tied up in managing your supply chain. This can be quite a significant number -

one not to overlook. This can also be expressed by the formula: stock days plus debtor days minus creditor days equals the cash-to-cash cycle. So, for example, a company that keeps its stock for on average 30 days, gets paid by its debtors on average within 30 days and pays its creditors on average within 30 days will have a cash-to-cash cycle of 30 days.

Companies that receive cash from their customers at the point of sale and that have their inventory under good control will have a short cash-to-cash cycle. A company could even have either a negative cycle or a cycle time of zero.

For example, if a business' receivables and payables are held in check at 30 days while inventory runs at Just-In-Time levels, then the cash cycle is zero – meaning that this company is in good shape with no working capital needs. And, of course, when receivable days are less than payables with JIT inventory, then the company will enjoy a positive cash-to-cash cycle – creating more cash on hand.

On the other hand, however, if a company puts payables down to 15 days and allows receivables to grow to 45 days, while inventory remains at steady levels, the cash cycle will be high. And. here, working capital will be constrained to compensate for inefficiencies.

PROCESSES AND PROCEDURES INVESTMENTS

Did you realise that working capital is the investment you are making in the inefficiencies of your processes and procedures plus your investment in your suppliers' and your customers' inefficiencies too? In other words, if you do not monitor inventory, accounts receivable, sales and marketing and accounts payable to ensure a healthy cash-to-cash cycle, then your working capital needs will not maintain a strong cash flow. The process will be out of control, and will not be optimized to create the greatest amount of effectiveness for the company.

Policies and Procedures Savings

So now you can see the relationship between your cash flow, your working capital and your cash to cash cycle. In order to increase your cash flow, you need to increase the velocity of your cash to cash cycle by reducing the inefficiencies found in your processes, your suppliers' processes and your customers' processes. The result is a decrease in your working capital and an increase in your cash. And, as we've seen, this can be a significant number – again, one that you shouldn't overlook.

INVESTMENT POLICY STATEMENT FOR TREASURY POOL

Under this policy, the Board of Regents authorized the Treasurer to manage the financial assets invested in the Treasury Pool within the described limits. The Treasurer is responsible for implementing an investment strategy in support of the "prudent" person standard, providing liquidity, safety, and yield to the institution.

Diversification of investments and appropriate time horizons contribute to the achievement of benchmark returns at acceptable levels of risk. The Treasurer's Office is well-positioned to forecast expected cash inflows and disbursements and to schedule investments to maximize earnings.

- Collection of the major portions of revenue is fairly predictable. State appropriations, letters of credit and tuition are received on a scheduled basis throughout the year. Gift fund and endowment income transfers from CU Foundation, investment earnings, credit card and auxiliary fund revenues and Federal contract receivables are also collected on a regular basis.
- Projection of expenditures is based on patterns that are well established and reasonably predictable. Approximately 65% of the University's total expenditures are regular, periodic payments, and 35% less predictable expenses, such as utilities, supplies, services, and equipment.

Investment earnings on most of the accounts in the Treasury Pool are unrestricted financial resources of the

University. A small number of accounts receive earnings in accordance with federal or state law. All uses of the earnings are budgeted as part of the Annual Budget Process in compliance with applicable University Administrative Policy and federal and state law.

All University monies are invested as part of the Treasury Pool except for certain monies which are not eligible or appropriate for inclusion in this Treasury Pool, such as endowment funds and proceeds from bond issues. In cases where pooling is either not permitted or appropriate, the Treasurer makes specific alternative arrangements to assure fiduciary oversight of those monies.

This revised *IPS* is based upon a Treasury Pool size of $358 million, which is the projected balance for 6/30/02. The percentages and dollars reported in the following parts apply to this base, and are shown here to demonstrate the results of the decision-making process. Annually, the size of the Pool is reviewed and, if appropriate, revised, and the percentages are reviewed, and if appropriate, revised, to ensure that dollars allocated to each segment meet the liquidity needs of the University.

The allocation percentages and dollars will change during the year as the size of the pool increases and decreases. This policy is brought back for revision by the Board of Regents when there are major shifts in the percentages allocated to each liquidity segment. The current sizes of the segments are reported to the Regents quarterly as part of the Treasurer's report to RAFAC.

Liquidity Requirements

The Treasury Pool is segmented into three categories by liquidity requirement in order to assure appropriate matching of investments with liquidity needs. At least annually, amounts assigned to the categories are reassessed. The three liquidity segments are:

- Daily Working Capital Segment;
- Contingency Segment;
- Non-Recurring Items Segment Assets held in the

Daily Working Capital segment are invested with the primary objectives of stability of principal and liquidity.

Such investments are restricted to high quality money market and other fixed income obligations with a maturity of one year or less. The determination of the amount of assets held in this segment is based on forecast expected cash inflows and disbursements and an examination of historical data from the most recent three fiscal years. The projected amount in this segment is about $60 million on July 1, 2002, and will represent 17% of Treasury Pool assets.

The dollars and percentage allocated to this segment will change within a year as the size of the pool increases and decreases. They may change annually based on the annual review conducted by the Treasurer with the Investment Advisory Committee.

The Contingency Segment serves as a buffer for the Daily Working Capital Segment. Shortfalls that occur will be met by the Contingency Segment, to protect against unplanned disbursements from the Non-Recurring Items Segment. The assets in the Contingency Segment are set at 33% of the Daily Working Capital Segment and represent approximately 6% of pool assets at July 1, 2002.

It is anticipated that the absolute size of the Contingency Segment will remain relatively constant during the fiscal year, and will include changes due to reinvested earnings. Annually, the percentage allocated to this segment, and the resulting dollars allocated, may change based on the annual review conducted by the Treasurer with the Investment Advisory Committee.

Investments are limited to high quality fixed income obligations with a maturity of five years or less. Through proper identification of the needs of the Daily Working Capital and the Contingency Segments, the remaining assets in the Treasury Pool are targeted for non-recurring expenditures. These assets, designated the Non-Recurring Items Segment, have a longer time horizon for investment. The projected amount in this segment on July 1, 2002 is approximately 77%

of Treasury Pool assets. This allocation percentage will change during the year, as the Daily Working Capital segment expands and contracts during a normal year, although the absolute dollars in the segment will remain relatively constant and typically include reinvested earnings and dividends.

This segment is invested to achieve meaningful additional returns, relative to the current asset mix, without taking on inappropriate levels of risk. Initially, 29% of this segment will be invested in certain types of equities, and 71% of this segment will be invested in fixed income instruments.

This allocation will change slightly during the year, as the performance of the different markets unfolds, and will be reviewed as part of the annual review process by the Treasurer and the Investment Advisory Committee. In summary, the first two segments are invested with the objectives of providing liquidity and safeguarding principal with a commensurate investment return.

The third segment is invested just as to a total return philosophy. In combination, the following investment objectives of the Pool will be met:

(1) liquidity for day to day operations;

(2) protection of the nominal value of assets; and

(3) generation of distributable earnings at a level that is commensurate with the time horizons of the investments.

Implementation

This policy, as updated, continues to use long-terr investments, including equities. Investments currently ı intermediate fixed-income vehicles will, after implementation, be invested using a slightly longer time horizon. Implementation of this updated policy will take less than one month.

Diversification

Each Segment of the Treasury Pool and each portfolio within the Non-Recurring Items Segment is diversified with respect to economic sector, industry, and specific issuer. Such diversification is intended to reduce risk. Securities issued by the United States government and its Agencies are not subject to diversification requirements due to their risk-free nature.

The Earnings Distribution

The Treasurer, in consultation with the Investment Advisory Committee, will develop a recommendation for maintaining undistributed investment returns in amounts which are considered to be reasonably adequate to dampen the effects of natural market cycles on the market value of invested assets and to protect the annual earnings distribution budget. The Treasurer will review this recommendation with appropriate University administrators during the annual budget process, and seek approval for funding.

Operating Procedures

The Treasurer reports on the investments and performance of the Treasury Pool to the Board of Regents through quarterly reports to the Regent Audit and Financial Advisory Committee. Reports include review and analysis of Treasury Pool assets in the three segments described in this policy statement. The Treasurer maintains a written statement of Operating Procedures that includes specific investment guidelines, performance measurement standards, and mutual fund and investment manager and securities lending programme provider selection criteria. This document governs the day-to-day operations of the staff of the Treasurer's Office. The Investment Advisory Committee reviews the Operating Procedures annually. At least annually, the Treasurer reviews the amounts assigned to each of the three distinct liquidity segments and discusses the rationale with the Investment Advisory Committee.

FINANCIAL POLICIES

INVESTMENT POLICY

Investments in the City shall be undertaken in a manner that seeks to ensure the preservation of capital in the overall portfolio and to meet the cash flow demands of City operations.

- To maintain the safety of public funds, the City shall diversify its investments to avoid incurring unreasonable and avoidable risk.
- The City's investment strategy shall provide sufficient liquidity to meet the City's operating, payroll, and capital requirements.
- The City's investment portfolio shall be designed with the intent of attaining a market rate of return throughout budgetary and economic cycles, while minimizing investment risk.
- Asset protection measures required by new Florida Statute changes have been incorporated.

Accounting and Reporting Policy

All financial transactions of the City shall be properly authorized, documented, and reported.

- All disbursements of funds shall be within budget limits, authorized at the appropriate level, and supported with proper documentation.
- Quarterly financial and performance reports shall be prepared and distributed to the City Council, City Manager, and Department Heads by the Administrative Services Department.
- An independent audit of the City's financial books, records, statements, and reports shall be conducted by a Certified Public Accountant annually.

Position Authorization and Attrition

Only positions authorized by City Council, funded in the budget, and operationally warranted shall be filled.

- Positions shall be authorized by City Council annually through the budget process or by budget amendments as needed and as funding exists.
- Vacant positions will be reviewed by the Department Head and the Human Resources Director before the position is filled to ensure the need and urgency of filling the position warrants immediate recruitment.

Grant Management

Outside sources of revenue through grant funding shall be maximized. However, careful consideration of departmental objectives and programming priorities shall be given before grant applications are prepared. Duplication of services shall be avoided and expanded levels of service shall be analysed thoroughly before proceeding with a funding request.

Budget Preparation and Adjustment

The annual City budget shall be planned and prepared to conform to State law and Palm Bay City Code.

- The legal level of authority shall be at the department level.
- The annual City budget shall be approved by September 27th proceeding the fiscal year which begins October 1 and ends September 30.
- During the development of the budget, the impact of the proposed budget on the next two fiscal years will be evaluated.
- Once the budget has been adopted, the City Manager may authorize the transfer of any unencumbered appropriation balance between general classifications of expenditures within a department.
- At the close of each fiscal year, the unencumbered balance of each appropriation shall revert to the respective fund from which it was appropriated.

Debt Management

Borrowing in the City shall be undertaken in a manner which seeks to ensure efficiency and equity for the taxpayers.

- Efficiency means getting the best return for a given commitment of resources.

  When the efficiency, with which government services are performed, can be greatly increased by substituting capital expenditures for current expenditures, debt shall be considered.
- Equity means that the beneficiaries from capital expenditures shall pay for them. Maturity of the debt

shall be approximately equivalent to the period over which the capital will be used.

Working Capital/Fund Balance

A working capital reserve shall be maintained in the General Fund to ensure adequate cash flow. This reserve should be an amount equal to ten per cent of budgeted operating expenditures.

- An adequate reserve will be maintained in the Building Fund for stabilization in the event of downswings in construction.
- Adequate fund balances and reserves shall be maintained in the Debt Funds to ensure timely payment of debt obligations when due.
- Adequate amounts of retained earnings shall be maintained in the Utility Funds to comply with bond covenants. Reserves are maintained at 15% of budgeted operating expenditures or at a level to comply with bond covenants.
- In the Employee Benefits Fund, two months claims anticipated cost shall be maintained as unreserved fund balance
- In the Risk Management Fund, the anticipated claims payable for the next fiscal year, as actuarially determined, shall be maintained as unreserved fund balance.

Preservation of Capital Assets

Sufficient funds shall be appropriated each year for the purpose of preserving and replacing capital assets that are vital to the ongoing delivery of government services.

- Specific schedules for routine capital maintenance of City facilities shall be developed and funded as revenues allow.
- Specific schedules for the replacement of vehicles and computer equipment shall be developed and funded as revenues allow.

THRUST TO GROWTH POLICIES

The world's perception about India is changing quite rapidly. And this is getting strongly reflected in the recent writings of leading commentators such as Peter Drucker and Jeffrey Sachs. India is now focussed on emerging as the economic powerhouse of the world. Economic performance this year supports this "spirit of change", though a number of structural reforms remain to be carried out. A deeper analysis of the underlying macro currents suggests that India can look forward to a strong expansion in the months ahead. This is vindicated by the latest DSE-ECRI Indian Leading Index Report, prepared by Prof Pami Dua and Dr Anirvan Banerji, which shows a sharp increase in the value of the index in March-September 2003.

In contrast to the global situation, India registered a robust performance accompanied by macroeconomic stability. The sharp turnaround in agriculture and its positive spin-offs on industry and services are fuelling an overall recovery by containing inflation. Government estimates, the total foodgrains production in FY-04 will increase by 20 per cent to touch 220 million tonnes from 183 million tonnes in FY-03. The rise in oilseeds output during the kharif season of 2003-04 is 63.6 per cent and that of cotton, 40.9 per cent. Only sugar recorded negative growth, with the output declining by 6.2 per cent; adverse weather condition in some parts of Maharashtra is said to be the cause.

Backed by rising rural incomes and low interest rates, the industrial sector staged a healthy recovery, growing 6.2 per cent in April-November 2003. The recovery has been fuelled by the manufacturing sector, which grew at 6.8 per cent. This growth has been broad-based, with capital and consumer goods sectors logging 8.8 per cent and 8.1 per cent respectively. In the core sector, the growth impetus continues to come from steel and cement, recording production increases of 7 per cent and 5.1 per cent respectively during April-November 2003. This comes on top of corresponding year-on-year increases of 10.7 per cent and 8.9 per cent, respectively. Similar buoyancy is observed for petro products output, with a 6.9 per cent growth in the first eight months of this fiscal. Backed by strengthening financial and IT-related activities and buoyant housing demand, the services sector grew by nearly 8 per cent in the first quarter of FY-04. A CII survey expects the services sector to grow by at least 7.5 per cent in FY-04, as, in eight of the past 10 years, the sector logged in excess of 7 per cent and often crossed even 8 per cent. And as per the latest CSO estimates, the sector has, on an average, grown at 8.6 per cent in the second quarter of 2003-04. Considering these sectoral trends, a real GDP growth of 7-7.5 per cent for the entire year cannot be ruled out.

Headline inflation has started moving up owing to rising oil and manufactured goods prices. But the Government has, to some extent, contained these pressures through increased edible oil imports and running down the foodgrain stocks. The total stocks were reduced from a record 63 million tonnes to 35 million tonnes in July 2003.

Though inflation is expected to go up because of manufactured products' prices and the cascading effect of the fuel price hike, the average annual inflation for 2004 is unlikely to exceed 5 per cent, thanks to the improved supplies of agricultural commodities. On the monetary front, there is sufficient liquidity cushion to support an expansion in credit demand or investment in securities by banks without putting pressure on yields.

As of December 2003, liquidity in the banking system is estimated at around Rs 3,45,965 crore. The accommodative stance of the RBI's Monetary Policy has been supported by strong capital inflows to sustain the soft interest-rate regime. This is apparent in the term structure of interest rates.

The yield on 91-day treasury bills declined to 4.2 per cent in mid-January 2004 from 5.6 per cent a year back, while yield on the 10-year bond declined to 5.26 per cent from 5.86 per cent. Commercial banks have cut their deposit rates for one-year maturity to 5-6 per cent from 6.5-7.5 per cent.

Also, effective January, banks have come out with new benchmark PLRs, which are 25-75 basis points lower than their earlier levels. However, a third of the bank loans today are contracted at rates well below the prime rate. Yet, the pace of credit flow to the commercial sector is quite slow due to reduced dependence of companies on bank loans, through more efficient working capital management, increased retained earnings and direct borrowings from the capital market.

Monetary expansion is effectively controlled by the RBI through sterilisation. As a result, broad money supply grew by about 10.1 per cent during April to end-December this year against 12.3 per cent a year ago.

Though the current point-to-point inflation rate at 6.1 per cent is higher than the 10-year benchmark yield of 5.26 per cent, it is unlikely that interest rates would reverse their trend till end-March, as inflationary expectations are still low and easy liquidity conditions are expected to continue, thanks to strong capital inflows.

The equity market is also on a high. The 2003-04 Budget gave the first boost by making dividends on mutual fund plans tax free in the hands of investors. Long-term capital gains on equities were waived to encourage long-term investments. This certainly became a "feel-good factor" for equity investors. Positive triggers came by way of plentiful rainfall, steadily rising corporate profitability, in the first two quarters of FY-2004, and foreign interest in common stocks. This helped the Sensex cross the 6,000 mark on January 2.

In the first nine months of this year, the net foreign purchases of common stocks exceeded $6 billion compared with $1 billion in the whole of FY 2003. While legal challenges have delayed the full privatisation of oil sector companies, their low valuations *vis-à-vis* the private companies, and strong earnings have fuelled the rally. In the initial stages of recovery, the IT sector lagged because of margin pressures and an appreciating currency, while sectors such as steel, aluminium, cement, auto, auto-ancillaries, pharmaceuticals, engineering and power resurged and fuelled the run-up.

The PE ratio of the benchmark BSE Sensex companies moved from around 13.2 in April 2003 to 19.7 in January 2004. However, the consensus value for this ratio with respect to one-year forward earnings is around 13-14. This will help attract FII money into the bourses. Further, the earnings momentum of the corporate sector is expected to continue in the next two quarters as well. Even if there is some diversion of funds away from the emerging markets in Asia owing to a gradual recovery in the US and the Euro zone, domestic players are likely to make good the foreign capital.

The country's foreign exchange reserves have climbed consistently throughout the year. The rise has, to a significant extent, been because of buoyant FII inflows. In fact, this source accounted for 11.1 per cent of the accretion during April-Sept 2003. The RBI has been working at eliminating interest arbitrages. Yield differential on 10-year paper of the US and Indian government securities has narrowed, from 240 bps in November 2002 to about 100 bps now.

But the prospects of the Indian economy are creating long-term demand for Indian paper and, as a result, inexorable flow of FII money. The rising rupee on the back of strong inflows and uncertainty over the US economy has had a sobreing impact on export figures. The cumulative figure for April-November has accordingly decelerated to 8.8 per cent. So far the central bank has effectively countered the upward pressures on the exchange rate to preserve external competitiveness.

The rupee, as a result, has appreciated only 5.1 per cent against the dollar. By end of fiscal 2004, the rupee is expected to remain between Rs 45 and 46, as there are factors working from both the sides. As industrial activity accelerates, imports will necessarily rise further and would affect net trade inflows and result in rupee depreciation. But the increased economic activity will ensure that the targeted levels for tax collections are met, and this would keep a check on fiscal deficit.

And this, in turn, will check to some extent the downward pressure on the rupee. Similarly, current trends in forward premia rule out significant weakening of rupee *vis-à-vis* dollar. Also, continued inflows of foreign funds backed by strong fundamentals would keep upward pressure on rupee value.

This optimistic outlook has given policymakers another opportunity to push forward the pending structural reforms.

While some progress has been made in indirect tax liberalisation, which has direct implications for productivity enhancement, the hitherto neglected sectors of agriculture and infrastructure are still lagging well behind other South-East Asian countries.

And if the fiscal deficit swells further, it could lead to insolvency. The current macro situation should be looked upon as an opportunity to aggressively follow pro-growth policies.

3

Cash Management System

CASH MANAGEMENT

Cash Management may be used to describe all bank accounts provided to businesses of a certain size, but it is more often used to describe specific services such as *cash concentration, zero balance accounting,* and *automated clearing house* facilities. Sometimes private bank customers are given cash management services.In United States banking, cash management, or treasury management, is a marketing term for certain services offered primarily to larger business customers.

The following is a list of services generally offered by banks and utilised by larger businesses and corporations:

- *Account Reconcilement Services:* Balancing a checkbook can be a difficult process for a very large business, since it issues so many checks it can take a lot of human monitoring to understand which checks have not cleared and therefore what the company's true balance is. To get around this, banks have developed a system which allows companies to upload a list of all the checks that they issue on a daily basis, so that at the end of the month the bank statement will show not only which checks have cleared, but also which have not. More recently, banks have used this system to prevent checks from being fraudulently cashed if they are not on the list, a process known as *positive pay*.
- *Advanced Web Services*: Most banks have an Internet-based system which is more advanced than the one

available to consumers. This enables managers to create and authorize special internal logon credentials, allowing employees to send wires and access other cash management features normally not found on the consumer web site.

- *Armored Car Services*: Large retailers who collect a great deal of cash may have the bank pick this cash up via an armored car company, instead of employees depositing the cash.
- *Automated Clearing House:* services are usually offered by the cash management division of a bank. The Automated Clearing House is an electronic system used to transfer funds between banks. Companies use this to pay others, especially employees. Certain companies also use it to collect funds from customers. This system is the subject of the ire of some consumer groups, because under this system all banks assume that the company initiating the debit is correct until proven otherwise.
- *Balance Reporting Services:* Corporate clients who actively manage their cash balances usually subscribe to secure web-based reporting of their account and transaction information at their lead bank. These sophisticated compilations of banking activity may include balances in foreign currencies, as well as those at other banks. They include information on cash positions as well as 'float'. Finally, they offer transaction-specific details on all forms of payment activity, including deposits, checks, wire transfers, ACH, investments, etc.
- *Cash Concentration Services:* Large or national chain retailers often are in areas where their primary bank does not have branches. Therefore, they open bank accounts at various local banks in the area. To prevent funds in these accounts from being idle and not earning sufficient interest, many of these companies have an agreement set with their primary bank, whereby their primary bank uses the

Automated Clearing House to electronically "pull" the money from these banks into a single interest-bearing bank account.

- *Lockbox services:* Often companies which receive a large number of payments via checks in the mail have the bank set up a post office box for them, open their mail, and deposit any checks found. This is referred to as a "lockbox" service.
- *Positive Pay:* Positive pay is a service whereby the company electronically shares its check register of all written checks with the bank. The bank therefore will only pay checks listed in that register, with exactly the same specifications as listed in the register. This system dramatically reduces check fraud.
- *Sweep Accounts:* are typically offered by the cash management division of a bank. Under this system, excess funds from a company's bank accounts are automatically moved into a money market mutual fund overnight, and then moved back the next morning. This allows them to earn interest overnight. This is the primary use of money market mutual funds.
- *Zero Balance Accounting:* can be thought of as somewhat of a *hack*. Companies with large numbers of stores or locations can very often be confused if all those stores are depositing into a single bank account. Traditionally, it would be impossible to know which deposits were from which stores. To help this problem, banks developed a system where each store is given their own bank account, but all the money deposited into the store account is automatically moved into the company's main bank account. This allows the company to look at individual statements for each store. US Banks at the present time, however, are almost all converting their systems so that companies can tell which store made a particular deposit, even if these deposits are all being done into one account. Therefore, zero balance accounting is being used less frequently.

- *Wire Transfer*: A wire transfer is an electronic transfer of funds. Wire transfers can be done by a simple bank account transfer, or by a transfer of cash at a cash office. Bank wire transfers are often the most expedient method for transferring funds between bank accounts. A bank wire transfer is a message to the receiving bank requesting them to effect payment in accordance with the instructions given. The message also includes settlement instructions. The actual wire transfer itself is virtually instantaneous, requiring no longer for transmission than a telephone call.
- *Controlled Disbursement:* This is another product offered by banks under Cash Management Services. The bank provides a daily report, typically early in the day, that provides the amount of disbursements that would be charged to the customers account. This early knowledge of daily funds requirement allows the customer to invest any surplus in intraday investment opportunities, typically money market. This is different from delayed disbursements, where payments are issued through a remote branch of a bank and customer is able to delay the payment due to increased float time.

In the past, other services have been offered the usefulness of which has diminished with the rise of the Internet. For example, companies could have daily faxes of their most recent transactions or be sent CD-ROMs of images of their cashed checks. These services can be costly but usually the cost to a company is outweighed by the benefits: cost savings, accuracy, efficiencies, etc.

UNLOCKING WORKING CAPITAL

Many sectors and European economies are experiencing slow growth, while high oil and energy costs are putting profit margins under pressure. In this environment, improving operational processes and ensuring an efficient supply chain can help to improve profitability and safeguard it for the future. And, with senior management more and more aware of the benefits of self financing, treasurers and finance professionals are under pressure to unlock working capital tied up in the supply chain for operational use or investment. CFOs and their treasury staff are achieving this mainly through an enterprise-wide tightening up of the 'working capital value chain'.

This involves operational improvements in diverse areas ranging from sales and accounts to warehouse managers and logistics. Treasury has a key part to play in reducing working capital requirements through best practice cash management – including centralising cash-flow and liquidity management – and making the business more cash-aware.

In the quest for competitive advantage, multinationals have great scope to unlock capital trapped in physical and financial supply chains. A recent study1 calculated that the top 100 Western European companies alone have around EUR 480 billion trapped in inefficient management of working capital. Similarly, there are huge amounts of capital held captive in the working capital chains of companies in the Americas and Asia.

Another study, conducted by BDRC on behalf of ABN AMRO2, found that 48% of companies have centralised their liquidity management – which means that large numbers still have the opportunity to do so, if it fits their business model. Forces encouraging multinationals down the path of reducing working capital requirements include not only the return of growth to the agenda, but also the current determination of boards and shareholders to impose more disciplined management of capital.

The emphasis on cash flow as a yardstick of performance is symptomatic of this, as is the importance shareholders place on return on capital employed. In addition, a natural trend towards late payment in the recent period of slow growth led to increasing focus on payment terms and reasons for late payment. Often, failure to pay or late payment is the result of poor client service or disputes on delivery, for example, non delivery or delivery errors. Just as the exercise of reducing working capital requirements has implications for many of the areas of the business, so its benefits spread beyond improved working capital ratios. Most importantly, the improvements in operational processes that lead to a reduction in working capital additionally tend to decrease costs. Consequently, there is an increase in profit. Therefore, there are multiple benefits in terms of value creation for shareholders.

For the treasurer, there is a role to play in reducing working capital requirements, even though implementation stretches across other areas of the organisation. Cash management is a prime responsibility of treasury and the starting point for building a broad working capital improvement programme.

Achieving Operational Reductions in Working Capital

For each multinational, the route chosen to reduce the working capital tied up in its operational supply chain will depend on its unique characteristics. Much depends upon the industry in which a company operates, and its power in relation to the entities with which it trades.

For example, a large retailer may have the power to improve the terms under which it pays its suppliers. Other types of companies may not have such power, and may have to seek efficiencies in operational processes, or inventory reductions and efficiencies. This is particularly the case in the commodity-based businesses, where continuing pressure on margins can only be compensated if operational cost can be reduced. Analysing where the opportunity for improvement lies requires detailed information regarding the flow of funds and goods in all areas of the business – it reaches to the core of a company's business processes.

When seeking operational reductions in working capital, there are three key areas. These are: Days Sales Outstanding (DSO), Days Payables Outstanding (DPO) and Days Inventories Outstanding (DIO). In the case of both sales (DSO) and payments (DPO), one of the opportunities for improvement lies in negotiation of more favourable terms, and this depends on who has the power in the business relationship. The first step is to analyse why some clients are paying later than others, using benchmarking techniques. Then, companies need to ensure that the benefits of negotiating extended payment terms are not outweighed by costs in areas such as loss of discounts, which can have a detrimental impact on profit.

Additionally, there are risks to reputation and to credibility with suppliers. In the case of DSO, it is important to identify the root cause of any weaknesses and to take a proactive approach to the management of receivables. Late payment may be the result of problems with invoicing, product delivery or ambiguous payment terms.

Automating the payments workflow through electronic straight-through-processing rather than inefficient manual processes can be part of the solution. Another possibility is to make sales and services responsible for booked revenues, instead of mandated ones.

Once internal processes have been analysed, banks can provide automated cash management options that can unlock working capital in the DSO cycle. But good information is essential, as it enables the identification of late payers and analysis of any reasons for payment delay.

In the case of DPO, there will likely also be improvements to be made to internal processes. Incorrect payments are often made as a result of incorrect invoice details, missed data, ambiguous terms and so on.

These problems can be minimised by, for example, automating workflow, having a consistent strategy and approach towards suppliers and payments, and having comprehensive and consistent access to invoice and transaction information. An additional strategy for reducing working capital is to take it off-balance sheet through asset securitisation or vendor financing programmes.

Cash Management in Working Capital Improvement

Cash management's role in reducing working capital requirements involves introducing the greatest possible efficiencies in cashflow management and liquidity management. The way treasurers go about this will depend on the nature of the organisation. Broadly speaking, the greatest opportunities for efficiencies exist among decentralised organisations where cash management can be centralised and a Shared Service Centre (SSC) established. Centralised organisations may already have highly efficient cash management practices, although this is not always the case.

Establishing an SSC should be a catalyst for the improvement of working capital management. From a treasury perspective this will also involve the introduction of a new treasury management system, rationalisation of banking relationships and benchmarking initiatives. One major benefit of such a reorganisation comes at no extra cost; the organisation as a whole will start talking to each other about improving its working capital, impacting and energising all levels and departments.

Cashflow Management

Cashflow management involves optimising transaction processes with the aim of minimising transaction costs and maximising control while improving information flow and reporting. How this is done depends on the company's business model. For example, a decentralised company – with local management and production–may approach this differently to a centralised company.

Obviously multinationals generally achieve the greatest efficiency gains through the introduction of a Shared Service Centre (SSC). By definition, an SSC has a big impact on the company's core processes. An SSC takes multiple tasks, processes, general ledgers and IT infrastructures, and reduces them to one process per task in one central location – although there are always some tasks that cannot be centralised. Harmonising procedures by introducing uniform enterprise resource planning (ERP) systems confers real gains in financial terms, but also in more accurate reporting. Introducing a true SSC can lead to considerable efficiencies if it is done well; at its best, it will provide insight into a company's 'end-to-end' receivables and payables process. For many companies, the

SSC may be one step too far. Instead, they may initially focus on centralising payment execution through a single 'payment factory', with local subsidiaries retaining their own Accounts Payable (AP) and Accounts Receivable (AR) management. Additionally, the payment factory will provide an interface to the company's banks. While a payment factory does not attain the full benefits of an SSC, it does lead to a reduction in transaction costs. Furthermore, centralising payments provides a better understanding of cashflows, which helps to improve liquidity management.

Liquidity Management

Once the maximum practicable efficiencies have been achieved in cashflow management, the treasurer can turn to the management of liquidity.

The aim is to achieve the lowest possible funding cost on debits and the highest possible return on invested liquidity. A reliable cashflow forecast is crucial to enable the company's cash balances to be managed with a longer horizon than several days. The daily cashflows from the operational/commercial side of the firm will result in daily balances in different currencies within different current accounts in different jurisdictions/regions. The cash manager's challenge is to achieve the highest possible return on these balances. Combining the individual account balances results in several short or long positions in different currencies.

This can be achieved by automatic concentration structures supplied by banks, or by manual transfers, currency conversion or physical swaps. The cash manager invests these balances in different instruments depending on the profile of the balances. We have defined three different profiles:

- Daily fluctuating operational cash;
- Short-term cash, which is not required for between a few days and three months;
- Long-term cash, which is not required for three months or more. Daily fluctuating cash is traditionally invested in deposit accounts, but a high yield current account might provide a more convenient option in some situations. Short-term cash

can be invested for a longer period in weekly deposits or money market funds. Long-term cash can be invested in management funds or commercial paper or other structured products with a longer investment horizon.

The selection of investment instruments depends, on the one hand, on treasury policy. A treasurer might, for example, be authorised to invest in deposits with an AA rated bank but might not be allowed to invest in an triple A rated money market fund.

On the other hand, liquidity investment is a trade-off between risk, return and liquidity. In general terms, a firm can only achieve a higher return than the inter-bank rate if more risk is taken. If invested funds are required to be liquid, which is mostly the case for operational cash balances, longer term instruments are not an option and yield enhancement cannot be achieved.

THE FOUR BASIC CASH MANAGEMENT STRUCTURES

How much opportunity a treasurer has for achieving efficiencies depends on a company's existing cash management structure. We have identified four stages in a company's evolution from a much decentralised organisation to a centralised cash management organisation. Broadly speaking, the less centralised the cash management model, the greater the gains the company can achieve. If a company already has a highly centralised model then it is likely there are few further gains to be made.

Decentralised Liquidity and Cashflow Management

If the cash management function is fully decentralised, every individual entity or branch of sufficient size manages its own cash positions without taking other operating companies cash position into consideration. This contrasts with the more centralised approach, where the regional cash manager is striving for synergies and economies of scale across several countries.

Centralised Liquidity and Decentralised Cashflow Management

Under this model, liquidity is managed centrally. The centralised cash management function operates with or without delegation to a local financial representative. The central cash manager manages the pot of liquidity in one currency from one centralised position. He/she gathers information on cash positions from the banks and the cashflow forecasts of local operations.

This kind of structure is seen mostly in single currency environments, for example Europe and the United States. In multi-currency environments like Asia, or Central and Eastern Europe, the cash manager may manage liquidity from a central location but invest the funds locally due to legal and FX restrictions. This, additionally, follows the single currency centre concept, meaning the funds remain in the home country of the currency. Organisations with this type of arrangement can gain further efficiencies by centralising their cashflow management functions.

Decentralised Liquidity and Centralised Cashflow Management

Cashflow management is handled by a transaction centre, which has a single pipeline to the bank for settlement by way of the appropriate local clearing mechanism. Liquidity management is conducted on a local level without taking the liquidity positions of other countries into account. Theoretically, this type of structure is feasible in multi-currency environments – but it is unlikely to be used in the euro-zone. The aim of this model is to achieve a major reduction in transaction fees, while leaving liquidity management in the hands of the local operating companies.

A payment factory is an example of such a structure. Many companies with the objective of reducing internal and external transaction costs, but with structural long cash positions, prefer a payment factory. For these companies, centralising operational liquidity balances on a daily basis would not provide major financial gains.

Centralised Liquidity and Centralised Cashflow Management

Here all activities are centralised. The SSC acts on behalf of the local operating companies, and provides full administration of both liquidity and cashflow. The SSC maintains a single pipeline to a pan-European bank, and agrees to specific service levels with the individual operating companies. This is the most efficient structure for optimising interest. Also, by handling the local operating companies' transaction processing, it has a direct and beneficial impact on the company's working capital position.

It is clear that cash management has a vital role to play in reducing working capital requirements. Decentralised organisations have the most to gain, as they are able to achieve considerable efficiencies through the introduction of a more centralised approach – perhaps through an SSC. When it comes to reducing the working capital requirement in operational processes, it is vital that this is not attempted without regard to other costs. Less favourable treatment of trading partners can have knock-on costs in the form of lost discounts, or erosion of reputation.

Looking forward, those multinationals with the most efficient internal processes for managing capital will have an advantage over others. Of course, this cannot compensate for being in a stagnant industry, or having uncompetitive products, but other things being equal the most efficient users of capital will be looked on most favourably by the shareholders who provide that capital. At the margin, the reward for using capital efficiently will, logically, be a lower cost of equity capital. It will obviously be beneficial to be an early adopter of working capital management, rather than a late joiner, within your own industry. A cash-aware company will be better placed to safeguard future growth and profitability in a market with shrinking margins.

WORKING CAPITAL MANAGEMENT FOR MNCS

A multinational enterprise to survive and succeed in a fiercely competitive environment must manage its working capital prudently. Working capital management in an MNC requires managing its current assets and current liabilities in such a way as to reduce funds tied in working capital while simultaneously providing adequate funding and liquidity for the conduct of its global businesses so as to enhance value to the equity shareholders and so also to the firm. While the basics of managing working capital are, by and large, the same both in a domestic or multinational organization, risks and options involved in working capital management in MNCs are much greater than their domestic counterparts. Further, working capital management in a multinational firm focuses on inter subsidiary transfer of funds as well as transfers from the affiliates to the parent firm. Besides, there are specific approaches to manage cash, receivables and inventories in MNCs. All these aspects are dealt with in this unit in this unit.

IN DOMESTIC AND MULTINATIONAL ENTERPRISES

Although the fundamental principles governing the managing of working capital such as optimization and suitability are almost the same in both domestic and multinational enterprises, the two differ in respect of the following:

- MNCs, in managing their working capital, encounter with a number of risks peculiar to sourcing and investing of funds, such as the exchange rate risk and the political risk.
- Unlike domestic firms, MNCs have wider options of procuring funds for satisfying their requirements or the requirements of their subsidiaries such as financing of subsidiaries by the parent, borrowings from local sources including banks and funds from Eurocurrency markets, etc.
- MNCs enjoy greater latitude than the domestic firms in regard to their capability to move their funds between different subsidiaries, leading to fuller utilization of the resources.
- MNCs face a number of problems in managing working capital of their subsidiaries because they are

widely separated geographically and the management is not very well acquainted with the actual financial state of affairs of the affiliates and working of the local financial markets. As such, the task of decision making in the case of MNCs' subsidiaries is complex.

- Finance managers of MNCs face problems in taking financing decision because of different taxation systems and tax rates.

In sum, through MNCs have some advantages in terms of lattitude and options in financing, the problems of working capital management in MNCs are more complicated than those in domestic firms mainly because of additional risks in the form of the currency exposure and political risks as also due to differential tax codes and taxation rates.

Intra Corporate Transfer of Funds

Intra corporate transfer of funds comprises transfer of funds from affiliates/ subsidiaries to the parent company and also transfer of funds as among affiliates. Such transfers may be in the form of royalties, fees, payment for acquisition of inputs and equipments, interest on loans, repayment of loans, dividends and repatriation of the original investments.

Royalty is paid to the owner in return for the use of patents, technology or a trade name. It represents a payment usually by an affiliate to the parent for getting the right to use the company's name or special processes, usually under a licensing arrangement. Royalties are usually stated as percentage of sales revenue so that the owner is compensated in proportion to the volume of sales.

Fees are paid in lieu of professional services and expertise, usually provided by the parent to the affiliates. License fees are usually based on a percentage of the value of the product or on the volume of production. Host countries are generally found to object to the payment of fees for the services of visiting executives or maintenance personnel on the ground of higher scale of compensation. This problem is generally noticeable in the case of US MNCs who charge significantly higher compensation for their services as compared to other countries. This problem can be minimized if scale of fees is specifically stated in a formal agreement between the parent and the affiliate at the outset. Transfer of funds by way of dividend payments from the affiliates to the parent company is dependent upon host country's policy of dividend payment, and dividend transfer policy of the affiliates.

Remittance of dividends is a classical method by which firms transfer profits back to owners-individual shareholders and parent firms. Policy regarding dividend payment is basically influenced by tax factor, political risk, foreign exchange risk, liquidity factor and joint venture consideration. Dividend transfer policy of an affiliate is impacted by tax laws of host country. Most countries levy tax on retained earnings and distributed earnings at different rates. Parent countries generally levy a tax on foreign dividends received but allow tax credit for foreign taxes already paid on that income.

In case of political uncertainty, parent firm may require affiliates to remit the entire locally generated funds not needed to finance their expansion programmes. Pursuance of stable dividend payout policy by the affiliate may be a good idea. This will avoid the possibility of the company being perceived as using dividend payment for transferring funds to parent company.

MNCs may decide to speed up the transfer of funds through dividend if exchange rate risk is perceived: This perception is usually part of a larger strategy of funnelling funds from weak currency to strong currencies. However, decisions to accelerate dividend payments ahead of the event should take into consideration interest rate differences and the likely impact on host country relations. Speeding up or slowing down payments is termed as "Lead and Lags"

Liquidity position of the affiliate also influences the dividend transfer policy of the parent. A fast expanding affiliate may not have adequate cash to remit a dividend equal to its earnings because profits of such firms are often tied up in ever-increasing receivables and inventories. Conversely, affiliates having large amount of cash collected from past receivables may decide to pay higher dividend so as to transfer funds to the parent. Conflicts of interest of joint venture partners may also affect dividend transfer policy of an MNC parent. An MNC desirous to position funds internationally may not be liked by independent partners or local shareholders because the latter perceive their benefits from the success of the particular Joint Venture rather than from the global success of the MNC.

They may object to reduction of dividends on the fall of earnings or rise in dividend on the surge of earnings and prefer to go for stable dividend policy: This is why many MNCs prefer 100% ownership of affiliates so as to avoid possible conflicts of interests with outside shareholders. Intra-corporate transfer of funds has a number of constraints with which a finance manager of an MNC must be familiar.

The greatest problem in this respect is political in nature which may range from limits to transfer of certain types of funds to outright blockage of funds and inconvertibility of currency. Sometimes due to foreign exchange problems being faced by host country, foreign exchange controls are clamped resulting in barrier to transfer of funds. This also creates problem of servicing of loans. However, by taking loans from an international banking institution, the problem of loan service can be eased because the host country may not take penal action against such an arrangement for fear of damage to their international credit standing.

Problem generally arises in most of the developing countries in respect of remittance of dividends by the affiliates to their parent. This is for the fact that these host countries prefer retention of larger proportion of the affiliates' earnings and their investment within the country. Magnitude of the problem can, however, be reduced if dividend transfer policy is spelt out at the outset and communicated to the host country's authorities.

Transfer Pricing

Transfer prices are the prices set on Kea company exchange of goods and sales. The pricing of goods and services traded internally is one of the most critical issues and assumes still greater importance in respect of intra corporate exchange of goods and services as among affiliates and the parent firm because it provides an effective weapon in the hands of an MNC to maximize its value.

The most important uses of transfer pricing are:

- To minimize the total tax liability;
- To reduce tariffs and avoid quantitative and administrative restrictions on imports;
- To position funds in locations that will suit the management's working capital policies;
- To avoid exchange control;
- To maximize transfer of funds from affiliates to the firm;
- To window-dress operations so as to improve financial health of an affiliate and establish its high credibility in the financial markets.

Transfer pricing is a very difficult decision to make. Even purely domestic firms do not find it easy to reach agreements on the best method for setting prices on transactions between related tots. In case of an MNC, the decision is further compounded by exchange restrictions on the part of the host country where the receiving affiliate is located, a differential taxation system and different tax rates between the two countries, and import duties and quotas imposed by the host country.

Most countries have transfer pricing guidelines similar to those in the U.S.A. An MNC finance manager has to strike satisfactory trade off between conflicting considerations of fund positioning and income tax. A parent company in its effort to funnel funds out of a particular country will charge higher prices on goods sold to its affiliate to the extent the host country government permits. In contrast, if a foreign affiliate is to be financed, the reverse technique of charging lower prices can be used.

A higher transfer price facilitates accumulation of funds in the parent's country. Transfer pricing also permits transfer of funds as among sister affiliates. Multiple sourcing of component parts on a global basis allows switching between suppliers within the corporate family as a device to transfer funds. Income tax consideration is an important factor which an MNC has to reckon with while setting a transfer price.

It is through transfer pricing mechanism that an MNC finance manager can maximize their worldwide corporate profits by setting transfer prices to minimize taxable income in a country with a high tax rate and maximize income in a country with a low income tax rate. A parent desiring to reduce the taxable profits of a subsidiary in a high tax country will set transfer price at a higher rate to increase the costs of the subsidiary, thereby reducing taxable income.

METHODS OF DETERMINING TRANSFER PRICES

The Organization for Economic Cooperation and Development (OECD) Committee has recommended three methods:

- Comparable Uncontrolled Price Method,
- Resale Price Method,
- Cost-Pitts Method for use by member countries. U.S. Internal Revenue code in its attempt to circumscribe freedom to set transfer prices has also provided for setting transfer price by these methods.

Comparable Uncontrolled Price Method

This method of setting transfer price is based on market forces and hence considered as the best evidence of aim's length pricing. However, there are practical problems involved in using this International Investment method because of differences in quality, quantity, timing of sales and proprietary trade marks

Resale Price Method

In the resale price method, considered as a second-best approach to arm's length pricing, first of all final selling price to an independent buyer is set and then an appropriate markup for the distribution subsidiary is subtracted. This markup represents the subsidiary's costs and profits. The price so set is then employed as the intra-company transfer price for similar items. However, it is not easy to determine an appropriate markup, particularly when the distribution affiliate adds value to the item through subsequent processing or packaging or both.

Cost-Plus Method

The transfer price under cost-plus method is determined by adding suitable profit markup to the seller's full cost comprising direct cost and overhead cost. Allocation of overhead cost in computing full cost poses problem and involves subjectivity, especially when joint products are involved. As such, this method provides enough scope for negotiation.

Re- Invoicing Centres

A re-invoicing centre is a separate corporate subsidiary that acts like a middle man between the parent and related unit in one location and all foreign subsidiaries in a geographic region. The re-invoicing centre takes title to all goods sold by one corporate unit to another affiliate or to a third-party customer, but the physical movement of goods is direct from the manufacturing plant to the purchaser.

The centre pays the seller and, in turn, is paid by the purchasing unit. The principal objective of these re-invoicing centres is to funnel the profits arising from these transactions to lower tax affiliates and away from the higher-taxed parent or affiliate. The U.S. tax system is a larger part of the reason that U.S. MNCs tend to conduct their currency risk management offshore.

These centres also often manage the MNC's currency risk exposures. Re-invoicing centre personnel can develop a specialized expertise in choosing which hedging technique is best at any moment, and they are likely to obtain more competitive foreign exchange quotations from banks because they are dealing in larger transactions. By guaranteeing the exchange rate for future order, the re-invoicing centre can set firm local currency cost in advance, enabling the distribution subsidiaries to make firm bids to unrelated final customers, and to protect against the exposure created by a backlog of unfilled orders. Finally, the re-invoicing centre can manage intra-subsidiary cash flows, including leads and lags of payments.

With a re-invoicing centre, all subsidiaries settle intra-company accounts in their local currencies. The centre needs only hedge residual foreign exchange rate changes. However, setting and operating re-invoicing centre involves cost. As such, benefit-cost analysis should be made while deciding about establishment of a re-invoicing centre.

At times, an MNC faces problem of repatriation restriction by host country government which places embargo on transfer of the earnings of the overseas subsidiary. Thus, funds which are not allowed to be repatriated permanently or temporarily are called "blocked funds". These funds represent cash flows generated by a foreign project that cannot be repatriated to the parent firm because of capital flow restrictions by the host government. There are various reasons for the host government for blocking the repatriable funds. One such reason is the grim foreign exchange crisis engulfing the host country.

In 18 Decisions and Working Capital Management such cases, the government may block repatriable Ends of overseas subsidiaries and limits foreign exchange to financing essential imports on other payments. Sometimes political factor is responsible for the blocking of funds repatriable by the foreign entities. Frequently, this occurs with change in national government which, out of political animosity, overturns the government's policies and places restrictions on the movement of the funds of the overseas units.

A firm may also face the ire of blockage of repatriable profits earned by its offshore subsidiary if it has been found flouting local laws and regulations and/or operating to the detriment of local interests. Blocking of funds can take several forms ranging from non-convertibility of the host currency to prior permission for repatriation of earnings. In between the two, blockage of funds may involve repatriation of only a portion of the funds, repatriation only after a certain time lag, a combination of restrictions on the proportion of funds to be repatriated and the time constraints and absolute ceilings on the total of funds that can be repatriated over a certain period of time. Prudent management of financial resources of multinational firms calls for effective utilization of funds blocked across the home turf A parent firm can make use of certain strategic arrangements for using these funds properly.

For example, the subsidiary may he directed by the MNC to set up a research and development division which incurs costs and possibly generates revenues for other subsidiaries. The parent firm may pursue strategy of transfer pricing in a manner that will increase the expenses incurred by the affiliate.

A host country government is likely to be more lenient on money being used to meet local expenses than on earnings remitted to the parent. Another strategic move could be the directive to the affiliate by the parent to borrow from a local bank rather than from the former and repay the interest and the principal out of as local earnings.

Charging fees and royalties at higher rate, leads and lags in making payments abroad and payment of dividends at higher rate to local stockholders, can he other direct measure which an MNC can take to repatriate blocked funds. The MNC can also instruct its affiliate to reinvest the blocked funds in the host country in a manner that avoids deterioration in their real value because of inflation or exchange depreciation. Tactics for transferring funds indirectly include:

- Parallel or back-to back loans
- Purchase of commodities for transfer abroad '
- Purchase of capital goods for corporate wide use
- Purchase of local services for worldwide use
- Hosting corporate conventions, vacations and so on

Two more methods which have been gaining popularity in recent years are increasing the value of the local investment base because the level of profit remittance often depends on the amount of a company's capital. One way to enhance an affiliate's capital is to buy used equipment at artificially inflated value. The other way is for an affiliate to acquire a bankrupt firm at a large discount from book value. The acquisition is then merged with the affiliate on the basis of the failed firm's original book value, thereby raising the affiliate's equity base.

MULTINATIONAL CASH MANAGEMENT

The basic principle to guide the management of cash balance holdings in international working capital management is, broadly, similar to the one applicable to domestic International Investment situation. That is, after carefully covering all the contingencies under contemplation, besides, regular requirements, the ideal cash balance holding should be zero (0).

However, such an ideal situation rarely exists even in case of domestic enterprise; in spite of massive application of computers and operations research techniques. This is as a result of problems in human perception which continue to hunt modern managers in their role as financial planners. That is, even the most perfect system of planning has some lacuna to warrant the retention of residual cash reserve.

Problem of Managing Cash in MNCs

Cash Management in an MNC is primarily aimed at minimizing the overall cash requirements of the firm as a whole without adversely affecting the smooth functioning of the company and each affiliate, minimizing the currency exposure risk, minimizing political risk, minimizing the transaction costs and taking full advantage of the economies of scale and also to avail of the benefit of superior knowledge of market forces. However, these objectives are in conflict with each other leading to increased complexity of the cash management. For instance, minimization of the political risk involves conversion of all receipts in foreign currencies in the currency of the home country.

This may, however, go against the interest of the affiliates who need minimum working capital to be kept in the local currencies to meet their operational requirements. Further, minimization of transaction costs involved in currency conversions calls for holding cash balances in the currency in which they are received. In another respect too, primary objectives are antagonistic to each other. A subsidiary, for example, may need to carry minimum cash balances in anticipation of future payments due to the time required to channelize funds to such a country.

Holding of such balances in excess of immediate requirements may ostensibly impringe on the objective to benefit from economies of scale in earning the highest possible rate of return from investing these resources. Another major problem which an MNC faces in managing cash is with respect to estimation of cash flows emanating out of operations of its affiliates.

This problem arises because of foreign exchange fluctuations. Similar problem arises in estimating cash inflows stemming out of future sales because actual volume of sales to overseas buyers depends on foreign exchange fluctuations. The sales volume of exports is also susceptible to business cycles of the importing countries.

Uncertainty arises with regard to cash collections from receivables because it is the quality of credit standards that will decide the value of goods sold to be received back in cash. Loose credit standards may cause a slow down in cash inflows from sales which could offset the benefits of augmented sales. In view of the problems leading to increased uncertainty in estimating cash flows, the management may be constrained to carry larger amount of cash balances so as to protect the firm against any crisis.

Cash management in an MNC is further complicated by the absence of effective tools to expedite transfers and by the great variations in the practices of financial institutions. As such, an international finance manager must exercise great prudence in forecasting cash flows of the affiliates.

Cash Flow Analysis: Subsidiary Perspective

Prudent working capital management of an MNC is dependent, inter alia, upon liquidity management of its affiliates. This, therefore, calls for estimating cash outflows and inflows periodically to ascertain excess or deficient cash for a period of time. 20 Decisions and Working Capital Management As noted earlier, cash outflow by the subsidiary occurs when the latter buys raw materials. Cash is also needed to meet the costs incurred in manufacturing goods. Cash inflow to the subsidiary takes place when sales proceeds are received in cash and receivables for the goods sold on credit are collected after sometime.

Cash outflow by subsidiary also comprises dividend payments and other fees to be made periodically to the parent. The level of dividends paid by subsidiaries to the parent is dependent on liquidity needs, potential uses of funds at various subsidiary locations, expected movements in the currencies of subsidiaries, and host-country government regulations.

Once estimates of cash outflows and inflows are made, the subsidiary will be in a position to know there is cash surplus or deficit for a particular period. If cash deficiency is expected, short-term financing is necessary. In case of excess cash, it must decide how the surplus cash will be used. A firm, it must be noted, may maintain liquidity without substantial cash balances.

CENTRALIZED CASH MANAGEMENT

So as to maintain adequate liquidity without jeopardizing profitability, an MNC and its subsidiaries carry minimum amount of cash balances to meet transactional and precautionary demands. While each subsidiary manages its working capital and reaches its own decision as to the appropriate level. In most of the cases the affiliates are better equipped to make a decision as to what constitutes adequate balance in view of their intimate knowledge of their circumstances.

However, there is a strong need to monitor and manage the cash flows between the parent and the subsidiaries and also between the individual subsidiaries. This task of international cash management should, therefore, be delegated to a centralized cash management group. Centralization, in this context, does not necessarily entail the pooling of overall liquid resources, although some degree of pooling would take place, but rather the centralization of reports, information and most importantly, the decision-making process as to cash mobilization, movement and investment outlets. An effectively designed and managed centralized system has the major advantage of holding of overall cash balances to the minimum, enabling the MNC to make fuller utilization of the idle cash and maximize earnings without risking liquidity throughout the system.

Besides, the centralized system permits the centre to make full utilization of a multilateral netting system, both inter-affiliate and between the MNC and other corporations so as to minimize transaction costs and currency exposure and enables the centre to employ optimally the various hedging strategies available to the firm so as to ensure enforcement of the MNC's foreign exchange exposure policies.

With centralized system of cash management, an MNC can take maximum advantage of the transfer pricing mechanism within the legal and administrative mechanism and thereby improve the profitability of the corporation. It may not be always possible for the centralized cash management division of an MNC to accurately forecast events that affect parent subsidiary or inter subsidiary cash flows.

It should, however, be adequately equipped to respond quickly to any event by considering any potential adverse impact on cash flows and take measures to avoid such an adverse impact. It should have sources of funds available to meet the cash needs and it must have suitable strategies to deploy the excess funds in the system.

TECHNIQUES TO OPTIMIZE CASH FLOWS

Cash flows can be optimized through:

- Accelerating cash inflows
- Minimizing currency conversion costs
- Managing inter-subsidiary cash transfers

Accelerating Cash Inflows

Cash inflows can be prompted through quick deposit of

customer's cheques, establishing collection centres, lock-box method and other devices.

Minimizing Currency Conversion Costs

Cash flow can also be optimized through Netting. Netting involves offsetting receivables against payables of the various entities so that only the net amounts are eventually transferred among affiliates. An MNC can also utilize multilateral netting with outside firms and agencies. This technique optimizes cash flow by reducing the administrative and transaction costs arising out of currency conversion.

It also reduces unnecessary float, funds that are in the process of being transferred among affiliates instead of being invested by the centre. The process of netting forces tight control over information on transaction between subsidiaries leading to greater coordination among all subsidiaries to accurately report and settle their various accounts.

Netting also makes cash flows forecasting easier since only net cash transfers are made at the end of each period, rather than individual cash transfers throughout the period. There are two kinds of netting. A bilateral netting system involves transactions between two units: between the parent and a subsidiary or between two subsidiaries.

A multilateral netting system usually involves a more complex interchange among the parent and several subsidiaries. Multilateral netting system is most useful to MNCs in reducing administrative and currency conversion costs. Such a system is highly centralized so that all necessary information is consolidated. With the help of the consolidated cash flow information net cash positions for each pair of units can be determined and the actual reconciliation at the end of each period can be done.

Managing Inter-Subsidiary Cash Transfers

Through techniques of leading and lagging, cash flows can be managed to the advantage of a subsidiary, If A purchases supplies from B and pays for its supplies earlier than necessary. This technique is called leading. Alternatively, if B sells supplies to A, it could provide financing by allowing A to lag its payments. The leading or lagging strategy can help in improving efficiency of cash utilization and thereby reducing debt. Some host governments prohibit this practice by requiring that a payment between subsidiaries occurs at the time at which goods are transferred. MNC management must, therefore, be aware of existence of such prohibitory laws.

Complications in Optimization of Cash Flow

The process of optimalization of cash flows in an MNC is complicated because of unique features of the company, government restrictions and characteristics of banking system. Optimisation of cash flow can be impeded because of the specific situations existing among subsidiaries of an MNC. For example, if one of the subsidiaries delays payments to other subsidiaries, the latter may have no option but to borrow until the payments are received. This problem can be overcome by the centralized approach that monitors all inter-subsidiary payments. Cash flow optimisation policy is also disrupted by government restrictions. For example, some governments ban the use of a netting system. In addition, some governments prohibit transfer of cash from the country, thereby, preventing net payments from being made.

Problem in efficient utilization of cash also arises due to insufficient banking services in a country. Banks in the USA, for example, are advanced in cash transfers but other countries' banks do not offer such services to MNCs. More often than not, MNCs want some form of zero-balance account system which allows the customer to use excess cash funds to make payments but earn interest until they are used. This kind of facility is not available in most countries. Some countries may lack in lock box facility. In many developing countries MNCs do not even get updated detailed position of their account. As a result, the management may find it too difficult to utilize the cash resources efficiently.

Investing Excess Cash

Investing surplus cash in liquid assets such as Euro currency deposits, foreign treasury bills and commercial paper, etc is one of the key functions of international finance manager. While making decision in this regard, many crucial issues merit thorough consideration. Some of these issues are:

- Should the excess cash of all subsidiaries be pooled together or remain separated?
- How can the effective yield expected from each possible alternative be determined?
- What does interest rate parity suggest about short-term financing?
- Will it be useful to diversify investment among currencies?
- These issues are discussed in the following paragraphs.

Separate or Centralized Approach

While handling the issue regarding deployment of surplus cash, an MNC has to decide if individual subsidiaries will make separate investments on their own or a centralized approach will be followed to pool the excess cash from each subsidiary which will then be converted into a single currency for investment purposes.

However, the advantage of pooling may be offset by the transaction costs involved in conversion in a single currency. Even then also centralized cash management could be useful. Alternatively, the short-term cash available in each currency could be pooled together so that there would be a separate pool for each currency.

The excess cash of subsidiaries in a particular can still be used to satisfy other subsidiary having deficiency in that currency. This strategy will save transaction costs of the MNC. If an MNC is left with excess cash and expects future cash outflows in foreign currencies which are to gain in value it may decide to cover such positions by making short-term deposits in those currencies, dovetailing the maturity of a deposit to the date of payment.

The remaining cash, if any, may be invested in domestic or foreign short-term securities keeping in view potential yield of the securities and possible exchange rate movements.

Determining the Effective Yield

For an international finance manager it is effective yield, not the interest rate, which is important because the effective yield considers both the interest rate and the rate of appreciation (or depreciation) of the currency denominating the deposit and can, therefore, be very different from the quoted interest rate on a deposit denominated in a foreign currency.

Suppose that an MNC X of the US has surplus cash of $2,000,000. It can invest it a one-year domestic bank deposit @ 6 per cent. The company finds that one-year deposit in Australian bank would fetch 9 per cent. The exchange rate of the Australian dollar at the time of investment is $0.68. Due to higher interest rate X decided to invest in Australia. The U.S. dollars are, therefore, converted to Aus $2,941,176 and then deposited in a bank.

After one year, X receives Aus $3,205,882 (equivalent to initial deposit plus 9percent interest on the deposit). X then converts it into U.S. dollars. Assume that the exchange rate at this time is $72. The effective yield could be negative if the currency denominating the deposit depreciates to an extent that more than offsets the higher interest accrued from the deposit.

Implications of Interest Rate Parity

Generally, it is believed that a foreign currency with a high interest rate would be an ideal short-term investment outlet for covered interest arbitrage. However, such a currency will normally exhibit a forward discount that reflects the differential between its interest rate and the investor's home interest rate.

This relationship is based on the theory of interest rate parity. Investors will not lock in higher return when attempting covered interest arbitrage if interest rate parity exists. Short-term investment may be feasible if interest rate parity exists but this has to be on an uncovered basis. In other words, short-term foreign investing may be more profitable than domestic investing but it cannot be guaranteed.

Diversifying Cash Across Currencies

In order to avoid the possibility of incurring substantial losses arising out of depreciation of a foreign currency, an MNC prefers to diversify its investible funds among various foreign currencies. To what extent a portfolio of investments denominated in various currencies will reduce risk would depend on the currency correlations. Ideally, the currencies represented within the portfolio will show low or negative correlations with each other. When currencies are likely to be affected by the same underlying event, their movements tend to be highly correlated, and diversification among these types of currencies does not substantially minimize exchange rate risk. 24 Decisions and Working Capital Management

MULTINATIONAL

Basic considerations influencing credit and collection policies of MNCs are the same as those of domestic firms. However, certain additional variables such as currency fluctuations, exchange restrictions, differential inflation rates, etc have also to be reckoned with by an MNC while managing receivables. In an MNC, receivables arise for a short period when goods are sold on cash against documents or sight draft and are in transit or for the time which lapses between the drawing of the draft and its payment by the importing firm or banker.

Receivables mainly arise when goods are shipped on open account, consignment shipments and shipments of goods and services between parent and affiliates, as well as among the latter. Besides, local sales on credit by subsidiary units give rise to receivables for the selling units, as well as for the MNC as a whole. While deciding about sales on credit to a particular firm, an MNC has to compare incremental benefits with incremental costs, as in the case of a domestic firm. In addition, an additional factor, viz., foreign exchange loss on sales on credit made by one of its subsidiaries has to be reckoned with. Another issue related to receivables management in an international firm relates to factoring of receivables. Decision on factoring should take into account its benefits and costs.

For example, factoring permits the exporter to quote more competitive terms or to ship goods on open account rather than insisting on cash terms or shipment against letter of credit. It relieves the exporting firm from the costs of credit investigation, assessing the political risk and collection.

The factoring agency is better equipped to assess these risks and can manage credit analysis and collection more efficiently and at lower costs. It is advisable to small firms who cannot afford the cost of credit investigation and risk evaluation to factor their receivables. Firms having occasional export sales to a few geographically dispersed countries can also hire the services of factoring agency. However, international factoring is still an expensive process. Factoring fees differ depending on the size, quality, and the annual turnover of the underlying receivables.

MULTINATIONAL INVENTORY MANAGEMENT

Fundamental decision rules determining the optimal level of stock of raw materials and components, work-in-process and finished goods are the same for both MNCs and domestic firms. Even the techniques employed to determine the level of required safety stocks are also the same in both the cases. However, MNCs have to face certain additional problems in managing inventories which a domestic firm does not experience.

These problems are the diverse inventories maintained in several widely separated locations, frequently changing import controls and tariffs, and supply disruptions due to strikes and political turmoil. Currency fluctuation risk complicates the task of inventory management in an international firm. The magnitude of safety stock, which is the function of an optimum solution equalizing stockout costs and the cost of carrying the safety stock, has to be revised upward in case of an MNC due to the higher frequency of estimated stockouts.

Likewise, lead time in case of an MNC has to be longer to guard against a. higher probability of unexpected delays in transit or delays in clearance from customs. At times, MNCs are constrained to source their raw materials and components on a worldwide basis. They may even decide to stockpile certain materials when their supplies are likely to be disrupted due to expected strikes, political crisis or other destabilizing factors.

In the same way, an affiliate may engage in anticipatory purchases of imports and components to guard against transfers or likely depreciation of domestic currency. However, the policy of stockpiling should keep in view the following variables:

- Expected rate of depreciation of the local currency against the parent currency
- Expected rise in the price of imported parts and components in terms of the suppliers′ currencies
- Holding cost of inventories
- Opportunity cost of local lands

4

Forecasting Cash Flows

CASH FLOW

A revenue or expense stream that changes a cash account over a given period. Cash inflows usually arise from one of three activities - financing, operations or investing - although this also occurs as a result of donations or gifts in the case of personal finance. Cash outflows result from expenses or investments. This holds true for both business and personal finance. An accounting statement called the "statement of cash flows", which shows the amount of cash generated and used by a company in a given period. It is calculated by adding noncash charges to net income after taxes. Cash flow can be attributed to a specific project, or to a business as a whole. Cash flow can be used as an indication of a company's financial strength.

In business as in personal finance, cash flows are essential to solvency. They can be presented as a record of something that has happened in the past, such as the sale of a particular product, or forecasted into the future, representing what a business or a person expects to take in and to spend. Cash flow is crucial to an entity's survival.

Having ample cash on hand will ensure that creditors, employees and others can be paid on time. If a business or person does not have enough cash to support its operations, it is said to be insolvent, and a likely candidate for bankruptcy should the insolvency continue. The statement of a business's cash flows is often used by analysts to gauge financial performance. Companies with ample cash on hand are able to invest the cash back into the business in order to generate more cash and profit. Cash flow is a term that refers to the amount of cash being received and spent by a business during a defined period of time, sometimes tied to a specific project. Measurement of cash flow can be used

- To evaluate the state or performance of a business or project.
- To determine problems with liquidity. Being profitable does not necessarily mean being liquid. A company can fail because of a shortage of cash, even while profitable.
- To generate project rate of returns. The time of cash flows into and out of projects are used as inputs to financial models such as internal rate of return, and net present value.
- To examine income or growth of a business when it is believed that accrual accounting concepts do not represent economic realities. Alternately, cash flow can be used to 'validate' the net income generated by accrual accounting.

Cash flow as a generic term may be used differently depending on context, and certain cash flow definitions may be adapted by analysts and users for their own uses. Common terms include operating cash flow and free cash flow.

CLASSIFICATION

Cash flows can be classified into:

- Operational cash flows: Cash received or expended as a result of the company's core business activities.
- Investment cash flows: Cash received or expended through capital expenditure, investments or acquisitions.
- Financing cash flows: Cash received or expended as a result of financial activities, such as receiving or paying loans, issuing or repurchasing stock, and paying dividends.

All three together are necessary to reconcile the beginning cash balance to the ending cash balance.

Benefits from Using Cash Flow

The cash flow statement is one of the four main financial statements of a company. The cash flow statement can be examined to determine the short-term sustainability of a company. If cash is increasing, then a company will often be deemed to be healthy in the short-term.

Increasing or stable cash balances suggest that a company is able to meet its cash needs, and remain solvent. This information cannot always be seen in the income statement or the balance sheet of a company. For instance, a company may be generating profit, but still have difficulty in remaining solvent.

The cash flow statement breaks the sources of cash generation into three parts: operational cash flows, investing, and financing. This breakdown allows the user of financial statements to determine where the company is deriving its cash for operations. For example, a company may be notionally profitable but generating little operational cash.

In such a case, the company may be deriving additional operating cash by issuing shares, or raising additional debt finance. Companies that have announced significant write downs of assets, particularly goodwill, may have substantially higher cash flows than the announced earnings would indicate. For example, telecoms firms that paid substantial sums for 3G licenses or for acquisitions have subsequently had to write-off goodwill, that is, indicate that these investments were now worth much less.

These write-downs have frequently resulted in large announced annual losses, such as Vodafone's announcement in May 2006 that it had lost £21.9 billion due to a writedown of its German acquisition, Mannesmann, one of the largest annual losses in European history. Despite this large "loss", which represented a sunk cost, Vodafone's operating cash flows were solid: "Strong cash flow is one of the most attractive aspects of the cellphone business, allowing operators like Vodafone to return money to shareholders even as they rack up huge paper losses." In certain cases, cash flow statements may allow careful analysts to detect problems that would not be evident from the other financial statements alone. For example, WorldCom committed an accounting fraud that was discovered in 2002; the fraud consisted primarily of treating ongoing expenses as capital investments, thereby fraudulently boosting net income. Use of one measure of cash flow.

OPERATING CASH FLOW

When analysts and the media refer to 'cash flow', they are most likely referring to "Operating Cash Flow". This is only one of the three types of cash flows. There are inherent problems in isolating only this type of flow, because businesses can easily manipulate the classification.

Common methods of distorting the results include:

- *Sales:* Sell the receivables to a factor for instant cash.
- *Inventory:* Don't pay your suppliers for an additional few weeks at period end.
- *Sales Commissions:* Management can form a separate company performance as its agent. The book of business can then be purchased quarterly as an investment.
- *Wages:* Remunerate with stock options.
- *Maintenance:* Contract with the predecessor company that you prepay five years worth for them to continue doing the work
- *Equipment Leases:* Buy it
- *Rent:* Buy the property.
- *Oil Exploration costs:* Replace reserves by buying another company's.
- Research and Development - Wait for the product to be proven by a start-up lab; then buy the lab.
- Consulting Fees - Pay in shares from treasury since usually to related parties
- Interest - Issue convertible debt where the conversion rate changes with the unpaid interest.
- Taxes - Buy shelf companies with Tax Loss Carry Forward's. Or gussy up the purchase by buying a lab or O&G explore co. with the same TLCF.

Example of a positive £40 cash flow

Transaction	In (Debit)	Out (Credit)
Incoming Loan	+£50.00	
Sales (which were paid for in cash)	+£30.00	
Materials		-£10.00
Labour		-£10.00
Purchased Capital		-£10.00
Loan Repayment		-£5.00
Taxes		-£5.00
Total	+£40.00	

In this example the following types of flows are included:

- *Incoming loan:* financial flow
- *Sales:* operational flow
- *Materials:* operational flow
- *Labour:* operational flow
- *Purchased Capital:* Investment flow
- *Loan Repayment:* financial flow
- *Taxes:* financial flow

Let us, for example, compare two companies using only total cash flow and then separate cash flow streams. The last three years show the following total cash flows:

Company A:
Year 1: cash flow of +10M
Year 2: cash flow of +11M
Year 3: cash flow of +12M

Company B:
Year 1: cash flow of +15M
Year 2: cash flow of +16M
Year 3: cash flow of +17M

Company B has a higher yearly cash flow and looks like a better one in which to invest. Now let us see how their cash flows are made up:

Company A:
Year 1: OC: +20M FC: +5M IC: -15M = +10M
Year 2: OC: +21M FC: +5M IC: -15M = +11M
Year 3: OC: +22M FC: +5M IC: -15M = +12M

Company B:
Year 1: OC: +10M FC: +5M IC: 0 = +15M
Year 2: OC: +11M FC: +5M IC: 0 = +16M
Year 3: OC: +12M FC: +5M IC: 0 = +17M

- OC = Operational Cash, FC = Financial Cash, IC = Investment Cash

Now it seems that Company A is actually earning more cash by its core activities and has already spent 45M in long term investments, of which the revenues will only show up after three years. When comparing investments using cash flows always make sure to use the same cash flow layout.

CASH FLOW FORECASTING

FORECASTING THE VIABILITY OF A FINANCIAL DECISION

Cash Flow forecasts help you to build a model of the way in which cash moves within a project or organisation. They help you to predict whether the sales or income you forecast will cover the costs of operation.

They also allow you to analyse whether a project will be sufficiently profitable to justify the effort put into it. Cash flow forecasts can also be useful for analysing your own personal finances. This is useful when you are about to make difficult financial decisions.

By carrying out a Cash Flow forecast on a spreadsheet package you can investigate the impact of changing factors within the forecast. If you have structured the spreadsheet correctly then you will be able to see, more or less instantly, the effect that changes will have.

Normally we structure Cash Flow Forecasts in a standard way. Other sorts of forecasting can be carried out with spreadsheets. A good way of structuring these is to firstly analyse the system being forecasted with a system diagram.

This system diagram will show the relationships between factors. You can then quantify these relationships, and build a model based on them. The structure of the model will depend on the system being modelled.

How to Use the Tool

Set Up Column Headings:

Decide the period of time over which you want to run your forecast, and the length of the periods within it. Typically the forecast will run over 1-2 years, with the periods as months. Head up one column with the title 'Cash Movement'. Then enter the periods of the forecast as the next column headings. This will give you column headings of, for example, Cash Movement, January, February, March, April.... etc.

Set Up Row Titles:

We organise rows into three main groups:

- *Income:* These rows show income expected during the period. Set up a separate row for each source of income. Examples might be:
  - Sales of ABC product
  - Sales of BCD service
  - Investment income, etc.

Where costs of operation are directly dependent on the amount sold, you may decide to deduct the direct cost of the sales made within this group of rows. Put in a subtotal at the bottom of the group.

- *Outgoings:* These rows show all of your costs, itemised by the type of cost. Examples might be:
  - Staff salaries
  - Payroll taxes
  - Stationery
  - Telephones
  - Etc.

Set up a subtotal at the bottom of this group.

- *Totals:* The next row shows the total of the income rows minus the total of the out-going rows for the month. This shows you your profit or loss for the month. Underneath this, put in a running total. In this row add your profit or loss for the period to the running total. This shows your financial position at the end of the period.

- *Estimate values:* By now you should have a table marked out with column headings and row titles. Now fill in the values of the cells on your table. An easy way of doing this is to fill in the first column, and then use the spreadsheet 'Fill... Right' function to copy values across. Then adjust values in the other columns appropriately.

When you are entering projections for sales for a new business, bear in mind you will not sell much until your customers have seen mention of your business several times. Your estimates for sales will be much more reliable if you base them either on previous years' revenues, on trial marketing, or on good quality market research. When you are entering values for costs, try, where possible, to base projections on costs from previous years. If this is not possible, base your estimates on real prices quoted. This keeps your estimates as realistic as possible.

- *Calculate:* On most modern spreadsheet packages this will happen automatically, providing you have set up totals correctly as described in part. As you enter and change the values of cells within the spreadsheet, you should see that the period totals and running totals change appropriately

Cash Flow Forecasting is a relatively simple technique for checking the viability of a project. Cost/Benefit Analysis is another. These are good techniques for decisions involving relatively small amounts of money. Where large sums are involved, project evaluation can become a complex and sophisticated art, which uses more formal techniques. The fundamentals of this are explained in Principles of Corporate Finance by Richard Brealey and Stewart Myers - this is something of an authority on the subject. The book is reviewed at the top of our right hand side bar.

Example: A motor home enthusiast has decided that he wants to set up a motor home hire company. He has researched the costs of set up, and estimated the number of weeks of hire he can sell during the year. Note that he has been quite optimistic in hoping to sell all the weeks of holiday available during the high season of July and August. He will charge the same price as his competitors for a holiday.

He works out the cash flow forecast: The enthusiast is very worried – although the business plan he wants to set up will return a small profit of just under $10,000 at the end of the year, he will be nearly $18,000 in the red at the end of March. Unless he has this amount of spare cash of his own and is prepared to tie it up in the venture, or he is willing to arrange a loan or overdraft facility, his proposed business model is not viable. He may just have saved a lot of time, money and stress by using a Cash Flow Forecast.

Cash Flow Forecasts are important tools for investigating whether a project or business is viable. They allow you to experiment with changing factors, to see the impact that this will have. Spreadsheet packages are invaluable for cash flow forecasting. We set up Cash Flow Forecasts in the following stages:

- Setting out column headings for periods during the forecast.
- Setting out three main groups of rows:
  - Income rows, with a subtotal
  - Expenditure rows, with a subtotal
  - Period total and running total rows
- Entering values within cells: Ideally you should do this from real data, or from formal market research information. If this is not possible, then you will have to use the best estimates you can make.
- Calculation

IMPORTANCE OF CASH FLOW

When planning the short or long-term funding requirements of a business, it is more important to forecast the likely cash requirements than to project profitability etc. Whilst profit, the difference between sales and costs within a specified period, is a vital indicator of the performance of a business, the generation of a profit does not necessarily guarantee its development, or even the survival. Bear in mind that more businesses fail for lack of cash flow than for want of profit.

Cash Flow vs Profit

Sales and costs and, therefore, profits do not necessarily coincide with their associated cash inflows and outflows. While, a sale may have been secured and goods delivered, the related payment may be deferred as a result of giving credit to the customer. At the same time, payments must be made to suppliers, staff etc., cash must be invested in rebuilding depleted stocks, new equipment may have to be purchased etc. The net result is that cash receipts often lag cash payments and, whilst profits may be reported, the business may experience a short-term cash shortfall. For this reason it is essential to forecast cash flows as well as project likely profits.

Calculating Cash Flow

Normally, the main sources of cash inflows to a business are receipts from sales, increases in bank loans, proceeds of share issues and asset disposals, and other income such as interest earned. Cash outflows include payments to suppliers and staff, capital and interest repayments for loans, dividends, taxation and capital expenditure. Net cash flow is the difference between the inflows and outflows within a given period. A projected cumulative positive net cash flow over several periods highlights the capacity of a business to generate surplus cash and, conversely, a cumulative negative cash flow indicates the amount of additional cash required to sustain the business. Cash flow planning entails forecasting and tabulating all significant cash inflows relating to sales, new loans, interest received etc. and then analysing in detail the timing of expected payments relating to suppliers, wages, other expenses, capital expenditure, loan repayments, dividends, tax, interest payments etc. The difference between the cash in- and out-flows within a given period indicates the net cash flow.

When this net cash flow is added to or subtracted from opening bank balances, any likely short-term bank funding requirements can be ascertained. If you need to produce regularly-updated cash flow projections, have a look at Cash flow Plan, our range of fully-integrated cash flow planners which generate projections for 12 months ahead and incorporate a roll-forward facility to simplify updating of projections. Details and free/trial version downloads.

Using a Computer to Forecast Cash Flow

With the aid of a computer and suitable software, a mathematical model can be used to prepare cash flow projections and project short-term banking requirements for a business. The use of a computer-based model reduces the tedium of carrying out numerous repetitive calculations and simplifies the alteration of assumptions and the presentation of results. A computer-based model can be constructed using a spreadsheet or acquired as a stand-alone package.

If constructing a spreadsheet model, be aware that it is not as easy as it might seem to build a friendly, robust and error-free planner. Invest-Tech's Exl-Plan can be used to compile 3-5 year cash flow projections by month for the first year, by quarter for the next two years and annually for the final two years. Also, have a look at Cashflow Plan, our range of fully-integrated cashflow planners which generate projections for 12 months ahead and incorporate a roll-forward facility to simplify updating of projections.

A cash flow model can be used to compile forecasts, assess possible funding requirements and explore the likely financial consequences of alternative strategies. Used effectively, a model can help prevent major planning errors, anticipate problems, and identify opportunities to improve cash flow or provide a basis for negotiating short-term funding from a bank. Generally, when seeking external funding, the time horizon covered by a set of projections should be equal to or greater than the period for which the funding is needed.

The greater the amount of funding required and the longer the period of exposure for the provider of these funds, the more comprehensive must be the supporting projections and plan. Typically, a computer model for short-term bank planning uses assumptions on sales, costs, credit, funding etc. to produce monthly cash flow projections for up to a year ahead. The initial assumptions can be readily altered to evaluate alternative scenarios.

For example, a model could be used to explore the extent to which future sales could be increased whilst holding bank borrowings within predetermined limits; to assess the effects on cash flow of varying sales, costs or credit terms; or to determine the likely short-term funding requirements for a business. Once assumptions on sales, expense payments etc. have been established, a model can be used to produce the cash flow projections which, in turn, indicate the likely future cash balances or banking requirements. However, the quality of these projections will be completely determined by the standard and reliability of the underlying assumptions. For example, if forecasts for sales, working capital or costs are unrealistic or inadequately researched, then the value of the model's output is greatly diminished. An impressive set of projections is of little benefit if it is unsupported by experience or research or based on mere speculation. In fact, they could be very damaging, or even destroy the business.

Planning to Project Cashflow

Before using a model for short-term cash flow forecasting, a manager or entrepreneur should:

- Decide the central purpose of the exercise.
- Identify the target audience
- Set the time intervals and horizon
- Sort out the level of detail required.
- Check that all the necessary key assumptions and data are to hand and have been adequately researched.
- Compile opening balances for all items which will involve cash flows within the forecasting period.
- Think through the likely impact of the critical assumptions on the cash flow projections. If necessary, prepare preliminary forecasts manually to confirm their overall direction and consider the underlying strategic issues relating to sales, funding, costs, stocks etc. As a guide, sales forecasts and debtor and creditor terms are likely to have the most profound impacts on short-term cash flows.

Planning Pitfalls when Forecasting Cash Flow

When preparing cash flow projections, be aware of the dangers of:

- Overstating sales forecasts
- Underestimating costs and delays likely to be encountered
- Ignoring historic trends or performances by debtors etc.
- Making unduly-optimistic assumptions about the availability of bank loans, credit, grants, equity etc.
- Seeking spurious accuracy whilst failing to recognize matters of strategic importance

These problems can arise as the result of a lack of foresight or knowledge, or because of excessive optimism. They can lead to under-estimation of the cash and other resources required sustaining or developing a business with potentially disastrous consequences. When forecasting bank requirements and preparing cash flow projections, realistic views should always be taken about future prospects. There is often merit in compiling "worst" case projections to complement "most likely" or "best" forecasts and to accept that the "worst" case might occur and to plan accordingly. Our software planners, Exl-Plan and Cashflow Plan, offer extensive facilities for doing sensitivity analyses.

Ways of Improving Cash Flow

Once the cash flow projections have been prepared, they should be critically examined and used as a management tool to control and improve the business's expected cash position. Issues which might be examined include the following:

30 + Ways of Improving Net Cash flow

- Increase sales.
- Reduce direct and indirect costs and overhead expenses.
- Defer discretionary projects which cannot achieve acceptable cash paybacks.
- Increase prices especially to slow payers.
- Review the payment performances of customers - involve sales force.

- Become more selective when granting credit.
- Seek deposits or multiple stage payments.
- Reduce the amount/time of credit given to customers.
- Bill as soon as work has been done or order fulfilled.
- Improve systems for billing and collection.
- Use the 80/20 rule to control inventories, receivables and payables.
- Improve systems for paying suppliers.
- Generate regular reports on receivable ratios and aging.
- Establish and adhere to sound credit practices - train staff.
- Use more pro-active collection techniques.
- Add late payment charges or fees where possible.
- Increase the credit taken from suppliers.
- Negotiate extended credit from suppliers.
- Make prompt payments only when worthwhile discounts apply.
- Reduce inventory levels and improve control over work-in-progress.
- Sell off or return obsolete/excess inventory.
- Utilize factoring, or discount facilities, to accelerate receipts from sales.
- Defer or re-stage all capital expenditure.
- Use alternative financing methods, such as leasing, to gain access to the use of productive assets.
- Re-negotiate bank facilities to reduce charges.
- Seek to extend debt repayment periods.
- Net off or consolidate bank balances.
- Sell off surplus assets or make them productive.
- Enter into sale and lease-back arrangements for productive assets.
- Defer dividend payments.
- Raise additional equity.
- Convert debt into equity.
- Make medium- and short-term cashflow forecasts and update them regularly

The Cash Flow Forecasting Model

The "Cash Flow Forecasting Model" generates a comprehensive cash flow forecast statement. It also provides a detail breakdown of Sales; Cost-of-Sales; Selling Expenses; General and Administrative Expenses; Other Operating Expenses; Non-Operating Expenses; Other Cash Inflows; and Other Cash Outflows. Forecasts cash flows allowing you to more accurately monitor your cash position identifying loan requirements and investment opportunities.

- Allows for more effective cash management. You can identify cash requirements months in advance resulting in improved bank relations. You can spot excess cash conditions allowing you to take advantage of short-term investments and reduce loan requirements.
- The model calculates item by item percentages for each category and of total sales. It calculates monthly averages and projects future period activity based on inflation and growth percentages provided by the user. This enables you to examine the validity and reasonableness of the numbers and their significance for further refinement or study.
- Allows you to evaluate your estimated and actual cash flow values and current financial position.
- Actual cash activity can be entered monthly during the period. This will allow you to perform a more effective cash management throughout the year.
- The model is designed to be used with any currency.
- The cash flow forecast covers five years. It consists of the first year by month; the second and third years by quarter; and the fourth and fifth periods by year.
- Multiple report formats simplify data entry as well as provide management review statements.
- Contains navigation and report printing macros for ease of operation.

Preparing a Cash Flow Forecast

A cash flow forecast shows the critical whens of cash coming in and cash going out during a certain month. Preparing a monthly cash flow forecast provides you with the opportunity, representing revenues and expenses, in the month the business expects to collect and spend the cash. A cash flow forecast does not show sales estimates or overhead expenses averaged across several months.

Used properly, this will provide you with the means to keep your business decision-making on track and your inventory purchasing in control. It will also serve as an early warning indicator when your expenditures are running out of line or your sales targets are not being met. As the manager of your cash, you will have enough time to devise remedies for anticipated temporary cash shortfalls and ample opportunity to arrange short term investments for the business' temporary cash flow surpluses.

The completed cash flow forecast will clearly show a bank loans officer what additional working capital, if any, the business may need, and will offer proof that there will be sufficient cash on hand to make the interest payments to support a revolving line of credit. If the performance projections are realistic, they will also provide support for the feasibility of a term loan for an equipment purchase or for a master marketing campaign.

Computer spreadsheet programmes such as Microsoft Excel, Lotus 123 or any of a variety of full-faceted business software can be very useful for cash flow worksheet development. Reliable cash flow projections can bring a sense of order and well-being to your business and more calm to your life. The most important tool owners/managers have available to control the financial aspects of their business is the cash flow worksheet.

Step One: Consider your Cash Flow Revenues

For new operations, the basis can be the average monthly sales of a similar-sized competitor's operations who is operating in a similar market It is recommended that you make adjustments for this year's predicted trend for the industry. Be sure to reduce your figures by a start-up year factor of about

50% a month for the start-up months. There are also publications available in libraries and book stores that discuss methods of sales forecasting.

For existing operations, sales revenues from the same month in the previous year make a good base for forecasting sales for that month in the succeeding year. For example, if the trend readers in the economy and the industry predict a general growth of 4% for the next year, it will be entirely acceptable for you to show each month's projected sales at 4% higher than your actual sales the previous year. Include Notes to the Cash flow to explain any unusual variations from previous years' numbers.

If you sell products on credit terms or with installment payments, you must be careful to enter only the part of each sale that is collectible in cash in the specific month you are considering. Any amount collected after 30 days will be termed Collections on Accounts Receivable and will be shown in the month in which it will be collected. It is critical to the credibility of your plan that any sales made should only be entered once the cash is received in payment. This is the critical test principle of the cash flow and should be applied whenever you are in doubt as to what amount to enter and when.

Step Two: Consider your Cash Flow Disbursements

Project each of the various expense categories beginning with a summary for each month of the cash payments to trade suppliers. Again, follow the principle that there should not be any averaging or allocating of these inventory purchases.

Each month must show only the cash you expect to pay out that month to your trade suppliers. For example, if you plan to pay your supplier invoices in 30 days, the cash payouts for January's purchases will be shown in February. If you can obtain trade credit for longer terms, then cash outlays will appear two or even three months after the stock purchase has been received and invoiced.

An example of a different type of expense is your insurance expenditure. Your commercial insurance premium may be $2400 annually. Normally, this would be treated as a $200 monthly expense. But the cash flow will not see it this way. The cash flow wants to know exactly how it will be paid. If it is to be paid in two installments, $1200 in January and $1200 in July, then that is how it must be entered on the cash flow worksheet. The exact same principle applies to all cash flow expense items.

Once total cash collections, total cash payments on goods purchased, and any other expected expenses have been estimated for each individual month of operation, it is necessary to link the cash flow status of each month to the cash flow status and activity of the preceding and succeeding months.

Step Three: Reconciliation of the Cash Revenues to Cash Disbursements

The reconciliation part of the cash flow worksheet begins by showing the balance carried over from the previous months' operations. To this it will add the total of the current month's revenues and subtract the total of the current month's expenditures. This adjusted balance will be carried forward to the first line of the reconciliation portion of the next month to become the base to which the next month's cash flow activity will be added and/or subtracted.

Making the Best Use of Your Cash Flow

Cash flow plans are living entities and must constantly be modified as you learn new things about your business and your paying customers. Since you will use this cash flow forecast to regularly compare each month's projected figures with each month's actual performance figures, it will be useful to have a second column for the actual performance figures right alongside each of the planned columns in the cash flow worksheet.

As the true strengths and weaknesses of your business unfold before your eyes, actual patterns of cash movement emerge. Look for significant discrepancies between the planned and actual figures.

For example, if the business' actual figures are failing to meet your cash revenue projections for three months running, this is an unmistakable signal that it is time to revise the year's projections. It may be necessary to delay the stock replenishment plan, or apply to the bank to increase the upper limit of your revolving line of credit. Approaching the bank to increase an operating loan should be done well in advance of the date when the additional funds are required. Do not leave cash inflow to chance.

Designing a Cash Flow Worksheet

There are a variety of ways a cash flow forecast can be structured. To gain the optimum benefit, it is recommended that it be structured to show only revenues from operations, and the proceeds from sales of company assets, if appropriate, in the revenues portion of the worksheet.

On occasion a prepared format will show a slot for proceeds of a term loan in this part; this may, however, take away from the value of the cash flow as an indicator of the business' operating performance and of the cash flow's ability to clearly show the real amount of working capital needs. If a fixed term loan amount is treated as revenue to the business, the balances carried forward each month cannot accurately reflect how the business is earning money

Your general format should allow a double width column along the left side of the page for the account headings, then two side by side vertical columns for each month of the year, beginning from the month you plan to open. From there, the cash flow worksheet breaks into three distinctive parts.

The first part is headed Cash Revenues. The second part is headed Cash Disbursements. The final part is headed Reconciliation of Cash Flow.

Possible "Cash Disbursements" sub-headings

Cash Disbursements

- Cash Payments to Trade Suppliers of main product lines

- Cash Payments to Trade Suppliers of auxiliary product lines
- Management Draws
- Full-time Salaries and Wages
- Part-time and Casual Salaries and Wages
- Sales Commissions and/or Royalties Paid
- Cash Dividends Paid
- Advertising and Promotion Expense Paid
- Professional Fees Paid
- Business Licenses Registrations and Permits Paid
- Patents, Trademarks and Distribution Agreement Fees Paid
- Rental of Premises Payments
- Rental Payments for Equipment and Furnishings
- Other Rental Payments
- Motor Vehicle Expenses Paid
- Insurance Premiums Paid
- Repair and Maintenance Expenses Paid
- Utilities Payments
- Communications Payments
- Postal Expense Payments
- Cash Payments on Store/Office Supplies
- Other Business Expenses
- Interest Payments on Term Loans/Mortgages
- Interest Payments on Operating Linev
- Federal Tax Payments
- Provincial Tax Payments
- Municipal Tax Payments
- Total Cash Disbursements.

Possible "Cash Revenues" sub-headings

Cash Revenues

- Cash Sales from main product lines
- Cash Sales from auxiliary product lines
- Cash from Services Provided
- Collection from Accounts Receivable
- Proceeds from Sale of Fixed Assets

- Other Operations Cash Revenues
- Total Cash Revenues

Example:

ITEM	April Planned	April Actual	May Planned	May Actual
Cash Revenues				
Total Cash Revenues	$40	$10	$75	$35
Cash Disbursements				
Total Cash Disbursements	$50	$60	$60	$70
Reconciliation of Cash Flow				
Opening Cash Balance	$0	$0	($10)	($50)
Add: Total Cash Revenues	$40	$10	$75	$35
Deduct: Total Cash Disbursements	$50	$60	$60	$70
Closing Cash Balance (carry forward to next month)	($10)	($50)	$5	($85)

Possible Reconciliation of Cash Flow sub-headings

Reconciliation of Cash Flow

- Opening Cash Balance
- Add: Total Cash Revenues
- Deduct: Total Cash Disbursements
- Surplus or Deficit on this Month's Operations
- Closing Cash Balance
-

Importance of Cash Flow Forecast

A cash flow forecast shows the critical when of cash coming in and cash going out during a certain month. Preparing a monthly cash flow forecast provides you with the opportunity to show dollar figures, representing revenues and expenses, in the month the business expects to collect and spend the cash. A cash flow forecast does not show sales estimates or overhead expenses averaged across several months. Used properly, this will provide you with the means to keep your business decision-making on track and your inventory purchasing in control.

It will also serve as an early warning indicator when your expenditures are running out of line or your sales targets are not being met. As the manager of your cash, you will have enough time to devise remedies for anticipated temporary cash shortfalls and ample opportunity to arrange short term investments for the business' temporary cash flow surpluses. The completed cash flow forecast will clearly show a bank loans officer what additional working capital, if any, the business may need, and will offer proof that there will be sufficient cash on hand to make the interest payments to support a revolving line of credit.

If the performance projections are realistic, they will also provide support for the feasibility of a term loan for an equipment purchase or for a master marketing campaign. Computer spreadsheet programmes such as Microsoft Excel, Lotus 123 or any of a variety of full-faceted business software can be very useful for cash flow worksheet development. Reliable cash flow projections can bring a sense of order and well-being to your business and more calm to your life. The most important tool owners/managers have available to control the financial aspects of their business is the cash flow worksheet. For new operations, the basis can be the average monthly sales of a similar-sized competitor's operations who is operating in a similar market.

It is recommended that you make adjustments for this year's predicted trend for the industry. Be sure to reduce your figures by a start-up year factor of about 50% a month for the start-up months. There are also publications available in libraries and book stores that discuss methods of sales forecasting. For existing operations, sales revenues from the same month in the previous year make a good base for forecasting sales for that month in the succeeding year. For example, if the trend readers in the economy and the industry predict a general growth of 4% for the next year, it will be entirely acceptable for you to show each month's projected sales at 4% higher than your actual sales the previous year. Include Notes to the Cash flow to explain any unusual variations from previous years' numbers. If you sell products on credit terms or with installment payments, you must be careful to enter only the part of each sale that is collectible in cash in the specific month you are considering.

Any amount collected after 30 days will be termed Collections on Accounts Receivable and will be shown in the month in which it will be collected. It is critical to the credibility of your plan that any sales made should only be entered once the cash is received in payment. This is the critical test principle of the cash flow and should be applied whenever you are in doubt as to what amount to enter and when. Project each of the various expense categories beginning with a summary for each month of the cash payments to trade suppliers.

Again, follow the principle that there should not be any averaging or allocating of these inventory purchases. Each month must show only the cash you expect to pay out that month to your trade suppliers. For example, if you plan to pay your supplier invoices in 30 days, the cash payouts for January's purchases will be shown in February. If you can obtain trade credit for longer terms, then cash outlays will appear two or even three months after the stock purchase has been received and invoiced.

An example of a different type of expense is your insurance expenditure. Your commercial insurance premium may be $2400 annually. Normally, this would be treated as a $200 monthly expense. But the cash flow will not see it this way. The cash flow wants to know exactly how it will be paid. If it is to be paid in two installments, $1200 in January and $1200 in July, then that is how it must be entered on the cash flow worksheet. The exact same principle applies to all cash flow expense items. Once total cash collections, total cash payments on goods purchased, and any other expected expenses have been estimated for each individual month of operation, it is necessary to link the cash flow status of each month to the cash flow status and activity of the preceding and succeeding months. The reconciliation part of the cash flow worksheet begins by showing the balance carried over from the previous months' operations. To this it will add the total of the current month's revenues and subtract the total of the current month's expenditures.

This adjusted balance will be carried forward to the first line of the reconciliation portion of the next month to become the base to which the next month's cash flow activity will be added and/or subtracted. Cash flow plans are living entities and must constantly be modified as you learn new things about your business and you're paying customers. Since you will use this cash flow forecast to regularly compare each month's projected figures with each month's actual performance figures, it will be useful to have a second column for the actual performance figures right alongside each of the planned columns in the cash flow worksheet.

As the true strengths and weaknesses of your business unfold before your eyes, actual patterns of cash movement emerge. Look for significant discrepancies between the planned and actual figures. For example, if the business' actual figures are failing to meet your cash revenue projections for three months running, this is an unmistakable signal that it is time to revise the year's projections. It may be necessary to delay the stock replenishment plan, or apply to the bank to increase the upper limit of your revolving line of credit. Approaching the bank to increase an operating loan should be done well in advance of the date when the additional funds are required. There are a variety of ways a cash flow forecast can be structured.

To gain the optimum benefit, it is recommended that it be structured to show only revenues from operations, and the proceeds from sales of company assets, if appropriate, in the revenues portion of the worksheet. On occasion a prepared format will show a slot for proceeds of a term loan in this part; this may, however, take away from the value of the cash flow as an indicator of the business' operating performance and of the cash flow's ability to clearly show the real amount of working capital needs.

If a fixed term loan amount is treated as revenue to the business, the balances carried forward each month cannot accurately reflect how the business is earning money. Your general format should allow a double width column along the left side of the page for the account headings, then two side by side vertical columns for each month of the year, beginning from the month you plan to open.

5

Receivables Management

AN OVERVIEW

One of the very important components of working capital is receivables. You all know it very well that working capital requires management of all the components of working capital very well. We know that business firms generally sell goods on credit, to facilitate sale especially from those customers who cannot borrow from other sources, or find it very expensive or difficult to do so. For the existence of firm it is essential to sell on credit. Finished goods sold on credit get converted into receivables which when realised generate cash.

The average balance in the receivables account would approximately be; average daily credit sales multiplied by average collection period. For example, if the average daily collection period were 40 days, the average balance in the receivables account would be Rs 1,20,000. Since receivables often account would be Rs. 1,20,00,000. Since receivable often account for a significant proportion of the total assets. You will agree that Management of receivables takes up a lot of the Finance Manager's time.

Can you all tell me why a firm in a first instance sell goods on credit should or what is the purpose of Receivables? The purpose of receivables can be understood if we can grasp the basic objective of receivables management. The objective of receivables management is to promote sales and profits until that point is reached where the returns that the company gets from funding of receivable is less than the cost that the company has to incur in order to fund these receivables. Hence, the purpose of receivables is less than the cost that the company has to incur in order to fund these receivables. Hence, the purpose of receivables is directly connected with the company's objectives of making credit sales, which are:

- Increasing total sales as, if a company sells goods on credit, it will be in a position to sell more goods than if it insists on immediate cash payment.
- Increasing profits as a result of increase in sales not only in volume, but also because companies charge a higher margin of profit on credit sales as compared to cash sales.
- In order to meet increasing competition, the company may have to grant better credit facilities than those offered by its competitors.

So this is the purpose of receivables, now you will agree with me that a firm does incur some cost on receivables, let us discuss the costs.

Cost of Maintaining Receivables

- Additional fund requirement for the company: When a firm maintains receivables, some of the firm's resources remain blocked in them because there is a time lag between the credit sale to customer and receipt of cash from them as payment. To the extent that the firm's resources are blocked in its receivables, it has to arrange additional finance to meet it own obligations towards its creditors and employees, like payments for purchases, salaries and other production and administrative expenses. Where this additional finances is met from its own resources or from outside, it involves a cost to the firm in terms of interest.
- Administrative costs: When a company maintains receivables, it has to incur additional administrative expenses in the form of salaries to clerks who maintain records of debtors, expenses on investigating the creditworthiness of debtors etc.
- Collection costs: These are costs, which the firm has

to incur for collection of the amount at the appropriate time from he customers.

- Defaulting cost: When customers make default in payment not only is the collection effort to be increased but the firm may also have to incur losses from bad debts.

Isn't that quite a lot? So the solutions are easy compare costs with the benefits and go for the best alternative. Management always requires decision-making. Now let us decide on what should be the size of receivables? What do you how to decide on that? The size of receivables or investment in receivables is determined by the firm's credit policy and the level of it sales.

The following aspects of receivables management are:

- Formulation of credit policy,
- Credit evaluation.
- Credit granting decision.
- Monitoring receivables.

Credit policy

The credit policy of a company can be regarded as a kind of trade-off betweens increased credit sales leading to increased in profit and the cost of having larger amount of cash locked up in the form of receivables and the loss due to the incidence of bad debts. In competitive market, the credit policy adopted by a company is considerably influenced by the practices followed by the industry. A change in the credit policy of a company, by extending credit policy of a company, by extending credit period to 30 days, when the other companies are following a credit period of 15 days can result in such a high demand for the company's product that it cannot cope with.

Further, other companies also may have to fall in line in the long run. It is assumed generally that such factors have already been taken into consideration before making changes in the credit policy of a company. The term credit policy encompasses the policy of a company in respect of the credit standards adopted, the period over which credit is extended to customers, any incentive in the form of cash discount offered, as also the period over which credit is extended to customers, any incentive in the form of cash discount offered, as also the period over which the discount can be utilized by the customers and the collection effort made by the company.

This is quite simple isn't it? So let us discuss the variables associated with credit policy. The various variables associated with credit policy are:

- Credit standards
- Credit period
- Cash discount
- Collection programme

All these variables underlying a company's credit policy influence sales, the amount locked up in the form of receivables and some of the receivables turning sour and eventually become bad debts. While the variables of credit policy are related to each other, for the purpose of clarity in understanding, we shall follow what is technically known as comparative static analysis by considering each variable independently, holding some or all other constant, to study the impact of a change in that variable on the company's profit. It is also assumed that the company is making profits and has adequate unutilized capacity to meet the increased sales caused by a change in some variables without incurring additional fixed costs like wage and salaries, rent, etc. We have to make assumptions as you all know very well.

Credit Standards

When a company is confronted with the question of the standards to be applied to customers before deciding whether to extend credit or not, application of very stiff standards for the classification of customers to whom credit can be extended and to whom it cannot be extended is likely to result in a low level of sales, less amount of money locked up in the form of receivables, virtually no bad debt losses and less amount to be spent for collection.

On the other hand, indiscriminate extension of credit without bothering much about the credit standards expected of the customers is likely to increase sales. But in its wake the company is more likely to be saddled with a large quantum of money locked up in the form of accounts receivable, higher incidence of bad debt losses and increases expenses on the collection front. In the United States, there are excellent professional credit rating agencies such as Dun and Brad Street whose services can be utilized for a consideration.

Let us assume for the time being that the company has rated the customers into four categories ranging from 'high', 'good', fair and limited in the descending order of credit rating. Let us also assume that the company has been foregoing sales from 'fair' and 'limited' categories. The company has been contemplating to increase its sales from its existing level by liberalizing or relaxing its credit standard to some extent. What course of action should it take: liberalize or not? The answer to the question lies in making a comparison of the incremental benefits associated with a liberalized policy and the associated incremental costs.

The decision to liberalize will be justified only when the net incremental benefits are positive. Before going into the analysis we have to reckon with the factor that the earlier customers may take a lenient view in their paying habit once they come to know that the lowly rated customers of the company are taking a longer period for payment than what they themselves have been taking to pay. With a view to facilitating the exposition it is assumed that the existing customer will into alter their paying habit even after liberalization of credit by the company and the company can meet the increase in sales demand without incurring additional fixed cost as stated earlier on. Let us now consider the items of incremental benefits and incremental costs under the simplified assumptions. A numerical illustration will help in understanding the incremental cost benefit analysis.

Example

The existing sales of Aditi Company are Rs. 2 crores. The current customers are drawn from companies having 'high 'or 'good 'credit rating. With partially liberalized credit standards the company's sale are likely to go up by Rs. 24 lakhs, the mix of new customers being 67 per cent and 33 per cent from the group rated 'fair' and limited respectively. The average collection period is likely to be 45 days and the incidence of bad debt losses 10 per cent for the new customers. The contribution to sales ratio for Aditi Company is 20 per cent and the cost of funds is 15 per cent.

Credit Period

The credit period refers to the length of time allowed to customers to pay for their purchases. It generally various from 15 days to 60 days. If a firm allows, 45 days of credit with no discount to induce early payment its credit terms are stated as net 45'.

Lengthening of the credit period pushes sales up by inducing existing customers to purchase more and attracting additional customers. At the same time it increases the incidence of bad debts loss. A shortening of credit period will tend to lower sales, as customers decrease investment in receivables, and reduce the incidence of bad debt loss.

Let us consider the impact of lengthening the credit period by means of an example.

Example

The Nitin Company's existing sales are Rs. 180 lakhs. It is currently extending a credit period of net 30days to its customers. The company is contemplating to increase it sales by Rs. 16 lakhs to be achieving by means of lengthening the existing period to net 45 days. The bad debt losses on additional sales are expected to be 5 per cent. Should the company go in for a policy change or not?

All companies invest in working capital. For many organisations the reality is that working capital is the poorest performing asset that the company holds. Poor performance can be reflected in both the size of the investment and in the associated costs in back offices, production facilities, distribution networks and customer turnover. At Alvarez and Marsal, we have found that it is not unusual for 20% and 40% of net working capital to contribute nothing towards achieving business goals.

Working capital may be reported on the balance sheet, but the roots of poor performance lie throughout an organisation's administrative and operational processes. Success in addressing these issues comes from employing an approach driven by a sound business case coupled with entrepreneurial leadership. For this reason, A&M helps drive change from within our client's organisation. Our approach centres on helping our clients make informed decisions and act swiftly to deliver both long and short term benefits. Resisting delay and taking decisive action based on reliable facts are keys to achieving sustainable improvements in working capital performance.

Operational and financial expertise gained across multiple sectors and geographies, coupled with high performing professionals who have a bias towards hands-on implementation is at the core of Alvarez and Marsal's working capital management capabilities. This unique blend enables us to partner with our clients at all stages of a working capital improvement programme, from identifying the benefits through developing solutions to working hand-in-hand to deliver results.

The Working Capital Group operates across four focused areas:

- Order to Cash and receivables management
- Payables and purchasing management
- Inventory and Supply Chain
- Cash management and treasury

Working capital could be defined as the portion of assets used in current operations. The movement of funds from working capital to income and profits and back to working capital is one of the most important characteristics of business. This cyclical operation is concerned with utilisation of funds with the hope that they will return with an additional amount called Income. If the operations of a company are to run smoothly, a proper relationship between fixed capital and current capital has to be maintained. Sufficient liquidity is important and must be achieved and maintained to provide the funds to pay off obligations as they arise or mature. The adequacy of cash and other current assets together with their efficient handling, virtually determine the survival or demise of the company. A businessman should be able to judge the accurate requirement of working capital and should be quick enough to raise the required funds to finance the working capital needs.

Working capital is often classified as Gross Working Capital and Net Working Capital. The former refers to the total of all Current Assets and the latter refers to the difference between Current Assets and Current Liabilities. The maintenance of a sound Working Capital position is an important function of the Finance Department of the organisation. With the magnitude of business rising with globalisation, the quantum of working capital to be managed is on the increase. No wonder, working capital management is talked about more today than ever before.

Importance of Short Term Funds Management

Long-term investment decisions and long-term financing decisions are characterized by the facts that they

- Generally involve large amounts of money,
- Are relatively infrequent occurrences.

Decisions that come under the heading "short-term finance" are equally important, because, while typical decisions often don't involve as much money, decisions are much more frequent. This is suggested in the results of a recent survey of CFOs.

Ranked Greatest Importance Average Time Allocated
Financial Planning 59% 35%
Working Capital Mgmt 27% 32%
Capital Budgeting 9% 19%
Long-Term Financing 5% 14%
Total 100% 100%

In defining short term finance, we focus on the cash flows connected with the operations of a company. Because the cash inflows and cash outflows are not synchronised, a company needs a temporary parking place for cash, which we can call a liquidity portfolio. This liquidity portfolio may consist of cash and marketable securities. Since cash flows for a company are uncertain, both in amount and timing, the amount of cash in temporary storage may not be adequate for all time periods. Thus, it is necessary to provide some backup liquidity for periods when the normal store of liquidity is insufficient. Also there is a need to move cash from one point to another within a company.

We need to have internal cash flows to connect these various inflows, outflows and sources of liquidity. The cash system of a company is the mechanism that provides the linkage between cash flows. The financial manager of the company has the responsibility, at least in part, to develop and maintain the policies and procedures necessary to achieve an efficient flow of cash for the company's operations. Short term financial management thus encompasses decisions about activities that affect cash inflows, cash outflows, liquidity, backup liquidity, and internal cash flows.

Many decisions of a company have a short term financial management aspect. For example, the decision to sell a bond issue in order to raise funds to finance an expansion in plant and equipment is clearly a long term decision. However, the decision on how to invest the proceeds from the bond issue until they are needed to pay for the construction is a short term financial decision. The use of a 1-year time horizon to separate short term and long term decisions is arbitrary and, in some cases, ambiguous.

To refine the definition of short term finance, it is helpful to examine the differences and interrelationships between the decisions that are classified as short term finance and those that are considered long term finance. Decisions usually classified as long term are difficult to reverse and essentially determine the basic nature of the business and how it will be carried out.

Short term financial policies take the results of these decisions as a starting point and concentrate on how they can be efficiently and economically carried out. We can think of short term decisions as being more operational. Once implemented they are easier to change.

COMPONENTS OF WORKING CAPITAL

The elements of working capital are as follows:

- *Current Assets*:
  - Cash
  - Bank Balance
  - Short term investments
  - Trade Debtors
  - Inventory
    - (a) Finished Goods
    - (b) Work in process
    - (c) Raw materials
    - (d) Stores and Spares
  - Pre-payments (Insurance, advances etc.)
- *Current Liabilities*:
  - Trade Creditors
  - Bank Overdraft or Cash Credit
  - Short Term Borrowings
  - Provision for taxes
  - Provision for dividends

If current assets is the source from which current liabilities are to be met during the course of business operations, then their strengths or weaknesses will have significant bearing on the short run liquidity of the company. The importance of preserving this short term liquidity need not be emphasised and hence the need to manage the working capital. Working parameters of a company influence the composition mix of various components of working capital. Whether the company is single product or multiple product? Whether the company does made-to-order work or it keeps stock in inventory? Whether it is a manufacturing company or a trading company? Whether it extends credit to its customers or does not?

Whether it gets credit from its suppliers or does not? These are some of the questions that the company has to answer before it can really decide what levels of working capital that the company needs. Single product companies normally operate with a lower quantum of working capital than multi-product or multi-process companies. Trading operations, which get the payments in cash everyday, will necessarily have to manage their funds in a different way than a defence contractor who gets his payment after six months of the completion of the job. The management of funds will be altogether different for an infrastructure contractor whose payment terms are divided over a number of years.

Investment in Current Assets

The size of the company's investment in current assets is determined by its short-term financial policies. There are three types of policies that the company can use: 1) Flexible policy, 2) Restrictive policy and 3) A compromise policy that lies between the two.

- A company keeping a flexible working capital policy means that the company is very liberal in its trade terms and has invested a large amount of funds in its operations. Flexible policy actions include:
  - Keeping large cash and securities balances
  - Keeping large amounts of inventory
  - Granting liberal credit terms
- A company keeping a restrictive working capital policy is basically investing the lowest amount possible in the operations. for Restrictive policy actions include:
  - Keeping low cash and securities balances
  - Keeping small amounts of inventory
  - Allowing few or no credit sales
- A company keeping a compromise working capital policy is realistically investing the money in the operations, neither has very large amount of cash nor runs always short of it like the restrictive policy does.

TYPES OF FINANCING POLICIES

A company that keeps a flexible policy keeps enough liquid assets that are sufficient to finance its peak requirements of working capital. This means that the company invests the excess money that it has when there is less than the peak demand. A company with a restrictive policy keeps enough liquid assets that are sufficient to meet the lowest level of working capital requirements. This means that the company borrows as the seasonal needs grow to fund its working capital needs. With a compromise policy, the firm keeps a reserve of liquidity which it uses to initially finance seasonal variations in current asset needs. Short-term borrowing is used when the reserve is exhausted. A restrictive policy is associated with higher risk and higher expected profitability. A conservative policy ensures higher liquidity and cover risk but is always accompanied by lower profitability.

The policy to be adopted is based on managements' perception of the risk with a view to maximise the utility value of the funds used in the working capital management. This means that the risk-return trade-off is to be kept in mind while formulating the WC policy. Flexible policy means that the company is carrying excess cash and hence bearing higher carrying costs than the other two policies.

Restrictive policy means that the company is out of cash many times and hence carries shortage costs like loss of orders, etc. As the level of working capital increases, shortage costs go down while the carrying costs increase. This means that there would be a point where the sum total of carrying costs and the shortage costs would be the lowest. This is the optimum level of current assets that the company should keep.

Factors Influencing Working Capital

In addition to the working parameters peculiar to a company that determine the quantum of required working capital, the following factors are also equally important:

- Profit levels
  - A company earning huge amounts of profits can add to the working capital pool a larger quantum of funds. Such companies should, however, guard against the temptation of expanding beyond necessity and tying up the funds in unproductive capital expenditure or allow unnecessary increase in overheads. Generally it is seen that companies with high profit levels become lax in management of funds and usually

mismanage by blocking funds excessively in stocks or debtors.

- Tax Levels and Planning
  - Income Tax laws provide for payment of advanced tax in installments. Excise and sales tax are payable at time of dispatch of goods from the factory premises and the point of sales respectively. Any working capital management must make adequate and timely provision for the same as all of them involve cash outlays.
- Dividend Policies and Retained Earnings
  - Dividend policy and retained earnings are directly related. There has to be a proper balance between the need to preserve cash resources and the obligation to satisfy shareholder expectations. Sometimes reserves are sacrificed for consistent dividends. Dividends once declared become a short time liability which has to be paid for in cash and this impact should be recognised in the working capital budget. On the other hand, it would be of little satisfaction to the general body of the shareholders to enjoy a liberal dividend at the expense of ploughing back the same for the growth of the company. Reserves in the form of retained earnings are a very important source of augmenting working capital.
- Depreciation Policy
  - The extent to which depreciation provision is made during the course of making the financial statements has a direct bearing on the dividend policy and retained earnings. This so because a higher quantum of depreciation would leave lesser profits resulting in reduced retained earnings and dividends. The quantum of depreciation can be made to vary by choosing different methods to provide for the use of assets. As provisions for depreciation are actually only book entries and represent no cash flow at that

time, they will have no bearing on working capital except to the extent they may hold back distribution of dividends.

- Expansion/ Diversification Plans
  - Addition of fixed assets to produce new products, resorting to multiple shifts, or marginally adding to the plant and machinery are some of the common known ways to expand or diversify. Either of them represent an increase in production which calls for a higher quantum of spending of current assets, e.g., you buy more raw material when you produce more and so on. In such situations, it is unwise to strain the internal resources for avoiding external funding.
- Price level changes in raw material and finished goods
  - Inflation has got a direct bearing on the working capital. It depends to a large extent on the companies ability to readjust its own prices to cover the increase in the cost. In case the product or service requires government approval or is administered as far as the price is concerned, inflation may have a very significant bearing on the working capital needs. Inflation could be either recessive or expensive. During recessive inflation the companies are unable to sell more products due to lack of demand which results in the reduction of production. Inventories pile up and fixed expenses need a drastic reduction.
- Operating Efficiency of the company
  - Operating efficiency of a company plays a major role in working capital management. An efficient company will have a shorter manufacturing period, long credit terms available from suppliers and minimal customers credit outstanding. If this is achieved then the quantum of working capital required will be naturally reduced.

THE WORKING CAPITAL CYCLE

The Working Capital Cycle is the length of time between a company's paying for material entering into stock and receiving the inflow of cash from sales. The movements in the cycle are different for different types of companies and are dependent on the nature of the company. The operating cycle is the time period from inventory purchase until the receipt of cash. The cash cycle is the time period from when cash is paid out, to when cash is received.

Receivables Management

If we are getting trade credit to fund our needs, we also have to extend trade credit to our customers. A company grants trade credit to protect its sales from the competitors and to attract the potential customers to buy its products at favourable terms. There are several affects of extending credit to the customers on various operating parameters of the company. These include:

- Revenue effects
  - As the customers are extended credit, payment for goods is received later giving the customers time to generate sales from the goods and pay back the company. This may allow the company to charge a higher price and also the quantity sold may increase.
- Cost effects
  - Extending credit means that the company has to maintain a credit department. This involves costs. Also collecting receivables has its own costs associated with it.
- The cost of debt
  - If the company has to extend credit it must finance these receivables from its own money or from borrowings. Both of these methods involve costs.
- The probability of nonpayment
  - The company always gets paid if it sells for cash but if it extends credit there is a probability that

the customer may not pay. This means that the company may not get its payments resulting in a loss to the company.

- The cash discount
  - Athere is higher probability that the company will get more cash upfront and vice versa. Extending trade credit creates receivables or book debts which the company expects to collect in the near future. The book debts or receivables arising out of trade credit have three characteristics:
- It involves an element of risk
  - This should be carefully analysed. Cash sales are riskless, but not the credit sales as the cash are yet to be received.
- It is based on economic value
  - To the buyer, the economic value in goods or services passes immediately at the time of sale, while the seller expects an equivalent amount of value to be received later on.
- It implies futurity
  - The cash payment for the goods or services received by the buyer will be made by him in a future period. The customers from whom receivables or book debts are due are called "debtors" and represent the company's claim or asset. Let us take up an example to emphasise the benefit of providing trade credit.

Example: A company is planning to extend credit to its customers. The choice is between one month and two month's credit. The first year's results under the three alternatives, of providing no credit and one and two months credit.

(Rupees) No credit One month's credit
Two month's credit
Sales 120,000 160,000 240,000
Debtors 13,333 40,000
Stocks
10,000 13,333 20,000

Total 10,000 26,666 60,000
Increase in working capital through
granting credit 16,666 50,000
Marginal contribution 30,000 40,000 60,000
Less: Cost of:
Credit control (6,000) (6,000)
Bad debts (1,600) (4,800)
Relevant comparable profits 30,000 32,400 49,000
Increase in profits 2,400 19,200

But the company requires a return of15% on the increase in capital employed; *i.e.* 2,500 7,500. The net advantage (or disadvantage) of the proposed changes in credit policy is therefore (Rs.100) Rs.11,700. Note that we have not shown an 'interest' charge on the increased working capital because in due course the increase in stocks and debtors will in effect be financed out of the improved profits, and no specific borrowing may be needed.

However, regardless of how the working capital is financed it must still produce the required rate of return. The example makes the fairly obvious points that giving credit involves cost, including the opportunity cost of additional capital employed.

In some cases these costs will cancel out or outweigh any gains from increased business like in the second alternative. In some cases the granting of credit may not increase the sales of the business but may be justified because it will prevent a loss of sales to a competitor.

There are two costs that we can associate with extending credit costs and opportunity costs. Credit costs are the cash flows that must be incurred when credit is granted. They are positively related to the amount of credit extended. Opportunity costs are the lost sales from refusing credit. These costs go down when credit is granted.

This means that there is a point where the sum totals of these two costs are minimum for the company. This point depicts the optimum credit policy that the company must follow. The discussion will suggest three ways of management control in connection with credit policy:

- Debtors expressed in relationship to sales - either as a percentage or as a number of weeks sales. This provides an overall confirmation that the business is effective in carrying out its own credit policy.

With a seasonal business, however, these calculations could be misleading. Another disadvantage of averages is that they may conceal the fact that some long-overdue debts are being compensated by quicker collections from other customers. For management control there is no substitute for a complete listing of debtor accounts, analysed by age, compiled every month.

- Bad debts as a percentage of sales value, or reported otherwise in detail.
- Credit control costs.

This means that credit control involves three types of action:

- Deciding the normal credit period to be allowed;
- Establishing credit limits for individual customers;
- Implementing the system.

Deciding the Credit Period:

If a business is offering a unique product or service, or one for which demand exceeds supply, there may be no need to offer credit terms at all. In other cases the starting point in deciding credit policy is a review of the credit terms offered by competitors, and from this basis the credit terms of the particular business will be developed.

Other factors that affect the length of the credit period are the following:

- Buyer's inventory and operating cycle
- Perishability and collateral value
- Consumer demand
- Cost, profitability and standardisation
- Credit risk
- The size of the account
- Competition
- Customer type

Long credit period may be offered to the customers if this will enable the business to capture a larger share of the available market, or the break into a new market. The initial effect of granting long credit periods may be adverse because of the extra costs involved but profits from increased volumes should more than offset the losses. If it does not there is no use in extending longer credit periods. Even otherwise it is necessary to look to the longer term where, among other possibilities, selling prices may be increased because smaller competitors have been eliminated in the 'credit war'. Shorter credit may be imposed if demand is inelastic, so that the quantity sold will not be affected simply by changes in credit terms.

Establishing Credit Limits

The fact that the business has a credit policy does not mean that credit terms will be granted to every customer. It is not always easy to decide whether a particular customer is 'credit worthy' in the sense that he has both the ability and the inclination to pay at the due date. Many companies require cash with order from new customers until their creditworthiness have been established. Five Cs of Credit that a bank looks at are the ones that you should also look at while granting credit:

- Character: Willingness to pay back the credit
- Capacity: Ability to pay back
- Capital: Financial reserves including cash
- Collateral: What assets could be pledged or are pledged to others that hinder payments
- Conditions: Relevant economic conditions

That means that in assessing the creditworthiness of a customer two things are absolutely necessary:

- Facts about his business, in particular whether it is profitable, whether it is generating or has access to sufficient cash to met its liabilities, and whether it has suitable assets available to cover the claims of unsecured creditors in the event of winding up. In brief, it is necessary to analyse the accounts of the business. It is helpful also if the customer will supplement these with the sort of information they do not give; e.g., any plans for future development, and the condition and market value of the assets owned by his business.

- Opinions about the business and the people running it, formed from either personal contacts (director level, or at any reliable and knowlegeable level) or obtained from third parties such as business associates, mutual acquaintances or employees changing jobs. There are other sources from which we can have information about the company as well as the industry that it is operating in:
  - Reports from the relevant trade protection association, if one exists;
  - Trade references from other companies with which the customer does business;
  - Bank references - these may not give a lot of information but they tend to use a series of standardised replies, and experience of these will indicate the relative credit grading of the customer in question;
  - Reports published in trade journals or the financial press dealing either with the customer company or with the type of business in which it is engaged.

In assessing the creditworthiness of overseas customers, reports from bankers are an important source of information. It is also necessary to weigh up the risks of the customer being prevented from paying either through political or exchange control restrictions. On all these matters the Export Credits Guarantee Department can usually give guidance. If the customer's creditworthiness appears to be established, the next stage is to decide the amount of credit to be given.

Theoretically there are three possible ways of doing this:

- The income or cash flow method, which requires knowledge of the amounts of cash becoming available to the customer, and how he proposes spending them, thus indicating his ability to pay the supplier's invoices - this method is possible between a bank manager and his client seeking an overdraft or loan, but seldom in business life;
- The capital structure method, under which the value

of uncharged assets in the customer's last balance sheet is established, and the credit limit will be a percentage of this value. This is a necessary calculation when the proposed value of future transactions will involve a major increase in the customer's total indebtedness, but it is not an indicator of liquidity, and is not particularly relevant to small transactions in the ordinary course of trade;

- The requirement method, which is almost always used in practice. If the customer is creditworthy then we should be able to rely on him to pay any amounts arising from the ordinary course of business. The amount of credit granted, therefore, is based on the value of business which the customer expects to place with the supplier each month.

The forecast monthly sales to the customer are multiplied by a number of months' credit laid down as company policy to give that customer's credit limit. If, for example, a customer proposed placing orders totaling Rs.1,500 per month with a supplier whose credit terms required payment by the end of the month following the date of invoice the credit limit granted him might be 2xRs.1,500 = Rs.3,000 outstanding on the ledger accounts at any time.

For customers of international repute it may be decided that no limitation of credit is necessary, but the financial difficulties faced by several major companies in recent years must be a warning against the automatic granting of unlimited credit.

Vetting Incoming Orders

The amount appearing on the customer's ledger account at any time will, of course, result from invoicing the orders he has placed, so that if the value of orders in any period were to exceed the original forecast this might not become apparent until after invoicing. At that time the outstanding balance on the ledger would suddenly be found to be in excess of the agreed limit.

To safeguard against this possibility an order register may be kept for each customer, showing the value of orders placed for delivery in particular months. Each incoming order will then be checked against the register to confirm that it will not cause the credit limit to be exceeded. This could be a cumbersome procedure, and normally it would only be used in respect of:

- New customers' whose compliance with credit limits has not been established;
- Customers who had consistently failed to adhere to their credit limits in the past. (It might be better in such cases to withdraw credit facilities completely).

All incoming orders should be checked to ensure that are placed on the customer's official order form and authorised by somebody purporting to have the power to place that type of order. Computerisation has made this task very easy.

Sales Invoicing

So far as the customer is concerned, the company's credit period does not begin until he receives an invoice. Even then his accounting procedures probably involve a monthly cut off date for the receipt of invoices, so that any invoice received after, the 28th day of the month will be treated as belonging to the succeeding month. It is important, therefore, that delays in invoicing be kept to a minimum. The causes of delay are nearly all within the control of the company, and may include:

- An inflexible routine in the sales invoicing department (perhaps invoices are issued only on certain days in the month);
- A requirement for approval or signature of sales invoices by members of the sales staff who are often away from the office;
- Failure to agree prices for special work; and
- For job work, and in other cases where prices are linked with costs, excessively slow procedures for calculating costs.

Debt Collection

There must be no slackness in pursuing the collection of debts. In most business purely formal reminders are ineffective, and therefore a waste of money, when an account has passed its due date there should be early personal contact with the customer either by telephone or a salesman's visit or by a letter addressed to a named person in the customer company. If necessary, there may be a follow up at the higher level of authority. And this should be followed by a threat to cut off supplies. The value of legal action against debtors needs to be assessed. When this stage is reached, the likelihood of the customer's paying is sharply reduced, and additional legal costs may never be recouped.

On the other hand, the action may deter potential future defaulters. From the point of view of the salesman every customer is valuable. From the financial director's standpoint the marginal contribution from goods sold to a late payer will be more profitable without sales to that particular customer. Overdue debts should be the subject of formal discussion between the sales and financial managers. The reasons for delayed payment should be noted, and decisions should be minuted on the action to be taken in each case and the people responsible for taking it. Although the salesman's job is not complete until his customer has paid the money due, it is often advantageous for the more rigorous collection procedures to be handled by finance staff, leaving the salesman free to exercise his persuasive influence with the customer's buying department.

Cost of Credit Control

The costs of credit control include the cost of:

- Assessing and reviewing creditworthiness;
- Checking incoming orders;
- Sales ledger keeping, and invoicing
- Debt collection.

These costs may occur in various departments of the business, but there should be some means of identifying them and collecting the total cost, which will have to be taken into account in reviewing the benefits of the credit policy.

Cash Discount

An alternative or supplement of a formal credit policy is

to offer discount for prompt payment. In considering this possibility it is important to bear in mind that:

- Customers who normally pay promptly will now become entitled to discount, although there will be no improvement in the timing of their payments'.
- Some late payers will nevertheless deduct discount from their settlements, and there may be some practical difficulty in recovering these incorrect deductions.

There are various other ways in which a business can speed up its collection of cash without requiring the customer to pay any earlier.

Personal Guarantees

An alternative form of protection against bad debts is to take a personal guarantee in support of the customer's account. The value of personal guarantees varies considerably and they are likely to present two problems.

- It may be more difficult to assess the creditworthiness of an individual guarantor than of the trade customer;
- The guarantor does not normally expect to be called upon to pay, and there may be difficulties in obtaining money from him when the need arises.

These problems do not occur to the same extent when the guarantor is another company, often the parent company in the customer's group. So the objective of the receivables management remains as the most effective way to receive the cash back without sacrificing the sales and future prospects of the company.

Payables Management

When the company gets the trade credit, it would like to pay back as late as possible, because these are the funds that require no interest payments and are free of cost.

Right. Wrong, these funds are not free of cost because the sale price of these already includes the cost of the time for which the credit is given.

Cost of Trade Credit

For purposes of measuring the true cost, or the effective annual rate of interest associated with use of trade credit as a discretionary source of short-term business funds, it is necessary to consider the effects of its use both when:

- A company fails to take its cash discounts but nevertheless pays within the net period, and
- A company fails to take its discounts and allows its payable to become overdue.

These two situations are the only ones that involve an actual cost to the debtor. If no cash discount is offered, then there is no cost for the use of credit during the "net" period, however long it may be. By the same token, if a discount is available and the buyer takes it, there is also no cost for the use of credit during the discount period. However, if a cash discount is offered and is not taken, there is an explicit opportunity cost for the use of third credit. For example, the Road Company purchases it raw materials on terms of 2/10 net 30. It thus has the option of using the funds for 20 days after the discount period if it "passes" the discount but pays on the final day of the net period. Road Co., however, must pay 2% of the privilege of using the funds for 20 days.

It is given by the equation:

R = C(365 D)

D (100-C)

where

C = the cash discount

D = the number of extra days Road has the use of the supplier's funds

R = the annual interest rate for the use of these funds

In our example, C = 2 per cent, D = 20: the effective annual interest rate for the company would be R = 2 (365) 37.24 per cent 20 (100-2) Thus, we see that passed discounts can transform trade credit from a normally easy sources of funds into a very expensive form of short-term financing.

Therefore, if other financing is available even though with high interest rates, say 20 or 24%, Road's financial administrator would be well advised to borrow in sufficient time so that it can take advantage of any cash discounts offered by its suppliers. Sometimes companies that are short of cash and lack reserve borrowing power may be forced to not only pass up cash discounts but also postpone payment beyond the net period.

This practice is referred to as "stretching" accounts payable or "riding" trade creditors. There are two types of costs incurred by a company that stretches its accounts payable:

- The explicit cost of discounts foregone, and
- The implicit cost of permitting its trade credit rating to deteriorate.

If a company rides its creditors excessively, so that its trade payable becomes noticeably delinquent, its credit rating among all suppliers in the trade will surely suffer. They will view the company as increasingly risky to sell to and may quickly begin to impose rather strict terms of sale, up to and including COD or CBD.

Proper Use of Trade Credit

As compared with other kinds of short-term business credit — bank loans, for example-trade credit is almost automatic. And because it may be much more readily acquired, business companies must exercise continuing care to avoid falling into the habit of using trade credit to excess.

Because suppliers regard the extension of trade credit as a part of their overall sales promotion programmes, they often extend trade credit to many marginally creditworthy companies-small, new companies and old, declining companies-that do not qualify for and consequently cannot obtain credit from other sources of short-term funds. It is also quite easy to get into debt through the use of trade credit.

A company needs only to order additional goods from its suppliers; and if it is occasionally late in making payment, the sales promotion aspect of trade credit extension may prompt suppliers to "look the other way," so that the company's credit reputation may suffer no immediate harm. Finally, trade credit is exceedingly useful and valuable precisely because business companies can usually obtain it when, as, and to the extent that it is needed. When inventory should be increased to anticipate the seasonal expansion of sales, for example trade credit will automatically finance a part of the increase. Then, as the seasonal sales convert into cash through collections, the company may use the funds to reduce trade payable.

For this reason, trade credit is often termed a "spontaneous" source of funds. Thus, a company's financial officer while assuring that his company benefits from the availability of trade credit in every legitimate way, should always maintain the business liquidity required to pay all his company's bills as they come due. Even considering the extremely high cost of passing discounts, he should certainly plan to pay all of his company's trade bills within the discount period. Doing so will have favourable results, not only on the company's credit reputation in the trade but, more important, on its current and long-run profitability as well. In a negative but equally significant sense, doing so will automatically avoid the possible financial over extension of the company that could result from its succumbing to the temptation to use trade credit excessively "because it is there".

Inventory Management

The financial decisions relating to stockholding have certain special features, but looking first at saleable stocks (finished goods) we can postulate that the object of holding stocks is to increase sales, and that the object of increasing sales is to increase profit. We can then create a simple model similar to that for debtors.

Example

The Retail Company Ltd makes cash sales from stock and obtains an average rate of marginal contribution of 25% on sales value. When it holds stocks equivalent to one month's cost of sales it achieves sales of Rs.10, 000 per annum. It is estimated that by doubling the stock available an increase of 25% in sales value could be achieved; alternatively, if three months' stocks were held then sales could be increased by 35% from the present level. The effect on profits of these two alternatives, including any relevant changes in costs.

This somewhat exaggerated example draws attention to three points which are relevant to any further discussion of the financial implications of stockholding policy:

Rs. No credit One month's Credit Two month's Credit

Sales 120,000 160,000 240,000

Debtors 13,333 40,000

Stocks

10,000 13,333 20,000

Total 10,000 26,666 60,000

Increase in working capital through granting

credit 16,666 50,000

Marginal contribution 30,000 40,000 60,000

Less: Cost of:

Credit control (6,000) (6,000)

Bad debts (1,600) (4,800)

Relevant comparable profits 30,000 32,400 49,000

Increase in profits 2,400 19,200

But the company requires a return of 15% on

the increase in capital employed; *i.e.* 2,500 7,500

The net advantage (or disadvantage) of the proposed changes in credit policy is therefore (Rs.100) Rs.11, 700

There are some points that you need to note here:

- There may be a point beyond which further increase in stock will not give rise to sufficient additional sales and gross profit to justify the additional costs involved.
- Purchase order processing costs per unit or Rs. value of purchases are likely to diminish as stock holdings are increased, because instead of having to frequent orders for the renewal of stocks, the company is now placing less frequent bulk orders *i.e.* one negotiation, one order and one progress action cover a large quantity of any particular item;
- Stock holding costs naturally increase with the size of stockholdings because:

- Stocks occupy space which has to be purchased, rented or converted from some other use - that space has to be equipped with racks or containers;
- People are required to put the stocks into the warehouse, to withdraw them when needed (picking and packing), to record them, check their conditions and ensure they are not lost;
- Stocks lose value if they deteriorate, are wasted in handling, pilfered, destroyed or allowed to become obsolete - it may be desirable to insure against some of these risks;
- Stocks tie up money, involving interest charges or opportunity costs.

Why should increased stocks give rise to increased sales? One reason would be that the business may offer a wider range of goods and it diversifies its range. Another could be that with the existing range the business was offering a better level of service; *i.e.* it was less frequently out of stock of an item when it was required.

Stock Service Levels

In deciding on an inventory policy it is necessary to define the level of service to be offered to the customer, in the sense of the percentage of order which can be satisfied immediately from stock. This will depend on the nature of the business. In some cases the company may be the monopoly supplier of certain goods, or may offer particular advantages of quality, reputation, reliability or after-sales services.

Where such distinguishing features exist, it is possible that the customers will be prepared to endure occasional delays in meeting their requirements, and it would not be necessary to hold sufficient stocks to ensure immediate delivery.

In other cases quick delivery may be an essential feature of success in achieving sales. This would be the case, for example, if there was strong competition for a limited market, or if the failure to supply a spare part for installed equipment would cause significant loss to the customer while the equipment was out of use. When the required level of service has been defined, the next problem is to decide how much stock is needed to meet that requirement. This will be the minimum holding, and not the average holding which will be influenced by the stockholding costs emphasised in the previous paragraph.

Pattern of Procurement and Stockholding

Assuming that an item is in constant demand there are no difficulties in obtaining supplies, it would be normal to take a supply into stock and then use it up steadily until it was exhausted, when a new supply would be obtained. Taking the example from the paragraph on control of stock where sales were to be Rs.1,35,000 per annum, assume, that this represents 1,35,000 units of an item of stock at Rs.1 each. If demand is steady, the monthly usage of this item would be 11,250 units.

Now it would be possible to buy all 1,35,000 units at the beginning of the year and to use them progressively.

- There would be only one purchase, so the related costs in the buying department would be low;
- The average stock holding would be 62,500 units, so there would be 62,500x12 = 7,50,000 unit-months to influence the costs of stock-holding.

An alternative action would be to buy twice during the year. This would double the procurement costs, but would reduce the average stockholding to 31,250 units so that stockholding costs would be determined by only half the previous number of unit-months. There is obviously a very large choice of procurement and stockholding patterns; what is needed is to find that pattern which keeps total procurement and holding costs at the lowest possible level. This means that carrying costs increase with the quantity of inventory on hand and as the inventory go down the carrying costs also go down.

But with the declining amount of inventory held restocking costs go up as there are more number of orders and more number of receipts of orders. As total costs are the sum of the carrying and restocking costs we need to find a level where it is minimum. As we know that total costs are a sum of these two individual costs. But this doesn't give us the optimum size of the inventory order. For finding the minimum costs we need to find the 'economic order quantity' for the particular item of stock under review. The effect of the combination of the various items of stock into the total business inventory.

Economic Order Quantity (EOQ)

The economic order quantity is defined as a point where the total costs of restocking and carrying costs are the lowest. EOQ is usually calculated by a formula based on differential calculus. Though as suggested, not derive the formula we need to understand its working.

There are four assumptions that we make in the EOQ model:

- Sales can be forecasted perfectly,
- Sales are evenly distributed throughout the year, and
- Orders are received as soon as they are placed.

This set of assumptions mean is pretty restrictive and as suggested, relax these assumptions slowly. Before we relax these assumptions there are two important things to note about the EOQ:

- Although a mathematically precise EOQ can be calculated, in practice there is likely to be a range of order quantities within which total costs remain at a low level. The choice of order quantity within this low-cost range may not significantly affect the overall financial plan.
- The key factor in the calculations is usually the cost of capital (interest on stockholdings). In times of high interest rates this is likely to outweigh all the other variables. The inventory holding costs will go up very steeply, and one's cease will be that stockholdings should be kept to the lowest figure possible having regard to any practical difficulties in obtaining frequent replacement supplies.

Optimum Order Quantity (OOQ)

The last comment is a reminder that suppliers do not like handling small orders. The purchase price per unit, therefore, may vary with the size of the purchase order, and this will require a modification to our EOQ calculation. The supplier might, for example, impose a 'minimum order value' so that for quantities this limit the cost per unit would, in effect, be higher than normal.

This would either impose a lower cut-off limit on the size of order placed, or would introduce an upward curve at the lower end of the holding cost line on the EOQ chart, since insurance and interest charges per unit would be relatively high until the small order limit was reached. For larger orders, on the contrary, there might be quantity discounts, and these would cause one or more downward steps at those points on the holding cost line where they began to operate. This possibility can result in minimum total cost which differs from the position of the EOQ as originally calculated. This point is sometimes distinguished as the 'optimum order quantity'.

Safety Margins in Stockholding

So far we have assumed that a company wills he placing purchase orders at regular intervals of time for a fixed quantity (the economic or optimal order quantity) of any particular item. The possibility of doing this depends on demand remaining constant from period to period and on supplies being available as and when required. Sales demand, however, could show fluctuations around the normal level, so that in a period of high demand the available stock could be used up before fresh supplies are due.

Similarly, in some periods deliveries from suppliers could be delayed so that even the normal sales demand could not be satisfied. Against both these contingencies, it is necessary to hold a safety margin of stock. If it were necessary to hold a safety margin sufficiently large to cover the simultaneous occurrence of a peak in demand and a delay in supplies, then the minimum stockholding would form the greater part of the total stockholding. Very little can be done to correct for random delays in supply, but it may be possible to anticipate changes in the trend of demand and to modify the purchasing procedure to meet them in one of the following ways:

- To order in economic order quantities but at varying time intervals according to the rate of demand currently being experienced, or anticipated in the near future - this is known as the fixed order quantity or re-order level system ;
- To order at regular intervals but in varying quantities determined by the current rate of demand - this is the fixed interval, or periodic review system.

Modified Ordering Systems

The re-order level system involves deciding a level of stockholding at which new purchase orders shall be placed. This will be decided in relation to the normal rate of issues during the normal purchasing lead time. The quantity to be ordered is constant, and an order for that quantity will be placed whenever stock falls to the pre-determined order level. The system thus responds quickly to variations in demand though there is a danger that in doing so it may reflect purely short term or random fluctuations in sales.

The operation of re-order level system includes the use of:

- A maximum stock level. This would correspond to the normal peak holding under stable conditions. If the stockholding exceeds the peak level this provides a warning that demand has been running below the rate expected when the EOQ was fixed. The stock controller should then review the correctness of his standard purchase order quantity
- A minimum stock level which is probably the amount of the safety margin.

The minimum stock level provides a warning of a potential out-of-stock position. When a stockholding falls to that level the stock controller will review his outstanding purchase orders and their due dates, and also the current trend of demand, and can then decide whether additional emergency procurement is necessary.

Under the periodic review system purchase orders are placed at fixed intervals of time but the quantity ordered can be modified to meet the rate of demand indicated by current experience. This gives an opportunity for analysing the trend of demand, and various techniques such as 'exponential smoothing' can be used in forecasting this trend.

The system does not respond rapidly to immediate needs, and it may therefore necessitate a larger safety margin than the re-order level system. It is, in fact, a common experience that the re-order level system gives slightly lower average stock levels, and it is sometimes thought to be the cheaper system to operate because reordering is triggered automatically at the re-order levels, however, requires reviewing in the light of changes in the rate of demand. Any system can appear cheap in the short run if it is operated in a slovenly manner.

Infrequent and Seasonal Demand

In most inventories it will be necessary to carry items which are slow moving in the sense that units of demand are separated by significant intervals of time. These items may have high individual value but because they are demanded infrequently they will probably contribute only a small percentage of the total annual value of sales.

The normal distribution of stockholdings would show that about 20% of the line items carried would contribute 80% of the total annual usage, though this relationship will vary between different types of business. It may be decided not to hold stocks of some slow-moving items, but to procure them as and when they are required.

If a stock is needed however the amount held will probably be limited to the quantity most likely to be next demanded, the occurrence of the demand being the signal for further procurement action. The quantity held may, however, be increased if the purchase price per unit is sufficiently lower for large quantities so as to offset any increase in holding costs for a larger stock holding. This could occur for example when the supplier imposed a minimum order value.

There should be a regular review of slow-moving items to identify stocks which have become technically obsolete or for which the demand has diminished to the point where stock holding is no longer justified. In some businesses (for example, ladies fashion wear), it is necessary to place orders for the full seasonal requirement well in advance of the demand occurring, with a high probability that repeat orders will not be obtainable.

In such instances the purchase and sale of each batch will be a separate project or venture dependent heavily on accurate forecasting of demand quantities and selling prices. In this case, the evaluation procedure applicable to stock holding for continuous demand will not apply.

Of a similar nature will be decisions like the following:

- To purchase goods in bulk in advance of demand arising in order to protect the business against anticipated price rises or shortages of supply;
- To purchase commodities forward at a fixed price for future delivery;
- To combine forward purchase options with forward sales options, so as to limit losses arising from price changes (including changes in currency exchange rates);
- To purchase foreign currency forward against specific overseas purchases, so as to minimise the effect of changes in exchange rates.

These are financial decisions quite separate from the routine problems of inventory control, and would be evaluated as investment projects.

THE TOTAL INVENTORY

The techniques described in the foregoing paragraphs all relate to single line items of stock; the assumption has been made that if each item is held at its own economic level then the overall holding of stock will be correctly balanced. This would be true provided that two conditions were satisfied.

- That there was enough space available to hold all the stocks required; and
- That enough money could be found to finance them.

Neither condition is likely to be fulfilled in practice, so some form of mathematical programme might be used to constrain the ideal unit quantities within the limiting factors. There are, however, a number of simple pragmatic approaches to inventory reduction, and these include:

- Modifying the service level offered, either generally or in relation to selected items;
- Letting the company's suppliers performance as stockholders (possibly by placing bulk orders with schedules of call-off dates linked to sales demand);
- Discontinuing those items which are the least profitable having regard to their marginal contribution and relevant fixed costs per unit of the limiting factor.

Raw Material Stocks and Work-In-Progress

So far, in considering inventory control we have been discussing saleable stocks, but the same principles apply to stocks of raw materials. The main difference is that demand for raw materials is not direct from the outside customers but indirect through the production plans of the factory using the raw materials. In considering the scheduling of production the 'Economic Batch Quantity' (EBQ) corresponds to the EOQ for purchased items.

Manufacture in small batches will be more costly than in larger batches because there will be greater repetition of planning and progress actions and of the setting up and breaking-down of machine tooling, and also because there will be less opportunity for an efficient momentum of work to be established.

However, these batch processing costs (like procurement costs of stocks) will change inversely to the holding costs of the work-in-progress (floor space, insurance, interest on capital, etc.). A big problem with work-in-progress is that work passes in sequence through a series of operations. What is an economic batch for lathe work may not be economic for drilling, milling or assembly operations.

Applying EBQ calculation to one operation in isolation can cause bottlenecks in the flow or production - creating excessive holdings of partly-completed work because it could be produced cheaply in a large batch, even though there will be no demand for that work for some time ahead. A similar problem is that of keeping skilled work people steadily occupied, since their wages are basically fixed in relation to time, even though outside customer demand may be seasonal or erratic. Because these problems are concerned with the uneven timing of cash flows they are best solved by the use of discounted cash flow techniques. If, however, there is a capability of a rate of production which is in excess of a steady rate of demand (internal or external) then the problem is to decide what is the economic length of a production run, the facilities then being switched to other work until the next run is required. As the number of items could be very large in case of raw materials it is necessary to find ways to selectively pay attention to those items that represent the highest value.

A categorisation method known as ABC analysis is used for the same purpose. The idea behind ABC analysis is that attention is focussed on the highest value items that are usually small in number categorised as A-category items and the lowest value items are categorised as C and are ordered in more quantities so that less attention is required there. For example, the A category items represent only 10% of total inventory items but represent 57% of the total value. While C category items represent 50% of the total items but only 16% of the value. By concentrating more on the A category items the company is able to manage its raw material inventory better.

Integrated Short Term Funds Planning

Short-term financial planning is concerned with the management of the company's short-term, or current assets and liabilities. The most important current assets are cash, marketable securities, inventories and accounts receivable. The most important current liabilities are bank loans and accounts payable. Current assets and liabilities are turned over much more rapidly than the other items on the balance sheet. Short-term financing and investment decisions are more quickly and easily reversed than long term decisions. Consequently, the financial manager does not need to look too far into the future when making them. The nature of company's short term financial planning problem is determined by the amount of long term capital it raises. A company that issues large amounts of long term debt or equity, or which retains a large part of its earnings, may find that it has permanent excess cash. In such cases there is never any problem paying bills, and short term financial planning consists of managing the company's portfolio of marketable securities.

Companies with permanent excess cash should look at the cost of funds and pay them out to the shareholders if they are earning less than the cost of funds. Other companies raise relatively little long term capital and end up as permanent short term debtors. Most companies attempt to find a golden mean by financing all fixed assets and part of current assets with equity and long term debt. This may even be required by the bank to be so. Such companies may invest cash surpluses during part of the year and borrow during the rest of the year. The starting point for short term financial planning is an understanding of sources and uses of cash. Companies forecast their net cash requirements by forecasting collections on accounts receivable, adding other cash inflows, and subtracting all forecasted cash outlays. If the forecasted cash balance is insufficient to cover day-to-day operations and to provide a buffer against contingencies, you will need to find additional finance.

It may make sense to raise long term finance if the deficiency is permanent and large. Otherwise you may choose from a variety of sources of short term finance. In addition to the explicit costs of short term financing, there are often implicit costs. The financial manager must choose the financing package that has lowest total cost (explicit and implicit costs combined) and yet leaves the company with sufficient flexibility to cover contingencies.

Short Term Financial Planning Model

Working out a consistent short term plan requires burdensome calculations. Fortunately much of the arithmetic can be delegated to a computer. Many large companies have built models to do this. Smaller companies do not face so much detail and complexity and find it easier to work with a spreadsheet programme on a personal computer. In either case the financial manager specifies forecasted cash requirements or surpluses, interest rates, credit limits, etc. and the model grinds out a plan. The computer also produces balance sheets, income statements, and whatever special reports the financial manager may require.

Smaller companies that do not want custom built models can buy general purpose models offered by accounting companies, management consultants or specialised computer software companies. Most of these models are simulation programmes. They simply work out the consequences of the assumptions and policies specified by the financial manager. Optimisation models for short term financial planning are also available. These models are usually linear programming models. They search for the best plan from a range of alternative policies identified by the financial manager. Optimisation helps when the company faces complex problems with many interdependent alternatives and restrictions for which trial and error might never identify the best combination of alternatives.

Of course the best plan for one set of assumptions may prove disastrous if the assumptions are wrong. Thus, the financial manager has to explore the implications of alternative assumptions about future cash flows, interest rates and so on. Linear programming can help identify good strategies, but even with an optimisation model the financial plan is still sought by trial and error. In defining short term finance, we focus on the cash flows connected with the operations of a company. Short term financial management thus encompasses decisions about activities that affect cash inflows, cash outflows, liquidity, backup liquidity, and internal cash flows.

Many decisions of a company have a short term financial management aspect. Components of Working Capital include: Cash, Short term investments, Trade Debtors, Inventory and Trade Creditors. Bank Overdraft or Cash Credit and Short

Term Borrowings are tow of the major ways of financing working capital. Working parameters of a company influence the composition mix of various components of working capital. Whether the company does made to order work or it keeps stock in inventory? Whether it is manufacturing company or a trading company? Single product companies normally operate with a lower quantum of working capital than multi-product or multi-process companies. The size of the company's investment in current assets is determined by its short-term financial policies.

A company keeping a flexible working capital policy means that the company is very liberal in its trade terms and has invested a large amount of funds in its operations. This means that the company borrows as the seasonal needs grow to fund its working capital needs. Flexible policy means that company is carrying excess cash and hence bearing higher carrying costs than the other two policies. As the level of working capital increases, shortage costs go down while the carrying costs increases. There are other factors Influencing Working Capital including: Profit levels, Tax Levels and Planning, Depreciation Policy and Operating Efficiency of the company. Operating efficiency of a company plays a major role in working capital management.

An efficient company will have a shorter manufacturing period, long credit terms available from suppliers and minimal customers credit outstanding. If we are getting trade credit to fund our needs, we also have to extend trade credit to our customers. This involves various costs including: Cost effects-Extending credit means that the company has to maintain a credit department.

6

Inventory Management

INVENTORY

Inventory is a list for goods and materials, or those goods and materials themselves, held available in stock by a business. Inventory are held in order to manage and hide from the customer the fact that manufacture/supply delay is longer than delivery delay, and also to ease the effect of imperfections in the manufacturing process that lower production efficiencies if production capacity stands idle for lack of materials.

BUSINESS INVENTORY

The Reasons for Keeping Stock

There are three basic reasons for keeping an inventory:

- *Time*: The time lags present in the supply chain, from supplier to user at every stage, requires that you maintain certain amount of inventory to use in this "lead time"
- *Uncertainty:* Inventories are maintained as buffers to meet uncertainties in demand, supply and movements of goods.
- *Economies of scale:* Ideal condition of "one unit at a time at a place where user needs it, when he needs it" principle tends to incur lots of costs in terms of logistics. So Bulk buying, movement and storing brings in economies of scale, thus inventory.

All these stock reasons can apply to any owner or product stage.

- Buffer stock is held in individual workstations against the possibility that the upstream workstation may be a little delayed in long setup or change-over time. This stock is then used while that change-over is happening. This stock can be eliminated by tools like SMED.

These classifications apply along the whole Supply chain not just within a facility or plant. Where these stocks contain the same or similar items it is often the work practice to hold all these stocks mixed together before or after the sub-process to which they relate. This 'reduces' costs. Because they are mixed-up together there is no visual reminder to operators of the adjacent sub-processes or line management of the stock which is due to a particular cause and should be a particular individual's responsibility with inevitable consequences. Some plants have centralized stock holding across sub-processes which makes the situation even more acute.

Special Terms used in Dealing with Inventory

- *Stock Keeping Unit* (SKU) is a unique combination of all the components that are assembled into the purchasable item. Therefore any change in the packaging or product is a new SKU. This level of detailed specification assists in managing inventory.
- *Stockout* means running out of the inventory of an SKU.
- "New old stock" (sometimes abbreviated NOS) is a term used in business to refer to merchandise being offered for sale which was manufactured long ago but that has never been used. Such merchandise may not be produced any more, and the new old stock may represent the only market source of a particular item at the present time.

Inventory Examples

While accountants often discuss inventory in terms of goods for sale, organizations - manufacturers, service-providers and not-for-profits - also have inventories (fixtures, furniture, supplies,) that they do not intend to sell. Manufacturers', distributors', and wholesalers' inventory tends to cluster in warehouses. Retailers' inventory may exist in a warehouse or in a shop or store accessible to customers. Inventories not intended for sale to customers or to clients may be held in any premises an organization uses. Stock ties up cash and if uncontrolled it will be impossible to know the actual level of stocks and therefore impossible to control them.

Whilst the reasons for holding stock are covered earlier, most manufacturing organizations usually divide their "goods for sale" inventory into:

- Raw materials - materials and components scheduled for use in making a product.
- Work in process, WIP - materials and components that have begun their transformation to finished goods.
- Finished goods - goods ready for sale to customers.
- Goods for resale - returned goods that are salable.
- Spare parts

MANUFACTURING

A canned food manufacturer's materials inventory includes the ingredients to form the foods to be canned, empty cans and their lids (or coils of steel or aluminum for constructing those components), labels, and anything else (solder, glue,) that will form part of a finished can.

The firm's work in process includes those materials from the time of release to the work floor until they become complete and ready for sale to wholesale or retail customers. This may be vats of prepared food, filled cans not yet labelled or sub-assemblies of food components.

It may also include finished cans that are not yet packaged into cartons or pallets. It's finished good inventory consists of all the filled and labelled cans of food in its warehouse that it has manufactured and wishes to sell to food distributors (wholesalers), to grocery stores (retailers), and even perhaps to consumers through arrangements like factory stores and outlet centres.

LOGISTICS OR DISTRIBUTION

The logistics chain includes the owners (wholesalers and retailers), manufacturers' agents, and transportation channels that an item passes through between initial manufacture and final purchase by a consumer. At each stage, goods belong (as assets) to the seller until the buyer accepts them. Distribution includes four components:

- *Manufacturers' agents*: Distributors who hold and transport a consignment of finished goods for manufacturers without ever *owning* it. Accountants refer to manufacturers' agents' inventory as "matériel" in order to differentiate it from goods for sale.
- *Transportation*: The movement of goods between owners, or between locations of a given owner. The seller owns goods in transit until the buyer accepts them. Sellers or buyers may transport goods but most transportation providers performance as the agent of the owner of the goods.
- *Wholesaling*: Distributors who buy goods from manufacturers and other suppliers (farmers, fishermen, etc.) for re-sale work in the wholesale industry. A wholesaler's inventory consists of all the products in its warehouse that it has purchased from manufacturers or other suppliers. A produce-wholesaler (or distributor) may buy from distributors in other parts of the world or from local farmers. Food distributors wish to sell their inventory to grocery stores, other distributors, or possibly to consumers.
- *Retailing*: A retailer's inventory of goods for sale consists of all the products on its shelves that it has purchased from manufacturers or wholesalers. The store attempts to sell its inventory (soup, bolts, sweaters, or other goods) to consumers.

High Level Inventory Management

It seems that around about 1880 there was a change in manufacturing practise from companies with relatively homogeneous lines of products to vertically integrated companies with unprecedented diversity in processes and products. Those companies (especially in metalworking) attempted to achieve success through economies of scale - the gains of jointly producing two or more products in one facility. The managers now needed information on the effect of product mix decisions on overall profits and therefore needed accurate product cost information.

A variety of attempts to achieve this were unsuccessful due to the huge overhead of the information processing of the time. However, the burgeoning need for financial reporting after 1900 created unavoidable pressure for financial accounting of stock and the management need to cost manage products became overshadowed. In particular it was the need for audited accounts that sealed the fate of managerial cost accounting. The dominance of financial reporting accounting over management accounting remains to this day with few exceptions and the financial reporting definitions of 'cost' have distorted effective management 'cost' accounting since that time. This is particularly true of inventory. Hence high level financial inventory has these two basic formulas which relate to the accounting period:

Cost of beginning inventory at the start of the period + inventory purchases within the period + cost of production within the period = cost of goods

Cost of goods – cost of ending inventory at the end of the period = cost of goods sold

The benefit of these formulae is that the first absorbs all overheads of production and raw material costs in to a value of inventory for reporting.. Manufacturing management is more interested in *inventory turnover ratio* or *average days to sell inventory* since it tells them something about relative inventory levels.

Inventory turn over ratio (also known as inventory turns) = cost of goods sold/Average Inventory=Cost of Goods Sold/ ((Beginning Inventory + Ending Inventory)/2) and its inverse

Average Days to Sell Inventory=Number of Days a Year/ Inventory Turn Over Ratio=365 days a year/Inventory Turn

Over Ratio This ratio estimates how many times the inventory turns over a year. This number tells us how much cash/goods are tied up waiting for the process and is a critical measure of process reliability and effectiveness.

So a factory with two inventory turns has six months stock on hand which generally not a good figure (depending upon industry) whereas a factory that moves from six turns to twelve turns has probably improved effectiveness by 100%. This improvement will have some negative results in the financial reporting since the 'value' now stored in the factory as inventory is reduced.

Whilst the simplicity of these accounting measures of inventory are very useful they are in the end fraught with the danger of their own assumptions. There are in fact so many things which can vary hidden under this appearance of simplicity that a variety of 'adjusting' assumptions may be used. These include:

ACCOUNTING PERSPECTIVES

THE BASIS OF INVENTORY ACCOUNTING

Inventory needs to be accounted where it is held across accounting period boundaries since generally expenses should be matched against the results of that expense within the same period. When processes were simple and short then inventories were small but with more complex processes then inventories became larger and significant valued items on the balance sheet. This need to value unsold and incomplete goods has driven much new behaviour into management practise. Perhaps most significant of these are the complexities of fixed cost recovery, transfer pricing, and the separation of direct from indirect costs.

This, supposedly, precluded "anticipating income" or "declaring dividends out of capital". It is one of the intangible benefits of Lean and the TPS that process times shorten and stock levels decline to the point where the importance of this activity is hugely reduced and therefore effort, especially managerial, to achieve it can be minimised.

ACCOUNTING FOR INVENTORY

Each country has its own rules about accounting for inventory that fit with their financial reporting rules. So for example, organizations in the U.S. define inventory to suit their needs within US Generally Accepted Accounting Practices (GAAP), the rules defined by the Financial Accounting Standards Board (FASB) (and others) and enforced by the U.S. Securities and Exchange Commission (SEC) and other federal and state agencies. Other countries often have similar arrangements but with their own GAAP and national agencies instead.

It is intentional that financial accounting uses standards that allow the public to compare firms' performance, cost accounting functions internally to an organization and potentially with much greater flexibility. A discussion of inventory from standard and Theory of Constraints-based (throughput) cost accounting perspective follows some examples and a discussion of inventory from a financial accounting perspective.

The internal costing/valuation of inventory can be complex. Whereas in the past most enterprises ran simple one process factories, this is quite probably in the minority in the 21st century. Where 'one process' factories exist then there is a market for the goods created which establishes an independent market value for the good.

Today with multi-stage process companies there is much inventory that would once have been finished goods which is now held as 'work-in-process' (WIP). This needs to be valued in the accounts but the valuation is a management decision since there is no market for the partially finished product. This somewhat arbitrary 'valuation' of WIP combined with the allocation of overheads to it has led to some unintended and undesirable results.

Financial Accounting

An organization's inventory can appear a mixed blessing, since it counts as an asset on the balance sheet, but it also ties up money that could serve for other purposes and requires additional expense for its protection. Inventory may also cause significant tax expenses, depending on particular countries' laws regarding depreciation of inventory, as in Thor Power Tool Company v. Commissioner. Inventory appears as a current asset on an organization's balance sheet because the organization can, in principle, turn it into cash by selling it.

Some organizations hold larger inventories than their operations require in order to inflate their apparent asset value and their perceived profitability. In addition to the money tied up by acquiring inventory, inventory also brings associated costs for warehouse space, for utilities, and for insurance to cover staff to handle and protect it, fire and other disasters, obsolescence, shrinkage (theft and errors), and others. Such holding costs can mount up: between a third and a half of its acquisition value per year.

Businesses that stock too little inventory cannot take advantage of large orders from customers if they cannot deliver. The conflicting objectives of cost control and customer service often pit an organization's financial and operating managers against its sales and marketing departments. Sales people, in particular, often receive sales commission payments, so unavailable goods may reduce their potential personal income. This conflict can be minimised by reducing production time to being near or less than customer expected delivery time. This effort, known as "Lean production" will significantly reduce working capital tied up in inventory and reduce manufacturing costs role of a cost accountant on the 21st-century in a manufacturing organization

By helping the organization to make better decisions, the accountants can help the public sector to change in a very positive way that delivers increased value for the taxpayer's investment. It can also help to incentivise progress and to ensure that reforms are sustainable and effective in the long term, by ensuring that success is appropriately recognized in both the formal and informal reward systems of the organization. To say that they have a key role to play is an understatement. Finance is connected to most, if not all, of the key business processes within the organization. It should be steering the stewardship and accountability systems that ensure that the organization is conducting its business in an appropriate, ethical manner. It is critical that these foundations are firmly laid. So often they are the litmus test by which public confidence in the institution is either won or lost. Finance should also be providing the information, analysis and advice to enable the organizations' service managers to operate effectively. The traditional preoccupation with budgets – how much have we spent so far, how much have we left to spend? It is about helping the organization to better understand its own performance. That means making the connections and understanding the relationships between given inputs – the resources brought to bear – and the outputs and outcomes that they achieve. It is also about understanding and actively managing risks within the organization and its activities.

FIFO VS. LIFO ACCOUNTING

When a dealer sells goods from inventory, the value of the inventory is reduced by the cost of goods sold (CoG sold). This is simple where the CoG has not varied across those held in stock; but where it has, then an agreed method must be derived to evaluate it. For commodity items that one cannot track individually, accountants must choose a method that fits the nature of the sale. Two popular methods exist: FIFO and LIFO accounting (first in - first out, last in - first out).

FIFO regards the first unit that arrived in inventory as the first one sold. LIFO considers the last unit arriving in inventory as the first one sold. Which method an accountant selects can have a significant effect on net income and book value and, in turn, on taxation. Using LIFO accounting for inventory, a company generally reports lower net income and lower book value, due to the effects of inflation.

This generally results in lower taxation. Due to LIFO's potential to skew inventory value, UK GAAP and IAS have effectively banned LIFO inventory accounting. In computer science, FIFO and LIFO correspond to the queue and stack data structures, respectively. In fact, the acronyms are commonly used to denote the corresponding data structures.

STANDARD COST ACCOUNTING

Standard cost accounting uses ratios called efficiencies that compare the labour and materials actually used to produce a good with those that the same goods would have required under "standard" conditions. As long as similar actual and standard conditions obtain, few problems arise. Unfortunately, standard cost accounting methods developed about 100 years ago, when labour comprised the most important cost in manufactured goods. Standard methods continue to emphasize labour efficiency even though that resource now constitutes a (very) small part of cost in most cases. Standard cost accounting can hurt managers, workers, and firms in several ways. For example, a policy decision to increase inventory can harm a manufacturing managers' performance evaluation.

Increasing inventory requires increased production, which means that processes must operate at higher rates. When (not if) something goes wrong, the process takes longer and uses more than the standard labour time. The manager appears responsible for the excess, even though s/he has no control over the production requirement or the problem. In adverse economic times, firms use the same efficiencies to downsize, rightsize, or otherwise reduce their labour force. Workers laid off under those circumstances have even less control over excess inventory and cost efficiencies than their managers. Many financial and cost accountants have agreed for many years on the desirability of replacing standard cost accounting. They have not, however, found a successor.

THEORY OF CONSTRAINTS COST ACCOUNTING

Eliyahu M. Goldratt developed the Theory of Constraints in part to address the cost-accounting problems in what he calls the "cost world". He offers a substitute, called throughput accounting, that uses throughput (money for goods sold to customers) in place of output (goods produced that may sell or may boost inventory) and considers labour as a fixed rather than as a variable cost. He defines inventory simply as everything the organization owns that it plans to sell, including buildings, machinery, and many other things in addition to the categories listed here. Throughput accounting recognizes only one class of variable costs: the operating expenses like materials and components that vary directly with the quantity produced. Finished goods inventories remain balance-sheet assets, but labour efficiency ratios no longer evaluate managers and workers. Instead of an incentive to reduce labour cost, throughput accounting focuses attention on the relationships between throughput (revenue or income) on one hand and controllable operating expenses and changes in inventory on the other. Those relationships direct attention to the constraints or bottlenecks that prevent the system from producing more throughput, rather than to people - who have little or no control over their situations.

National Accounts

Inventories also play an important role in national accounts and the analysis of the business cycle. Some short-term macroeconomic fluctuations are attributed to the inventory cycle.

Distressed Inventory

Also known as distressed or expired stock, distressed inventory is inventory whose potential to be sold at a normal cost has or will soon pass. In certain industries it could also mean that the stock is or will soon be impossible to sell. Examples of distressed inventory include products that have reached its expiry date, or has reached a date in advance of expiry at which the planned market will no longer purchase it (e.g. 3 months left to expiry), clothing that is defective or out of fashion, and old newspapers or magazines. It also includes computer or consumer-electronic equipment that is obsolescent or discontinued and whose manufacturer is unable to support it.

IMPACT ON FIRMS' PERFORMANCE

A firm is required to maintain a balance between liquidity and profitability while conducting its day to day operations.

Liquidity is a precondition to ensure that firms are able to meet its short-term obligations and its continued flow can be guaranteed from a profitable venture. The importance of cash as an indicator of continuing financial health should not be surprising in view of its crucial role within the business. This requires that business must be run both efficiently and profitably. In the process, an asset-liability mismatch may occur which may increase firm's profitability in the short run but at a risk of its insolvency.

On the other hand, too much focus on liquidity will be at the expense of profitability and it is common to find finance textbooks begin their working capital parts with a discussion of the risk and return tradeoffs inherent in alternative working capital policies. Thus, the manager of a business entity is in a dilemma of achieving desired tradeoff between liquidity and profitability in order to maximize the value of a firm. Small businesses are viewed as an essential element of a healthy and vibrant economy. They are seen as vital to the promotion of an enterprise culture and to the creation of jobs within the economy.

Small Medium-Sized Enterprises (SMEs) are believed to provide an impetus to the economic progress of developing countries and its importance is gaining widespread recognition. Equally in Mauritius the SMEs occupy a central place in the economy, accounting for 90% of business stock (those employing up to 50 employees) and employing approximately 25% of private sector employees.

Storey (1994) notes that small firms, however, they are defined, constitute the bulk of enterprises in all economies in the world. However, given their reliance on short-term funds, it has long been recognized that the efficient management of working capital is crucial for the survival and growth of small firms. A large number of business failures have been attributed to inability of financial managers to plan and control properly the current assets and current liabilities of their respective firms. Working capital management (WCM) is of particular importance to the small business. With limited access to the long-term capital markets, these firms tend to rely more heavily on owner financing, trade credit and short-term bank loans to finance their needed investment in cash, accounts receivable and inventory. However, the failure rate among small businesses is very high compared to that of large businesses.

Studies in the UK and the US have shown that weak financial management - particularly poor working capital management and inadequate long-term financing - is a primary cause of failure among small businesses. The success factors or impediments that contribute to success or failure are categorized as internal and external factors.

The factors categorized as external include financing (such as the availability of attractive financing), economic conditions, competition, government regulations, technology and environmental factors. While the internal factors are managerial skills, workforce, accounting systems and financial management practices.

Some research studies have been undertaken on the working capital management practices of both large and small firms in India, UK, US and Belgium using either a survey based approach to identify the push factors for firms to adopt good working capital practices or econometric analysis to investigate the association between WCM and profitability. Specific research studies exclusively on the impact of working capital management on corporate profitability of the small manufacturing companies are scanty, especially for the case of Mauritius.

The financial management of small firms in developing countries and in particular, Mauritius, a small island developing state is altogether an ignored area of research. Keeping this in view and the wider recognition of the potential contribution of the SME sector to the economy of developing countries, our study is a modest attempt to measure and analyse the trend of working capital investment and needs of small manufacturing firms.

This study, therefore, attempts to assess the impact of WCM on profitability of a sample of small manufacturing companies and its results are expected to contribute to the existing literature on working capital and SMEs. The study objectives are to examine the working capital management of the sample firms, and in particular to:

- To examine the impact of accounts receivables days, inventories days, accounts payable days and cash conversion cycle on return on total assets; and
- To analyse the trend in working capital needs of firms and to examine the causes for any significant differences between the industries.

Nature and Importance of Working Capital

The working capital meets the short-term financial requirements of a business enterprise. It is a trading capital, not retained in the business in a particular form for longer than a year. The money invested in it changes form and substance during the normal course of business operations.

The need for maintaining an adequate working capital can hardly be questioned. Just as circulation of blood is very necessary in the human body to maintain life, the flow of funds is very necessary to maintain business. If it becomes weak, the business can hardly prosper and survive. Working capital starvation is generally credited as a major cause if not the major cause of small business failure in many developed and developing countries.

The success of a firm depends ultimately, on its ability to generate cash receipts in excess of disbursements. The cash flow problems of many small businesses are exacerbated by poor financial management and in particular the lack of planning cash requirements. *The Management of Working Capital* While the performance levels of small businesses have traditionally been attributed to general managerial factors such as manufacturing, marketing and operations, working capital management may have a consequent impact on small business survival and growth.

The management of working capital is important to the financial health of businesses of all sizes. The amounts invested in working capital are often high in proportion to the total assets employed and so it is vital that these amounts are used in an efficient and effective way. However, there is evidence that small businesses are not very good at managing their working capital. Given that many small businesses suffer from undercapitalization, the importance of exerting tight control over working capital investment is difficult to overstate. A firm can be very profitable, but if this is not translated into cash from operations within the same operating cycle, the firm would need to borrow to support its continued working capital needs.

Thus, the twin objectives of profitability and liquidity must be synchronised and one should not impinge on the other for long. Investments in current assets are inevitable to ensure delivery of goods or services to the ultimate customers and a proper management of same should give the desired impact on either profitability or liquidity. If resources are blocked at the different stage of the supply chain, this will prolong the cash operating cycle. Although this might increase profitability (due to increase sales), it may also adversely affect the profitability if the costs tied up in working capital exceed the benefits of holding more inventory and/or granting more trade credit to customers.

Another component of working capital is accounts payable, but it is different in the sense that it does not consume resources; instead it is often used as a short term source of finance. Thus it helps firms to reduce its cash operating cycle, but it has an implicit cost where discount is offered for early settlement of invoices.

Review of previous studies Although working capital is the concern of all firms, it is the small firms that should address this issue more seriously. Given their vulnerability to a fluctuation in the level of working capital, they cannot afford to starve of cash. The study undertaken by revealed that small firms tend to have a relatively high proportion of current assets, less liquidity, exhibit volatile cash flows, and a high reliance on short-term debt.

The recent work of Howorth and Westhead (2003), suggest that small companies tend to focus on some areas of working capital management where they can expect to improve marginal returns. For small and growing businesses, an efficient working capital management is a vital component of success and survival; *i.e* both profitability and liquidity. They further assert that smaller firms should adopt formal working capital management routines in order to reduce the probability of business closure, as well as to enhance business performance.

The study of Grablowsky (1976) and others have showed a significant relationship between various success measures and the employment of formal working capital policies and procedures. Managing cash flow and cash conversion cycle is a critical component of overall financial management for all firms, especially those who are capital constrained and more reliant on short-term sources of finance. Given these peculiarities, Peel and Wilson (1996) have stressed the efficient management of working capital, and more recently good credit management practice as being pivotal to the health and performance of the small firm sector.

Along the same line, Berry *et al* (2002) finds that SMEs have not developed their financial management practices to any great extent and they conclude that owner-managers should be made aware of the importance and benefits that can accrue from improved financial management practices.

The study conducted by De Chazal Du Mee (1998) revealed that 60% enterprises suffer from cash flow problems. Narasimhan and Murty (2001) stress on the need for many industries to improve their return on capital employed (ROCE) by focusing on some critical areas such as cost containment, reducing investment in working capital and improving working capital efficiency.

The pioneer work of Shin and Soenen (1998) and the more recent study of Deloof (2003) have found a strong significant relationship between the measures of WCM and corporate profitability. Their findings suggest that managers can increase profitability by reducing the number of day's accounts receivable and inventories. Studies on working capital management and financial management of small firms have focused on the US, UK and some other developed countries like Belgium and Australia.

Methodology

The primary aim is to investigate the impact of WCM on corporate profitability of Mauritian small manufacturing firms. This is achieved by developing a similar empirical framework first used by Shin and Soenen (1998) and the subsequent work of Deloof (2003). We extend our study by also analysing the trends in working capital need of firms and to examine the possible causes for any significant differences between the industries. Our study focuses exclusively on the small manufacturing firms operating in five major industry groups which are both registered and organised as proprietary/private companies. This restriction places a limit on the number of firms qualifying for the study and is further narrowed down following the revised Companies Act of 2001 which requires firms with a given turnover threshold to file only an aggregated financial statements.

Thus the empirical study is based on a sample of 58 small manufacturing companies. The data has been collected from the financial statements of the sample firms having a legal entity and have filed their annual return to the Registrar of Companies. The sample was drawn from the directory of Small Medium Industrial Development Organisation (SMIDO), a database for registered manufacturing firms operating in diverse activities and for which data was available for a 6 years' period, covering the accounting period 1997-98 to 2002-03. The companies qualified for the two conditions are further grouped into industries based on the classification as listed in the 2003 directory. Thus the data set covers 58 firms from five industry sub-sectors: food and beverages, leather garments, paper products, prefabricated metal products and wood furniture.

This has given a balanced panel data set of 348 firm-year observations for a sample of 58 firms. For the purpose of this study, profitability is measured by Return on Total Assets (ROTA), which is defined as profit before interest and tax divided by total assets. The operating income measure of profitability used in the study of Deloof (2003) is not appropriate for this study. The SMEs is characterised by a low fixed assets base and relied to a large extent on accounts payable to fund its gross working capital. Thus a comprehensive measure of profitability is best captured by computing the return on total assets which is equal to the total liabilities of the firms, made up mainly of equity capital and current liabilities. Some firms have significant fixed financial assets and were thus excluded from the calculation of ROTA.

The Explanatory Variables

The efficiency ratios, namely accounts receivable, inventory and accounts payable have been computed. The Cash Conversion Cycle (CCC) is used as a comprehensive measure of working capital as it shows the time lag between expenditure for the purchases of raw materials and the collection of sales of finished goods.

The longer the cycle, the larger the funds blocked in working capital. The return on assets is a better measure since it relates the profitability of the business to the asset base. There are many ways of managing return on assets but, in principle, key levers are, of course, profit increase and assets reduction. The latter has become more important to many businesses as the former becomes more elusive.

Control Variables

In order to account for firm's size and the other variables that may influence profits, sales a proxy for size (the natural logarithm of sales), the gearing ratio (financial debt/total assets), the gross working capital turnover ratio (sales/current assets) and the ratio of current assets to total assets are included as control variables in the regressions. The regressions also include the ratio of current liabilities to total assets to measure the degree of aggressive financing policy, with a high ratio being relatively more aggressive.

Return on total assets is on average 5.6% with paper products industry having the highest return of 11%. The leather and garments industry reported a negative operating profit margin, which could be explained by their high foreign exchange risk exposure and the high labour costs. Typical to the SME sector, the firms have relied mostly on short-term financing, with the metals industry being more aggressive, with an average of 82%. On average firms collect their receivables after 65 days while they take on average 116 days to pay suppliers. The average CCC is 105 days, implying that typical to the manufacturing sector firms turnover their stocks on an average of 3.3 times a year.

This shows the influence of leather and garments, metals products and wood and furniture industries holding inventories for more than 150 days, with a maximum value of 1688 days. Mean sales value for the sample companies is 10 million rupees, with only the paper products industry having a value twice the amount. On average about 22% of all assets are financed with financial debt. It is also noteworthy that the average firm in the sample has a gross working capital turnover ratio of 3.1, thus indicating a lower operational efficiency.

Working Capital Analysis

The major components of gross working capital include stocks (raw materials, work-in-progress and finished goods), debtors, cash and bank balances. The composition of working capital depends on a multiple of factors, such as operating level, level of operational efficiency, inventory policies, book debt policies, technology used and nature of the industry. While inter- industry variation is expected to be high, the degree of variation is expected to be low for firms within the industry.

A comparison of inventory composition of industries over the years shows only slight improvement for the food and beverages and the paper products industries. It is interesting to note the consistent improvement in trade debtors share of current assets in all the industries and except for the food and beverages, it represents less that 30% of total current assets.

Thus it can be deduced that the companies have monitored the accounts receivable reasonably well and this could be partly due to their need for generating funds from the operating activities instead of relying from outside funds. Except for the paper products, the other four industries have a greater reliance on short-term funds and this is even more in 2003. The prefabricated metal product is financing 85% of its assets out of current liabilities and this over-reliance may be a threat to the industry's survival. In terms of liquidity, all the four industries, food and beverages, garments, metal products, wood and furniture are having less liquid assets to meet their current obligations and if this becomes permanent, it may affect supplies of materials and thus production.

The proportion of liquid assets to total assets is above 70% for the wood and metal industries, indicating a low fixed assets base. This implies that these two industries can operate with a relatively low investment in fixed assets as compared to the other industries like printing and garments where the production tend to be heavily mechanised. Another plausible reason could be that the Mauritian small manufacturing firms have been more concerned about current operations than about longer term issues like capacity and technology.

Weinraub and Visscher (1998), also report industry-wise differences in the level of aggressiveness with respect to working capital investment over time. Pearson correlation coefficients for the variables used to assess the impact of working capital management on profitability, measured by return on total assets. ROTA is significantly positively correlated with OPM and capital-turnover ratio, but negatively correlated with the measures of WCM, except for the cash conversion cycle.

This positive relation for CCC is consistent with the view that resources are blocked at the different stage of the supply chain, thus prolonging the operating cycle. This might increase profits due to increase sales, especially where the costs of tied up capital is lower than the benefits of holding more inventories and granting more trade credit to customers.

Also the small manufacturing firms may be able to obtain trade credit from the suppliers and this is supported by the higher proportion of current liabilities to total assets for all the industries except for the paper products. However, care must be exercised while interpreting the Pearson Correlation coefficients because they cannot provide a reliable indicator of association in a manner which controls for additional explanatory variables. Examining simple bivariate correlation in a conventional matrix does not take account of each variable's correlation with *all* other explanatory variables. Our main analysis will be derived from appropriate multivariate models, estimated using fixed effects framework and pooled OLS. The different analyses have identified critical management practices and are expected to assist managers in identifying areas where they might improve the financial performance of their operation.

The results have provided owner-managers with information regarding the basic financial management practices used by their peers and their peers attitudes towards these practices. The working capital needs of an organization change over time as does its internal cash generation rate. As such, the small firms should ensure a good synchronization of its assets and liabilities.

This study has shown that the paper and printing industry has been able to achieve high scores on the various components of working capital and this has positively impact on its profitability. On this premise this industry may be referred as the 'hidden champions' and could thus be used as best practice among the SMEs.

Further, this research concludes that there is a pressing need for further empirical studies to be undertaken on small business financial management, in particular their working capital practices by extending the sample size so that an industry-wise analysis can help to uncover the factors that explain the better performance for some industries and how these best practices could be extended to the other industries. This would also assist policy-makers and educators to identify the requirements of, and specific problems faced by small firms in Mauritius, especially as more emphasis is placed on the sector by the government.

This study has come at an opportune time where the Mauritian government is deploying resources to help the SME sector so that the latter can positively contribute to the Mauritian economy. This analysis has been constrained by the sample size and the nature of the data, which could have well affected the results. Further studies will aim at increasing the sample size for still better and consistent panel estimates. Many pharma could focus on increasing sales and investing in new markets, without worrying too much about housekeeping. Times have changed and in future, domestic economies will play a far greater part in maintaining profitability in the industry.

One area where pharma could create value is in working capital management. Structure and Structure and Marc Loneux from working capital consultancy REL, the largest US and European pharrna companies have up to US$25 billion tied up in working capital that could be liberated through better management. The same companies could a further billion by reducing costs and implementing better business practice.

His comments are based on research conducted by REL on pharma's practices in this field. Like performance management, working capital management has been a priority for older industries with lower margins, but has been largely ignored by pharmaceutical companies. However, it is now widely recognised that operating efficiencies will be a major contributor to the long-term value growth in the industry.

At the end of 2004, the net operating working capital of the 18 largest pharmaceutical companies in the world (by sales, 13 US and five European) was US$79 billion. US firms had between US$6.4 billion and US$16 billion tied up in working capital. European companies have between US$4.6 billion and US$0.3 billion that could be liberated. Dealing with this excess would increase the market value of the US companies by between (0.8 per cent and 2.1 per cent.

Of the European firms included in the survey, better capital management could increase their value by between 0.9 per cent and 1.8 per cent. The smallest pharma companies in the US, together with Roche in Europe, offer the greatest potential for creating market value. Although there is a specific working capital model for every business sector, there are general principles that can be applied everywhere. One of The largest US and European pharma companies have up to US$25 billion tied up in working capital these is close collaboration between producers, sellers and wholesalers. This creates a win-win situation, giving manufacturers a better view of demand, and allowing both parties to manage their inventories more effectively. The automotive industry, in particular, has provided good collaborative models, as has the computer manufacturer Dell, which produces computers only when they are ordered and has negotiated very good payment terms with its suppliers.

Pharma has begun to implement better inventory-management practice over the past two years, with some firms entering inventory management agreements with their wholesalers. As a result, parts of the industry have levelled the quarterly volume fluctuations that once made it difficult to streamline production and reduce inventories. Improving working capital management also creates savings elsewhere. "We are talking about improved collection, improved logistics and supply chain, further consolidation, more efficient buying and so on,".

When you implement best practice in working capital, you can cut the number of collectors and people involved in wholesaling and logistics. You can also reduce write-offs in receivables because your inventories are lower. A more general strategy for pharma is "optimising the commercial". Focusing better on the product mix, ensuring that companies make the most of what they have out there, withdrawing or postponing launches in order to maximise the model.

Such strategies could prove a problem with governments and other healthcare providers, who are seemingly ready to oppose what they regard as manipulation of the market. It appears that pharma industry leaders are increasingly focused on engaging with external agents - governments, healthcare providers and patients - to develop a more collaborative working model.

Loneux acknowledges these difficulties, but thinks public-private collaborations pioneered by the likes of Bill Gates and GlaxoSmithKline are the way forward, ensuring people get medicines they can afford with a decent return for pharma.

Asked about the cost-effective ness of outsourcing admin, sales and marketing roles, Loneux is sceptical. He believes this will have a negligible impact on costs and that possible savings in R&D are limited by the quality constraints placed on pharma manufacturing - companies can't place the work just anywhere.

Moreover outsourcing is often done to serve local demand. Although many companies are opening up in India, where there is a growing market, demand is still largely concentrated in Europe and the US. "There is some outsourcing in India by the big ones. After the research was carried out, REL showed its work to some of the major pharma companies. Loneux comments

7

Planning for Working Capital Investment

FACTORS INFLUENCING WORKING CAPITAL PERFORMANCE

In practice, though, working capital management has become the Achilles' heel of scores of finance organizations, with many CFOs struggling to identify core working capital drivers and the appropriate level of working capital. From the perspective of the Chief Financial Officer, the concept of working capital management is relatively straightforward: to ensure that the organization is able to fund the difference between short-term assets and short-term liabilities.

As a result, companies can be limited in their ability to weather unforeseen or adverse events and ensure that cash is readily available where it is needed, regardless of the circumstances. By understanding the role and drivers of working capital management and taking steps to reach the "right" levels of working capital, companies can minimize risk, effectively prepare for uncertainty and improve overall performance.

For most CFOs, the greatest challenge with respect to working capital management is the need to understand and influence factors that are out of their direct control, in order to obtain a complete picture of the company's needs. The CFO's span of control can be limited in terms of functional silos, though corporate finance may well have some powers of influence over operating units. While organizations generally concentrate on the right processes, such as cash, payables and their supply chain, they are less likely to take into account various internal and external constraints that can dictate how effectively those processes are executed.

For example, the legal and business environments can have a significant impact on performance. Similarly, internal considerations—such as organizational structure, shared systems, autonomous business units, multinational operations and even information technology—can impact working capital, creating barriers that can hinder a CFO's ability to truly understand, and therefore manage, the company's needs. The human factor is another important consideration.

If management is focused purely on top-line growth, insufficient attention may be applied to cash flow management and forecasting. A hard-line focus on year-end or quarter-end results can produce a flattering, but inaccurate, picture of working capital performance and lead to counter-productive behaviour. Consider the impact on working capital of a year-end sales push, where production has been building up inventory (which may not be the appropriate inventory) to meet this artificial demand, and the quality of receivables deteriorates during the early part of the following year. While there is no magical solution for effecting robust working capital management, there are a number of prerequisites for gaining control of the complex process.

CASH FLOW FORECASTING

Proper cash flow forecasting is essential to successful working capital management. To do this effectively, organizations must take into account internal and external working capital drivers and consider the sensitivity of those drivers to changes in the business or market. Various questions need to be asked: How will unforeseen events impact working capital requirements? What if a sudden market downturn or upturn occurs? What if the company loses a major customer? What happens if a major competitor takes a significant action to improve its market position? Since each of these could have a sizable impact on the business, organizations must assume that the only certainty will be uncertainty, and prepare accordingly. In addition to assessing the cash flow impact of potential events, companies should consider the possibility of having to make additional working capital investments. That's because events could affect non-operational cash requirements such as investments, credit ratings and the ability to service debt, as well as inventory, payables and receivables. Companies must implement contingency plans that take a holistic view of the organization in the context of a variety of different challenging situations.

This will help minimize the adverse effects of unforeseen events and provide financial flexibility in uncertain times by having working capital as a ready source of cash. How can you manage uncertainty? The three fundamental approaches are: control it, predict it, react to it. The most successful approaches are based around one approach, but contain elements of all three. Market-leading companies, perhaps not surprisingly, are in the best position to manage uncertainty, often enjoying the ability to control supply, minimize inventory and apply payment pressure on customers.

Companies with less influence, however, must rely more heavily on a strategy of prediction. To properly prepare for events and improve or maintain performance during times of uncertainty, organizations must develop an objective, business-driven view of the role of working capital. Without real insight into true working capital drivers, a company may be able to produce a reasonably good consolidated forecast, but find that accuracy drops considerably when it comes to producing divisional, operating unit or even a product-line forecast.

Beyond Balance Sheets

The most effective programmes for both improving working capital performance and forecasting are those that look beyond the local organization and consider the broader corporate environment. Corporate investment and financing arrangements, for example, may provide for cash to be delivered by one location, but utilized at others. Restrictions on the repatriation of cash, internal inefficiencies in moving cash, delays driven by banks and sometimes-inadequate access to information can make the process problematic. Cash generated in one country, for example, many not have the same value to the organization as cash generated in another. As a result, companies must plan global working capital improvement initiatives in the context of the ultimate use for the cash, rather than simply managing local balance sheets.

IMPROVING WORKING CAPITAL MANAGEMENT

Successfully improving working capital management requires a multi-pronged approach. Companies must seek granular detail to identify the underlying drivers of working capital. This requires separating perception from reality and pinpointing impediments to efficient cash flow, such as poor links between production and billing or clumsy treasury operations. Companies must also adopt an entrepreneurial mindset. They must performance quickly to drive change by combining operational and financial skills, and expand their thinking beyond the finance organization to gain a more complete view of overall operations.

Rather than wait for the perfect solution, they must identify and implement strategies that result in quick wins, generating short-term cash to fund longer-term projects. Having the right people in place can also make or break the effort. Companies need to identify individuals who can be responsible for setting targets and performance levels and be held accountable for delivering. These professionals should be encouraged to challenge the status quo and drive change, using cross-functional teams.

Measured Approach

Finally—and this is where many projects fail—companies must remove emotion from the analysis process. All initiatives must be business-case driven, and projects without measurable results or those not contributing to overall goals should be abandoned. Companies must agree on success criteria, prioritize based on contributions to these criteria and continuously measure performance. While working capital forecasting is critical to a company's ability to make informed strategic business decisions, many CFOs struggle with the process because of a lack of control and real insight into the underlying drivers of their working capital needs. By empowering the entire organization to understand the company's true working capital needs, companies can successfully reduce their financial risk, prepare for uncertainty and create a ready cash reserve that will provide flexibility and security during difficult times.

CORPORATE WORKING CAPITAL MANAGEMENT

Several recent business studies suggest that corporations, on average, over-invest in working capital. For example, REL Consultancy Group has for years conducted an annual survey of corporate working capital management practices for CFO Magazine, which CFO Magazine then reports.

The *REL 2005 Working Capital Survey* concludes that U.S. corporations had roughly $460 billion unnecessarily tied up in working capital. Similarly, the results of a study arguing that poor working capital management practices cost IT companies billions of dollars annually. Do US corporations over-invest in working capital? If so, to what extent is this due to agency problems? We address both of these questions in this study. To see how important the efficiency of a corporation's working capital management can be, we use an example given in Shin and Soenen (1998).

Shin and Soenen (1998) point out that Wal-Mart and Kmart had similar capital structures in 1994, but because Kmart had a cash conversion cycle of roughly 61 days while Wal-Mart had a cash conversion cycle of 40 days, that Kmart likely faced an additional $198.3 million per year in financing expenses. Such evidence demonstrates that Kmart's poor management of its working capital contributed to its going bankrupt. As their 2005 U.S. survey report points out, there is a high positive correlation between the efficiency of a corporation's working capital policies and its return on invested capital. Using data on a panel of U.S. corporations from 1990 through 2004, we find evidence of a significantly negative relationship between firm value and investment in working capital that is consistent with over-investment in working capital.

An additional $1 million investment in working capital is associated with a roughly 119 to 129 thousand dollar reduction in firm value. To put this in perspective, a firm that under-utilizes debt by $1 million, can increase firm value by roughly $140 thousand at current rates by increasing its interest tax shield. Consequently, it is clear that working capital management decisions have corporation valuation effects of the same magnitude of corporate capital structure decisions – and so probably warrant just as much attention.

Turning to what influences a firm's management of working capital, we find that a firm's working capital policy is influenced by its industry's working capital policies, its size, its expected sales growth, the proportion of outside directors on its board, the current compensation of its CEO, and its CEO's share ownership. Consequently, managerial incentives and the monitoring of management are significant influences on a firm's working capital management performance.

Shin and Soenen point out that a corporation's working capital is the result of the time lag between the expenditure for the purchase of raw materials and the collection from the sale of finished goods. As such, it involves many different aspects of corporate operational management: management of receivables, management of inventories, use of trade credit, etc. Consequently, there are streams of research on individual aspects of working capital management (cash and marketable securities, e.g. Mauer, Sherman and Kim, trade credit, e.g. Rajan and Peterson etc.).

However, Schiff and Lieber, Sartoris and Hill, and Kim and Chung (1990) all emphasize the need to consider the joint effects of these individual policies, particularly with respect to inventory and credit decisions. For this reason, we only discuss the prior literature that focuses on overall working capital management. With respect to the effect of working capital management on firm value, we find no direct evidence. While Schiff and Lieber (1974), Sartoris and Hill (1983), and Kim and Chung (1990) model the effects of working capital management practices on firm value, they do not provide evidence on whether firms actually do maximize their value by their working capital management choices.

The study that comes nearest to addressing this issue is the study by Shin and Soenen (1998), which examines the relation between different accounting profitability measures and net trade cycles, a summary efficiency measure of a firm's working capital management. Shin and Soenen's study implies, without providing direct evidence, that firms that manage their working capital more efficiently (*i.e.*, shorter net trade cycle) experience higher operating cash flow and are potentially more valuable.

However, this last implication does not necessary follow because firms that have longer net trade cycles are also investing in short-term assets which may pay off in subsequent periods. Further, their evidence does not speak to whether the market sees firms as over-investing in net working capital. So the question as to whether firms over-invest in net working capital on average is unanswered by prior research.

As for the determinants of working capital practices, we find even less prior evidence on which to draw. Nunn uses the PIMS database to examine why some product lines have low working capital requirements, while other product lines have high working capital requirements. In addition, Nunn is interested in "permanent" rather than temporary working capital investment as he uses data averaged over four years. Using factor analysis, he identifies factors associated with the production, sales, competitive position, and industry. Reinforcing the role of industry practices on firm practices, Hawawini, Viallet, and Vora examine the influence of a firm's industry on its working capital management.

Using data on 1,181 U.S. firms over the period 1960 to 1979, they conclude that there is a substantial industry effect on firm working capital management practices that is stable over time. From these studies, we conclude that sales growth and industry practices are important factors influencing a firm's investment in working capital. There are models to describe how working capital management practices influence firm value, there is practically no evidence that firms manage their working capital so as to maximize their value. Further, there is little evidence on what factors influence a firm's management of working capital, particularly whether agency cost issues are concerns.

Sample and Sample Data

To address these questions, we examine samples of U.S. public corporations from 1990 through 2004. We begin by identifying all U.S. corporations with Compustat and CRSP data over this time period. Next, we exclude all firms in financial service industries as working capital has a very different meaning in these industries. This sample is what we examine when we study the effect of investment in net working capital on firm value. To study what influences working capital management performance; we add data from a number of different data sources, which reduces our sample in different analyses. First, we use the Investor Responsibility Research Centre (IRRC) Governance database to obtain data on certain corporate governance features over the 1990 through 2004 time period.

The availability of these data underlies our choice of time period to study. Specifically, IRRC collects data on governance provisions in effect for at least 3,155 major US corporations consisting of the S&P 1500 firms and other companies selected "primarily on the basis of market capitalization and high institutional ownership levels" over the years 1990 to 2004. As the original IRRC data is biennial and sometimes triennial, we use the filling method adopted by Gompers Ishii and Metrick (2003) and lately followed by Bebchuk Cohen and Ferrell (2004) in building our sample for all the years over the sample period.

We say the maximum number because the number of firms with IRRC data is larger than the number of firms with S&P Execucomp data and the number of firms with IRRC's Directors data. We use the IRRC's Directors database to collect information on the board of directors of sample firms. We use S&P Execucomp database to collect information on CEO compensation and share ownership. The use of these data further in our analysis of what factors influence a firm's working capital performance

Capital Cash Flow Analysis

While earlier examples focused on the costs associated with investment in working capital, they do not address the potential benefits. Clearly a company has to have stock on hand in order to make some sales. Further, competition between firms may require them to provide customers with interim financing in the form of trade credit – which becomes a receivable to the supplier. Thus, the net effect of investment in working capital is not as straightforward as earlier examples suggest. To discern if firms over-invest in working capital, we use the capital cash flow valuation model used in Kaplan and Ruback (1995) as our guide.

Like Kaplan and Ruback, we add the firm's current cash balances and use a net working capital definition that excludes investment in cash balances. This approach is particularly valuable in our context as it allows us to separate out cash management issues, which have been the focus of a separate literature and Pinkowitz and Williamson, from working capital management issues. Based upon this DCF valuation model, we develop two regression models to ascertain the relationship between firm investment in net working capital and its market value. Thus we are able to address the question of whether or not the market sees firms as over-investing in net working capital.

Regression Model 2

Our first regression model follows the DCF valuation approach taken in Kaplan and Ruback (1995). However, the analysis ignores incremental investment in cash and marketable securities. Whether such incremental investment should be included or excluded is unclear because some formulations of the DCF valuation framework use definitions of working capital that includes cash and marketable securities and some do not. To estimate these two regression models, we use Compustat data. The first variable, MVF(t), represents the market value of the firm computed as in Fama and 8 French (2002). Specifically, we start with total assets, subtract the book value of equity and add back the market value of equity as of the end of fiscal year.

To estimate, CASH(t), we use the cash and marketable securities balance of the firm at the same point in time as we measure its market value. We do this to be consistent with the way that Kaplan and Stein measured cash balances in their valuation model. To estimate *OCF*(*t*+1), we use the two approaches described in Kaplan and Stein (1995), and like their paper, we only report the results based on the second approach as the results are similar. Specifically, we start with net income; add back depreciation and amortization expense, interest expense, and the proceeds from the sale of fixed assets.

To estimate *INVL*(*t*+1), we use the firm's investment in long-term assets (PPE) from its cash flow statement. Using changes in PPE as an alternative measure does not change our ceases and so we only report results using this measure. To estimate *INVS*(*t*+1), we use a definition of net working capital that is consistent with the one in Kaplan and Stein's paper. Specifically, we use current assets minus cash and marketable securities, minus accounts payable, and minus accrued expenses. There are two important points to note about this definition. First, we are separating out investment in cash and marketable securities.

Second, we are focused on the investment in current assets that must be financed with non-spontaneous or outside sources of financing. This definition is consistent with our valuation model. To estimate *INVC*(*t*+1), we compute the change in the balance of cash and marketable securities between fiscal years. It is important to note that we estimate for the fiscal year subsequent to the date on which we measure the value of a firm and its cash balances. We do this to be consistent with our valuation model. The next issue that we have to confront is how to specify the data generating process for our regression models. It should be fairly obvious that MVF(t) is a nonnegative random variable. While some researchers have scaled MVF(t) by the book value of assets to create an estimate of Tobin's q. We do not take this approach, though as suggested, see that it does not later, as it introduces additional problems when there is more variation in book values of assets than in any of the explanatory variables. One 9 alternative is to take the logarithm of the dependent variable and use OLS to estimate a linear regression on it. Unfortunately, as Manning (1997) explains, this is not always appropriate, and can lead to biased estimates of the marginal effects of the explanatory variables.

Consequently, we follow the recommendation of Hardin and Hilbe and use a generalized linear model approach with a log link assumption. Specifically, we adopt a general estimating equation approach (a GMM approach) using the logarithm link function, $ln(E(y|x))$, and estimate the standard errors using the Rogers/Huber/White estimators adjusted for clustering at the firm level. Both models give fairly similar results. Current cash balances, operating cash flow, and investment in fixed assets are all positively priced. The last inference suggests that additional investment in fixed assets for most firms increases their value.

Interestingly, all these inferences are consistent with those that would be derived from estimates reported in either Faulkender or Wang (2005) or Pinkowitz and Williamson (2005). More importantly, for our study, we find that the coefficient on the investment in working capital variable is significantly negative. Following the interpretation of equation (4), this result implies that at the margin, firms tend to over-invest in working capital on average. As well as various annual REL Working Capital Surveys.

Apparently, the market recognizes this over-investment and discounts firms for it. Evaluated at the mean values of the explanatory variables, an additional $1 million investment in working capital is associated with a roughly $129 thousand reduction in firm value. To put this in perspective, a firm that under-utilizes debt by $1 million, can increase firm value by roughly $140 thousand at current rates by increasing its interest tax shield.11 Consequently, it is clear that working 9 capital management decisions have corporation valuation effects of the same magnitude of corporate capital structure decisions – and so probably warrant just as much attention.

The analysis provides evidence that on the margin, firms appear to over invest in net working capital on average. It is important to note that this result does not suggest that the value of net working capital is negative, but rather the incremental value of working capital is negative as we only examine investment at the margin. Since our valuation model is not typically that used in empirical corporate finance, we use the valuation framework proposed in Pinkowitz and Williamson (2005), which is an extension of the valuation framework proposed in Fama and French (1998), to explore the robustness of our results.

To implement this approach we use Compustat data for the sample firms in our prior valuation analysis to compute the following variables taken from Pinkowitz and Williamson (2005). *M* is the market value of equity following Fama and French's (1998) definition. *E* is earnings before extraordinary terms, plus interest, deferred tax credits and investment tax credits. *NA* is assets minus cash. *NNA* is *NA* minus accounts receivable and inventory. *RD* is research and development expense. *I* is interest expense. *DIV* is common cash dividends. *C* is cash and marketable securities. *NWC* is account receivable plus inventory minus accounts payable. Following Pinkowitz and Williamson, we divide each of these variables by total assets for the period, so that X(t) is the level of variable X in year t divided by the level of assets in year t. In addition, we compute dX(t) as the change in the level of X from year t-2 to year t divided by total assets in year t.

And finally, we compute dX(t+2) as the change in the level of X from year t to year t+2 divided by total assets in year t. Pinkowitz and Williamson argue that if the firm is not at some optimum, then changes are important to include to capture movements towards or away from the optimum. While we are dubious of this interpretation, we follow their example. While

Pinkowitz and Williamson uses the methodology of Fama and MacBeth (1973) to estimate their regression models, we use the panel data approach advocated in Peterson (2005) as it appears superior to the Fama and MacBeth methodology. Thus all our standard errors are estimated using Roger estimators adjusted for clustering on the firm level.

Our results for their base specification are somewhat different than theirs as our estimated coefficient on the level of cash variable is 0.701, rather than 0.97 as in their study. This difference may be due to the difference in time period studied: their regression covers 1950 to 1999, while ours covers 1990 through 2004. Other than differences in numerical values, our estimates share the same signs as their estimates. Building on this base specification, we next estimate a regression model with net assets reduced by investment in accounts receivable and inventory and then add a variable for investment in net working capital, defined by accounts receivable plus inventory minus accounts payable as this mimics our prior definition of net working capital.

The negative and significant coefficient on the level of net working capital investment is consistent with our prior estimated valuation model result in that it suggests that firms on average over-invest in net working capital. Before reaching a cease on how much, we next estimate a specification that includes prior and future changes in net working capital investment and report. The reported results suggest that prior and future investment in net working capital increase firm value. Such estimated coefficients suggest that Pinkowitz and Williamson interpretation of their change variables is somewhat questionable as we should not observe a negative sign on the coefficient associated with the current level of investment in net working capital if their interpretation was correct.

Nevertheless, we can estimate the total effect of investment in net working capital on firm value by evaluating its effect through current, past and future investment in net working capital. Evaluated at our sample averages, the total effect is that an additional $1 million investment in net working capital overall reduces firm value by roughly $119,326. What is striking about this estimate is that it is close to the $129,000 estimate that we derive from our prior valuation analysis. Given this consistency, we conclude 12 that our valuation analysis suggests that the market views firms as over-investing in net working capital on average.

That corporations over-invest in net working capital, the next question is why. One obvious possibility is that managers do not expend the effort necessary to minimize net working capital because of incentive compatibility problems, or agency problems. Prior literature suggests that there are three likely sources of misalignment: (1) CEO incentives, (2) board incentives, and (3) the structure of corporate governance. As suggested, explore each of these possibilities, but before we do we must first develop a basic model to identify potential control variables. Thus, we conduct this analysis in a series of steps.

We first develop a core model, and then we explore the influence of board characteristics, CEO compensation and ownership, and finally corporate charter provisions on a corporation's efficiency in managing its working capital. As our dependent variable in these regressions, we use a firm's cash conversion cycle (*i.e.*, the inventory conversion period plus the receivables collection period minus the payables deferral period using Compustat data) as our measure of the efficiency of its working capital management. While there are alternatives, such as Shin and Soenen's NTC measure, the cash conversion cycle measure (CCC) is standard in many corporate finance textbooks and is used in the *REL Working Capital Surveys* as a summary measure.

Consequently, we follow industry and textbook practice and use this measure for the efficiency of a firm's overall working capital management. Note that we winsorize this and all of our accounting and compensation variables at the 1% level to avoid distortions due to outliers. For our core model, we conjecture that the following factors are significant influences on a firm's working capital management. First, prior research such as Hawawini, Viallet, and Vora (1986) suggests that industry practices are significant determinants of a firm's working capital management practices. The working capital 13 policies of say a software company are going to be quite different from those of a retail shoe company. Consequently, it is important to control for the influence of industry practices on a firm's working capital practices.

To do this, we use the median cash conversion cycle of firms within a firm's industry, *CCCM*, to proxy for the typical working capital practices within such industry. For our identification of a firm's industry we use the Fama and French (1997) 48 industry delineations. Second, firm size may influence the efficiency of a firm's working capital management. Larger firms may require larger investments in working capital because of their larger sales levels. Or, alternatively, larger firms may be able to use their size to forge relationships with suppliers that are necessary for reductions in investments in working capital.

Current supply chain management practices require a lot of coordination between companies and are typically easier for a larger firm to implement than for a smaller firm to implement. Thus, firm size is likely to influence the efficiency of a firm's working capital management, though the direction of the effect is an open question. We use a firm's total assets, *TA*, as our proxy for its size.

Third, the proportion of a firm's assets accounted for by fixed assets might exercise an influence on a firm's working capital performance. For example, the inventory problems of an automobile parts manufacturer are likely to be quite different from that of a software manufacturer. Further, the receivables problems of these types of companies are also likely to be different. To measure this variable, we take the ratio of a firm's property, plant and equipment to its total assets, and name it *PTA*.

Fourth, based upon Nunn's (1981) evidence, we expect firm sales to influence a firm's working capital management. In this connection, and consistent with our earlier regression results, we expect a firm's expected future sales to influence its working capital investment, and so its cash conversion cycle. For example, a firm might build up inventories in anticipation of future sales growth, and as a result, may also increase its use of trade credit. To proxy for such growth, we use the firm's percentage sales growth over the future two years and name this variable, *FSG*. Finally, some might argue that firms with some degree of market power are able to work deals with suppliers and customers that give them an advantage over competitors. To capture this possibility, we compute the Herfindahl-Hirschman index using sales data for each firm's industry, again using Fama and French's (1997) 48 industry delineations.

The more concentrated the industry the more likely this will influence the cash conversion cycles of firms within it. We denote this variable as *HHI*. To determine the relevance of the above core factors to the efficiency of a firm's working capital management, we regress the firm's cash conversion cycle, *CCC*, on these above factors.

Before conducting this analysis, we must address the specification of the data generating process as *CCC* is a non-negative random variable. While we would prefer to use the same data generating process specification used in our valuation analysis, it does not appear appropriate for these data. A Hausman type test indicates that a random effects model is inappropriate in this case, and so we use a fixed effect model on a logarithmic transformed dependent variable and estimate Rogers/Huber/White standard errors adjusted for firm level clustering.

These results suggest that firms do not use their size or market power to reduce their cash conversion cycle. If anything, they use their position to relax their efforts. Of the factors examined, industry practices are the main determinant of a firm's working capital practices. In addition, positive future sales growth is associated with increased investment in net working capital.

And finally, firms with more tangible long-term assets reduce their investment in net working capital. These results, we now add the board characteristics of a firm to our core regression model to extend it. We use two characteristics to capture the essential features of a corporation's board: its size measured by the number of directors (*DIR*), and its proportion of outsiders on the board (*POD*). Prior literature leads us to expect that larger boards might be lax in monitoring management and so be associated with longer cash conversion cycles than other firms in their industry.

Conversely, prior literature suggests that more outsiders on the board lead to greater monitoring of management, which we expect will result in shorter cash conversion cycles for these firms. These results suggest that board size is not a significant influence, but that board composition is. The greater the proportion of outsiders on the board, the better the performance of the firm's working capital management. This result is consistent with the monitoring role of outsider directors.

Continuing this line of inquiry, we now include the compensation and share ownership of the CEO in our expanded regression model. The more the CEO is paid, the more likely they will have incentives to reduce a firm's cash conversion cycle. Consequently, we expect the firm's cash conversion cycle to be negatively correlated with the CEO's total current compensation. We measure such compensation that comprises of CEO's salary and bonus using the Execucomp database and denote it as *TCCOMP*. Note that we exclude their current period stock option grants from this measure and only focus on their current non-stock compensation.

We exclude their current stock option grants because we instead focus on their total unexercised stock option holdings. Stock options granted in the past might be just as important an influence as current stock option grants in our attempt to capture managerial incentive alignment with shareholder interests. Consequently, it might be better to recognize a CEO's total unexercised stock option position. To estimate this quantity, we use the Execucomp database to estimate the dollar value of the CEO's unexercised stock options and denote this variable as *TUO*. Finally, we can expect the CEO's current shareholdings to influence the management of the firm's cash conversion cycle. For this reason, we construct the proportion of stocks held by the CEO and call it *CEOPS*. Unfortunately, the effect of this variable is less clear as it could either create incentives for the manager to tightly control this cycle, or if it could create incentives for managers to expend less effort on this activity if they have the power to avoid the expenditure of such effort.

While both CEO compensation components have a negative influence on their firm's cash conversion cycle, only the total current compensation component has a statistically significant effect. In some ways this is consistent with our earlier expectation that a firm's investment in working capital primarily influences its performance in the current and near future periods. Consequently, we should expect current CEO compensation to have a greater influence on the firm's cash conversion cycle, while we might expect their unexercised stock options to influence their long-term investment decisions.

Interestingly, the CEO share ownership is significantly positively related to their firm's cash conversion cycle. So, the incentive effect of stock ownership appears to be dominated by other effects of CEO stock ownership. Expanding our regression model further, we now include a consideration of the firm's corporate charter provisions. Such provisions have figured prominently in recent literature on cash management as result of Gompers, Ishii, and Metrick's (2003) evidence on the relationship between these corporate characteristics and equity returns.

To begin this analysis, we follow Harford, Mansi, and Maxwell and simply include Gompers, Ishii and Metrick's governance index, *GINDEX*. The reported evidence does not suggest that these firm characteristics are significant influences on a corporation's working capital performance. Whether this cease is correct is somewhat unclear as the GINDEX assumes that all of charter provisions have the same influence on a firm's cash conversion cycle and that assumption has been subject to criticism in recent governance literature. For example, executive severance agreements such as golden parachutes can give management an incentive to agree to a takeover, while poison pills ostensibly are intended to deter takeovers. More importantly, some provisions (e.g., advance notice requirements) are intended to primarily influence internal changes in corporate governance, while other provisions (e.g., supermajority requirements for a merger) are intended to solely deter external changes in corporate control without any impact on internal governance.

Consequently, we create several indices which group governance features by intended purpose. Our component indices are: internal provisions, external provisions, compensation and liability provisions, minority voting provisions, and state laws. The rationale for each is as follows. Primarily influences its performance in the current and near future periods. Consequently, we should expect current CEO compensation to have a greater influence on the firm's cash conversion cycle, while we might expect their unexercised stock options to influence their long-term investment decisions.

Interestingly, the CEO share ownership is significantly positively related to their firm's cash conversion cycle. So, the incentive effect of stock ownership appears to be dominated by other effects of CEO stock ownership. Expanding our regression model further, we now include a consideration of the firm's corporate charter provisions. Such provisions have figured prominently in recent literature on cash management as result of Gompers, Ishii, and Metrick's (2003) evidence on the relationship between these corporate characteristics and equity returns. To begin this analysis, we follow Harford, Mansi, and Maxwell and simply include Gompers, Ishii and Metrick's governance index, GINDEX.

The reported evidence does not suggest that these firm characteristics are significant influences on a corporation's working capital performance. Whether this cease is correct is somewhat unclear as the GINDEX assumes that all of charter provisions have the same influence on a firm's cash conversion cycle and that assumption has been subject to criticism in recent governance literature. For example, executive severance agreements such as golden parachutes can give management an incentive to agree to a takeover, while poison pills ostensibly are intended to deter takeovers.

More importantly, some provisions (e.g., advance notice requirements) are intended to primarily influence internal changes in corporate governance, while other provisions (e.g., supermajority requirements for a merger) are intended to solely deter external changes in corporate control without any impact on internal governance. Consequently, we create several indices which group governance features by intended purpose. Our component indices are: internal provisions, external provisions, compensation and liability provisions, minority voting provisions, and state laws.

The rationale for each is as follows. The internal provisions index, INTERNAL, includes provisions that limit the constitutional rights of shareholders, like staggered boards, limitations on shareholder rights to amend charter and bylaws, and advance notice requirements. Therefore, the internal provisions index focuses on provisions that primarily influence internal governance or changes in the internal control of a firm. The external provisions index, EXTERNAL, which is constituted of provisions like poison pills, supermajority requirements to approve mergers, fair price, and anti-greenmail, focuses on provisions that are primarily used to thwart external control contests (*i.e.*, takeover bids).

The compensation and liability provisions index, *C&L*, focuses on provisions that primarily influence directors' legal liability costs, or compensation received by officers and directors in the event of a control change. The minority voting provisions index, *MVP*, focuses on shareholder voting rules, mainly cumulative and confidential voting rules. The state laws index, *SLAWS*, focuses on anti takeover provisions endorsed state law. Because these anti takeover statutes are often implemented by default in all firms incorporated in a particular state, and are sometimes redundant with the presence of firm level anti-takeover defences, it is not clear that they add much. The regression results from substituting these component indices for the GINDEX. While the negative sign on both the internal provisions index and the compensation and liabilities index are consistent with the arguments in Baranchuk, Kieschnick, and Moussawi (2005) in that such provisions help managers to maximize the value of potential growth options in their establishments, neither coefficient is statistically significant.

Further, none of the coefficients of the different corporate charter indices are statistically significant and so we conclude that the corporate charter characteristics of a corporation do not significantly influence its working capital management performance. Overall, our evidence for the compensation and governance variables suggest that monitoring of management and managerial compensation are more important influences on a firm's management of its working capital.

Several recent business studies suggest that US corporations, on average, over invest in working capital. If correct, and if recognized by the market, then one should observe a negative relation between investment in working capital and firm value. We address this issue by examining data on samples of U.S. corporations from 1990 through 2004. We find that on average firms have over-invested in their working capital in the sense that additional investment in working capital is associated with a reduction in firm value. Such a cease appears consistent with the various annual surveys by REL Consultancy for the *CFO Magazine* on corporate working capital performance.

Apparently the market recognizes this over-investment and discounts firms for it. However, one can also view the flip side of this evidence and explain why firms like Wal-Mart suggest that their working capital management practices are a source of their value. Given this evidence, we then turn to the question of what factors influence the efficiency of a corporation's working capital management. We find that the inefficiency of a firm's working capital management is positively correlated with firm size and uncorrelated with its industry's concentration. We interpret these results as suggesting that firms are not using their market power at the margin to improve the efficiency of their working capital management practices. Instead, they tend to follow the practices of their industry. Further, they tend to invest in working capital in anticipation of future sales growth. Expanding this analysis to include different firm governance features, we find evidence that the larger the proportion of outsiders on a firm's board, the better its working capital management performance.

Such evidence is consistent with the monitoring of management role of outside directors. Taking the CEO's compensation and stock ownership also proves important. The larger the CEO's current compensation the better the firm's working capital management performance. However, the larger the CEO's share of the firm's stock, the contrary behaviour is shown. Finally, taking corporate charter features in account, we find no evidence that any such features are significant influences on a corporation's working capital management practices.

Consequently our evidence appears to emphasize the role of board monitoring of management and management's compensation in its control of the firm's working capital. One question that is raise by our study is what determines industry practices, as it is clear from our firm level analyses that industry practices are a critical determinant of firm practices. We defer this issue to future research.

8

Working Capital Control and Banking Policy

CAPITAL CONTROL

In economics, capital control is the monetary policy device that a country's government (*i.e.,* sovereign power) uses to regulate the flows into and out of a country's capital account, *i.e.,* the flows of investment-oriented money into and out of a country or currency. The decade since the Asian Currency Crisis in 1997-1998 has rekindled debate over the wisdom of developing markets having capital controls. As globalization advanced with the formalization of the World Trade Organization and Uruguay Round of General Agreement on Tariffs and Trade (GATT), developing countries were urged by the International Monetary Fund and others to liberalize their capital controlled environments.

As it became clear that countries doing this, including Malaysia, Thailand and Mexico, essentially ceded control of their economies to external forces, namely international capital movements, hot money and capital flight; and countries that did not, like China and India, retained control and were not nearly as vulnerable to the volatility of international capital movement, some argued that capital controls were advisable for smaller economies to use, and to transition away from them only over long, general evolutionary timelines. Malaysia is an example of a country that switched regimes, from open in the late 1990s, to closed. Economists supporting capital controls in certain cases were not only from the left, but also liberal economists like Jagdish Bhagwati and news publications like The Economist.

Banking Policy and Trends Policy Measures

The major policy measures taken in the current financial year as part of the annual monetary and credit policy statement, including its mid-term review. These include freedom for banks to lend at interest rates below their respective PLRs to exporters and other creditworthy borrowers (including public enterprises), permission to formulate fixed deposit plans offering higher and fixed interest rates to senior citizens, flexibility in the composition of working capital as between cash credit and loan components, reduction in exposure limits for borrowers, revised guidelines for exposure of banks to capital market, and guidelines for investment in non-SLR securities through the private placement route. The initiatives specially aimed at strengthening the operational efficiency of banks relate to the Voluntary Retirement Plan, the Banking Service Recruitment Boards, Credit Information Bureau, and enlargement of the reach and scope of the electronic funds transfer facility.

Voluntary Retirement Plan (VRS)

VRS was implemented by 26 out of 27 public sector banks in 2000-2001. Indian Banks. Association (IBA), the total staff strength in public sector banks at the end of March 2000 was 8, 63,188 out of whom 1, 26,714 or 14.7 per cent applied for VRS. About 80 per cent of the number of applications were accepted, and the staff relieved under VRS until December 31, 2001 were 1, 01,300.

This constituted 11.7 per cent of the total staff strength at the end of March 2000. Banks were advised by the Reserve Bank to treat the ex-gratia payment as deferred revenue expenditure (DRE), which would not be reduced from Tier I capital. The position will be regularised by the end of the accounting year in which the DRE gets totally wiped out. The maximum period of deferment has been fixed at five years, including the year of acceptance of VRS applications by the banks.

Banking Service Recruitment Boards

In pursuance of the announcement made by the Finance Minister in his Budget speech, the Banking Service Recruitment Boards (BSRBs) have been abolished. Accordingly, banks have been advised to frame their own recruitment strategies, with the approval of the respective Boards, to meet future requirements.

While framing such strategies, banks are required to ensure, inter alia, that the recruitment policy is transparent and fair, with due representations of the members of SC/ST and minority communities in selection committees. Banks have also been advised to ensure that reservations in posts and related concessions/relaxations in fees and marks, as laid down by the Government of India, are strictly followed.

Electronic Funds Transfer (EFT)

EFT facilitates transfer of funds electronically within and across cities and between branches of a bank and across banks. EFT is operated by RBI, and is available for funds transferred across 13 major cities in the country as on January 11, 2002. With effect from October 1, 2001, large value transactions upto Rs. 2 crore have been permitted under EFT. Transfer of funds on a "same-day" basis was implemented effective from January 2, 2002 at the four metro centres with three settlements per day.

SMALL AND MEDIUM ENTERPRISES (SMES)

Problems Facing the SSI Sector

The SSI sector confronts several problems despite its strategic importance in any industrialisation strategy and its immense potential for employment generation. The problem which continues to be a big hurdle for the development of the sector is lack of access to timely and adequate credit. The Abid

Hussain Committee on SSIs (1997) examined the problems of the SSI sector and recommended a package of policies to restructure the industry in the context of current global economic changes. The Expert Committee was of the view that the existing institutional structure for delivering credit to SSEs needs a thorough overhaul.

It endorsed the recommendations of the Nayak Committee and urged the RBI to implement the same. The Committee recommended restructuring of financial support through SFCs and SIDCs, tapping of other sources of funding for SSEs, extending credit rating servcies to small units, and addressing the credit needs of tiny units to ensure that they are not bypased by the commercial banking system. The overall credit availability for SSIs during 1991-1996 amounts to only 13% of the value of production.

The Nayak Committee had recommended a desirable norm of 20% of the value of production to be made available by way of working capital through term-lending institutions and commercial banks A norm of 75% was set for fixed capital assets whereas actual availability is only 55%. Lack of finance has been one of the major causes of sickness in the SSI sector, blocking access to technological modernisation and other growth possibilities. There is an urgent need to enlarge flow of credit to the SSI sector from institutional sources.

The creation of a facilitating environment for SSIs will centre on access to credit. The Ninth Five Year Plan estimates additional working capital funds at Rs. 1420 to 1460 billion for the small sector. Lowering interest-rates, specifying a time-frame to clear loan applications and adherence to norms set down by the Nayak Committee are some of the minimum measures that need to be taken. Legislative measures have a role to play with regard to funding and financing of small scale units. There are measures which can basically ensure that impediments to credit availability are removed. These measures include:

- Right to reasonable credit from commercial banks as per RBI guidelines framed after consultation with representative Board

- Protection against non-normative demands for security
- Appeal and enforcement by Ombudsman/Board
- Access to public funds by way of debentures, deposits, securities
- Government guarantee for loans from banks

The measures to support Marketing and Competitiveness are as follows:

- State to exempt from contract security
- Prompt return of contract securities in case of others
- Prompt payment measures
- Protection against undue bundling of contracts by the state
- Protection against restrictive and monopolistic trade practices
- Ombudsman/arbitral services for enforcement

IMPACT OF WTO

The emerging challenges to the small-scale sector are to come from the impact of the Agreements under WTO to which India is a signatory along with 134 member countries. The setting up of the WTO in 1995 has altered the framework of international trade towards non-distortive, market-oriented policies. This is in keeping with the policy shift that occurred worldwide since the early 1980s in favour of free market forces and a tilt away from State regulation/intervention in economic activity.

This is expected to lead to an expansion in the volume of international trade and changes in the pattern of commodity flows. The main outcomes of WTO-stipulated requirements will be brought about through reduction in export subsidies, greater market access, removal of non-tariff barriers and reduction in tariffs. There will also be tighter patent laws through regulation of intellectual property rights under the TRIPS Agreement which lays down what is to be patented (both products and processes), for what duration (20 years instead of the present 7 years under India's 1970 Patent Law), and on what terms. The responses by trading countries and the reframing of domestic economic policies which will result from the impact of WTO and the repercussions on the global economy of all these changes are highly uncertain as they involve several unforeseeable factors. However, there are certain indications of the shape of future trade patterns. Increased market access to imports (of around 3% of domestic production to be raised to 5%) will mean opening up the domestic market to large flows of imports. The removal of quantitative restrictions (QRs) on imports has been speeded up to 2001.

At present 714 items are in the restricted category but imports of these items will soon be freed from all restrictions as announced in the recent EXIM policy. Increased market access under WTO requirements will also mean that our industries can compete for export markets in both developed and developing countries. But the expected surge in our exports can come about only if the SSI sector is restructured to meet the demands of global competitiveness which is the key to the future of small industries in the present context.

BANKING SYSTEM REFORMATION

SITUATION APPRAISAL

Monetary policy of the Belarusian authorities is distinguished by its unique character among the post-socialist countries of Central and Eastern Europe. Using, in contravention of the current legislation, "a printing press" as a source of covering low-effective public expenditure and levying thus enormous inflation tax on the population, the Government and the National Bank have achieved dubious economic growth and retained unproductive employment. As a result the country's economy has turned up in the financial and technological deadlock.

The following can be furnished to dramatize this thesis. Within the last six years net domestic ruble credit of the National Bank increased about 120 times, ruble money mass - approximately 210 times, official exchange rate of the Belarusian ruble decreased 111 times while consumer prices went up 161 times. These figures are undoubtedly indicative of the fact that "soft" monetary policy advocated by the present-day economic ideologists as presuming point-like public support to some branches at the expense of credit emission by the principle "emission to finance production of the goods does not lead to inflation" has appeared invalid.

Unique character of the monetary policy in Belarus is stipulated by the following causes. First, this is incredible economic incompetence of the Belarusian ruling elite as well as its total dependence upon the Head of the State. For some years the Government and the National Bank took and implemented decisions in the monetary sphere that were far away not only from the generally accepted practice in the civilized countries but also common sense. That concerns first of all the policy of covering public expenditure by credit emission of the National Bank, actual refusal of positive real interest rate, and attempts of administrative regulation of inflation and exchange rate.

Instead of real evaluation of financial possibilities of the country and use of budget resources, the authorities engaged in developing numerous programmes without effective facilities of implementation. Second, this is deep-rooted disrespect of own country that turned into chronic inferiority complex not allowing the majority of political elite representatives to get rid of the "provisional men" feeling. Out of ten years of its existence the Belarusian monetary system had perspectives of independent development for about one and a half years (end of 1994 - beginning of 1996). All other years passed under the sign of either a portion of the Russian money system (91-93) or pending fast "unification" (ruble zone of "new type", attempts to eliminate the Belarusian ruble in April of 1994, preparation and signing of the agreement on union state in 1996, etc.).

As a consequence long-term goals and benchmarks were absent in the monetary policy, facilities of its implementation were weak, qualified specialists left for commercial structures, relations with the international financial organizations were actually broken. Third, this is absence of the market reforms in the real sector of economy that would have forced the political power to pursue general economic and monetary policy facilitating the development of private business. Specifics of slow reformation of the real sector shown by the absence of systematic approaches and integrity in the introduced economic transformations have resulted in the fact that private sector has not received adequate development, and consequently middle class capable of sounding its economic interests has not been formed.

Shadow and semi-criminal business took the advantages of the effected economic policy. Economy of the country turned up eventually dependent on economic position of the public sector enterprises. In this situation all attempts, initiated by the specialists, to suggest and accomplish market plans of the monetary sphere were doomed to fail. Fourth, this is typical of the former USSR republics and extremely die-hard relapse of socialist attitude to legality when the laws are applied commensurate with their usefulness for a particular office holder. In case of the monetary system this principle can be emphasised by the following example.

The Law on The National Bank in effect from 1991 to 2000 stipulated that the latter could grant credits to the Government "for a term, as a rule, up to 6 months". Nevertheless, accretion of long-term credit amounts made up 122.6 billion rubles in 2000 alone (credits to cover budget deficit would be referred afterwards to the increase of domestic national debt). The Law on Banks explicitly barred the Government to interfere into activity of the banks. But that did not inhibit the Government to force the banks to provide credits to the Agro-Industrial Complex.

Such a queer way to interpret the laws has led to the fact that the enterprises and banks acted, as far as they could, in the same manner and avoided transparency of their operations at the money market. As a result steady and negative attitude was formed to the policy of the monetary authorities, and this is inadmissible in the pursuit of stabilization of the national monetary unit. Fifth, this is voluntarism in the formation of priority tasks of the economic policy and their misbalance. The

State lived beyond its income. Target parameters of volume indices (volume of housing construction, volumes of industrial output by the branches, etc.) passed over to the line ministries and departments were established arbitrary without taking available financial recourses of the State into account. Economic policy turned into a hostage of the populist political goals such as attainment of the GDP physical volume of 1990 in 2000.

Economic policy aimed at the growth of production at any expense by monetary expansion has brought about higher rates of inflation. Since 1997 the parameters of credit emission by the National Bank and growth of money mass in national currency invariably exceeded the target figures approved every year in the Major Directions of the Monetary Policy. The situation was aggravated by directive maintenance of the Belarusian ruble exchange rate at the overestimated level with introduction of mandatory surrender of the foreign currency receipts. That resulted in the appearance of multiple exchange rates and shadow foreign exchange market, more numerous barter deals, foreign currency deficit to pay for critical import, and a number of other adverse consequences.

For instance, share of housing construction in the total amount of credit emission of the National Bank made up 59% in 1999 and 38% in 2000 whereas this share is to total 90% as indicated in the forecast of the social and economic development for 2001. The housing construction credits were extended at a reduced interest rate of 5% per year (while average monthly inflation, for example, in 1999 was as high as 11%) and for long terms (up to 40 years). A narrow circle of people who got the opportunity to build dwellings under such conditions, was indirectly subsidized at the expense of other people who carried the burden of inflation tax. Weak and shadowed to a large extent economy could not generate a strong and civilized banking system.

The state of the Belarusian banking system within last five years can be characterized in the most general way by the following features. First, this is its chronic financial weakness. Assets of the Belarusian banks do not demonstrate noticeable tendencies to increase, and are in the state of deep stagnation. During the five-year period they decreased in currency calculation by 6%. The residue of credits on 01.01.2001 amounted to about 95% as compared with analogous index on 01.01.1996. Per cent of doubtful loans was on steady uprise - 17.9% of the balance of credit arrears on 01.01.2001 in comparison with 13.2% five years earlier.

Second, this is differentiation of the commercial banks by major indices. A privileged position and demonstrate unconditional support of the public sector of economy. Their share of resources amounts to 80-90% by main articles of the aggregated balance of assets and liabilities of the banking system. The share of Joint Stock Saving Bank "Belarusbank" exceeds in some cases the official index of monopolization - over 35%.

From the economic point of view this means that the most effective private business is limited in credit support by the banking system while the authorized banks being actually public, cannot expect significant preferences from external financial markets. As a result the banks and real sector are not able to feed each other, and are doomed to financial weakness.

Third, this is formality in observing the regulations of safe banking activity. The National Bank performed insurance of the deposits of the population only in the authorized banks. Up to 2000 the regulations of obligatory reserve formation were always lowered in practice - amount of reserves made up frequently only 5-6% with the official reserve norm of 16-18%.

Fourth, this is insufficient transparency of the banks. Over last nine years no trustworthy bank was set up in the country, and the information on financial position of the banks is accidental and published as a rule in non-public editions with small circulation. Therefore confidence of the enterprises and population to the banking system that is needed to accumulate free financial resources under the conditions of reliability and return is at the extremely low level in the present situation. It is no wonder that economic agents prefer to use any opportunity to export capital out of the country.

The problems of the Belarusian banking system together with the current monetary policy make any perspectives of its development indefinite. As a consequence that leads to financial isolation of a rather numerous group of the banks within the small and poor state and inevitable liquidation of the majority of them. The Belarusian authorities will have to face a new problem in 2001 - inconsistency between the declared rigid monetary policy and financial requirements of the unreformed real sector. Some indications were felt in 2000 when the National Bank merely tried to limit the rate of credit emission. With the statistical GDP growth of 5.8% the investments dropped by 3.4%, income on the sale of products - by 14.9%, profitability reduced by 2.3%, specific weight of loss-making enterprises increased by 6.4 per cent points to 23.5% of all enterprises. More rigid monetary policy will bring about bankruptcy of many enterprises and associated banks. That occurred at the stage of financial stabilization in practically all post-soviet republics.

General Conditions

Main directions and measures of the monetary policy for a middle-term period were suggested proceeding from the following circumstances:

- Beginning from February 2000 the Government and the National Bank pursue more weighted and considered monetary policy that includes limitation of credit emission by the National Bank to cover budget deficit, transfer to positive real interest rates, cancellation of the majority of currency market limits, and abolition of multiple currency exchange rates.
- Signature of the agreement with the Russian Federation on the transfer to common money unit in 2005 and monitoring programme with the IMF for a period of April-September 2001 (provided the agreement has been realised) forces the President Administration and the Government to take a number of certain measures towards reformation of the real sector of economy (liberalization of pricing,

privatization of public sector, bankruptcy of loss-making enterprises, lift of the barriers for the development of small and medium business).

Nevertheless, despite definite successes in the monetary sphere achieved in 2000, growth rates of prices are still at the inadmissibly high level.

The first objective source of inflation in the Belarusian economy has not been removed - high level of money mass growth. Failure to pay and deficiency of working capital of the enterprises in the real sector of economy caused by low economic efficiency generate constant demand for financial resources. In order to avoid bankruptcies of the loss-making enterprises and reduction of employment the Government, in the absence of other sources (foreign credits and private investments), meets the requirements predominantly at the expense of emission crediting.

The National Bank has to carry on emission financing of current cash gaps and deficit of the republican budget on the whole. Besides, methods of extra-economic character are used to force the commercial banks to continue crediting of the public programmes in the field of the Agro-Industrial Complex at their own resources.

The current macroeconomic policy must be based on the following principles:

- Systematic approach - mutual consistency of the measures and parameters of monetary, fiscal, foreign economic, structural, and institutional policy. The policy of financial stabilization should be accompanied with active privatization, and should produce conditions for restructuring of the real sector of economy, for creation of stimulating institutional environment to develop private business and attract foreign investments;
- Balanced targets of macroeconomic policy - radical inventory and review of the volume targets in the public programmes (housing construction, Agro-Industrial Complex, etc.) in order to make them consistent with the financial possibilities of the State.

TASKS OF THE MONETARY POLICY

Principle objective of the monetary policy is to form confidence on the part of business and households in the national money unit in the near future.

To attain this objective the following tasks have to be solved:

- To reduce the rate of inflation to 25% in the first year, 15% in the second, 5-10% in the third, and keep it afterwards at a level not exceeding 5% per year;
- To maintain positive real interest rate of all financial instruments denominated in the national currency. Attractive deposit policy will make it possible to increase specific weight of time ruble deposits in the money mass, which are the main source of credit resources for the needs of the real sector of economy. Owing to higher confidence in the national currency dollar-filling of the economy will be reduced, structures of the broad money mass will be improved by higher specific weight of the national currency in its total volume, monetization coefficient will be increased;
- To introduce the regime of floating exchange rate and secure convertibility of the Belarusian ruble in current operations. Activities of the National Bank should be limited by ironing out local, market fluctuations of the exchange rate and speculative misbalances in the currency demand and supply. Expediency of this exchange rate regime is determined by the fact that it corresponds to a great extent to the interests of small countries with transitional economy having export-oriented structure since the level of business activity and load of the available producing capacities directly depend on the demand for domestic products in the world market. This regime will make it possible to ensure competitiveness of the domestic goods due to the tendency of real exchange rate to reach an effective level. Taking moderate inflation within the period of stabilization into account (unlike the regimes with fixed exchange rate) burdensome currency interventions may be avoided.

- To set up a regulative base for the system of non-public financial institutions capable of servicing internal and external payment transactions as well as insuring safety of the money accumulations of the enterprises and savings of the households;
- To bring expenditure and revenue of the republican budget into balance.

Directions of Implementation

- Consecutive reduction of the accretion of net crediting of the budget deficit by the National Bank and its complete discontinuation by the third year of reforms. Positive effect consists in eliminating the major inner source of inflation and lowering the national currency exchange rate. Besides, the Government will be called "to live within its means".
- Reduction of the growth rate of net internal ruble credit of the National Bank to average 2-3% per month at the beginning of reforms and afterwards to 15-20% per year. That will generate rigid budgetary restrictions for all economic entities.
- Regulation of the growth rate of aggregate internal credit (ruble and foreign currency) in order to support the medium-term economic programme of the Government in proportion to expected growth of GDP.
- Securance of steady annual growth of net foreign assets of the National Bank to reach complete coverage of the national currency money base at the current exchange rate. In the given case the requirement for annual growth of foreign currency reserves has primarily psychological character that increases confidence in the current monetary policy.
- Preparation of the conditions (accumulation of net foreign assets and permanent control over the growth of ruble money mass) to tie up the Belarusian ruble to Euro with subsequent integration of the country into European Economic Community. The Authorities will

have to demonstrate adherence of the country to the European vector of development and to accept economic rules of the civilized market behaviour.

- Limitation of the growth rate of broad ruble money mass to average 2-3% per month in the first year of reforms and subsequently to 3.5-5% per year. As the rate of inflation goes down preconditions will appear to increase the coefficient of monetization of GDP.
- Successive reduction of the norm of obligatory reserves to 5-10% with total abolition of all privileges to the commercial banks. That will allow, first, to decrease the cost of ruble and foreign currency credits for the real sector of economy, and, second, provide the banks with the possibility to maintain sufficiently attractive interest rate on time deposits.
- Elimination of all restrictions in the domestic currency market to reach internal convertibility of the national money unit with subsequent transfer of the Belarusian ruble to convertibility on current operations.
- Regulative promotion of settlements in the Belarusian ruble within CIS and close neighbours - Poland, Baltic countries, Russia - to free the resources of convertible currencies for investment projects.
- Maintenance of the refinancing and interest rates in the money market at the level exceeding current level of inflation to stimulate saving and to promote investment process.

The measures must be executed in package. They will make it possible to augment confidence in the national money unit, to gradually edge out dollar as means of saving and circulation, to considerably increase foreign currency reserves of the National Bank. Furthermore, the suggested monetary policy is a prerequisite of integration of Belarus into the European Community.

THE BANKING SYSTEM REFORM

Principle purpose of reformation and restructuring of the banking system is to form a community of credit and financial institutions that are able to accumulate free internal and external financial resources with their profitable disposition, and to render all banking services to domestic and foreign customers. Main problems of the Belarusian banking system consist in its general financial weakness (as against 01.04.2001 it had assets totaling only 2 billion dollars out of which own resources were less than 17%, 44% - resources of the customers, and 10% - those of the National Bank). About half of all assets of the banking system are disposed as credits to the legal entities, majority of which are low-efficient and loss-making enterprises of the public sector. Total amount of doubtful, overdue and prolonged credits make up 19.2% out of the loans provided.

About 8.7% of the assets are disposed in the low-profit public securities. Deductions to obligatory reserves make up 4.7%. The banking system of Belarus does not practically possess financial instruments that are able to ensure accumulation of money resources in real calculation. Concentration of approximately 78% of all assets in six authorized semi-public banks that have to service public programmes associated with crediting of the low-efficient Agro-Industrial Complex and housing construction, produces a rather negative effect on the financial position of the banking system. The privileges on obligatory reserves and interest rates granted in return, do not permit to effectively regulate the money market by the market instruments and bring about certain distortions in its work.

Financial rehabilitation of the banking system must include two directions:

- Arrears of the real sector enterprises to the banks should be restructured;
- Recapitalization of the banks should be performed through attraction of additional financial resources to the banking system.

Restructuring of doubtful to redeem arrears of the enterprises to the banks can be implemented by two means: by conciliation procedures and by compulsory measures. In case the enterprise refuses to strike a conciliation agreement, the bank will have a right to initiate the procedure of bankruptcy irrespective of the form of property of the given enterprise in accordance with the current legislation (the Law on bankruptcy). Recapitalization of the banks during the period of common recovery of the economy may include the following measures:

- For the purpose of operational safety of the attracted resources extraordinary provisional measures are to be taken in all commercial banks to restore general liquidity of the banking system.
- Aggregate own capital of the Belarusian banks is to be significantly enlarged within first two years after beginning of the radical reforms.
- Spectrum of crediting and financial institutions is to be widened by setting up specialized non-banking institutions (investment, mortgage, leasing companies, societies of mutual crediting, etc.) assuming that some banks that do not have possibilities to enlarge their own capital, will be transformed into such institutions.
- A group of leading Belarusian banks is to be encouraged to get acknowledgement at the international financial markets including corresponding credit rating.
- International rules of accounting are to be used by the Belarusian banks. Main statistics on the commercial banks are to be passed over to independent analytical centres for systematic processing and publication of domestic bank rating.
- Transactions in the active accounts of the banks that fail to form reserves on doubtful credits are to be restricted (as against 01.04.2001 a sum of doubtful credits amounting to 153 billion rubles was covered by reserves only by 84% without prolonged and overdue credits, if such credits are taken into consideration - 57%).
- All banks with overdue arrears on extended credits in excess of 5% out of all granted credits, are to work

out a plan of own rehabilitation including a schedule of expected conciliation agreements with the borrowers and initiation of the procedure of bankruptcy.

The banks should be encouraged to develop a set of measures aimed at own financial rehabilitation:

- To adopt within 2-3 years a practice of preservation of the general licenses only for the banks having international rating;
- To work out a facility of coercive sale of the controlling block of stock of those banks that regularly fail to observe prudential norms and jeopardize the safety of the entire banking system. This right should be entrusted a banking supervision department or bank restructuring agency;
- To establish ultimate specific weight of the enterprise shares in the bank assets so that to encourage the banks to restore liquidity as fast as possible.

The Government and the National Bank should undertake in short order the following actions:

- Legal and actual restoration of sovereignty of the National Bank from the executive power as essential necessity of developing a modern banking system responsible before creditors and depositors.
- Withdraw the resources of the State and the National Bank from the equity capital of the commercial banks, primarily from Belarusbank and Belagroprombank, with their subsequent sale at free auctions. This is required, first, to make the conditions equal for all banks, and, second, to exclude possibility of non-market pressure of the Authorities and the National Bank on the money market through independent of them banks.
- Restoration of the specialized Saving Bank servicing exclusively the households and working in the money market. That will allow to raise the safety of household savings and to strengthen the market of long-term money resources.
- Reorganization of Belagroprombank by means of its

division into six (by number of regions) local land banks with transfer of the controlling block of shares to local authorities. That will allow development of regional financial markets around local land banks in the future.

- Creation of the third level of crediting and financial institutions - specialized non-bank crediting and financial institutions with limited license commissions and without the right to maintain settlement accounts of the legal entities and physical persons (investment, trust, mortgage and other companies, societies of mutual crediting, credit unions, etc.). As a result additional resources will be attracted to the money market including the ones from the "gray" economy. Specialization and better-quality crediting and financial services will be ensured, too.
- Setting of a special non-public fund as stock company to insure deposits of the households and time deposits of the legal entities. The fund will be replenished by proportional unrequited contributions of the banks and non-bank crediting and financial institutions. That will increase confidence in the banks and thus enlarge their resource base.
- Restriction of operations in the active accounts of the banks that fail to form reserves for doubtful credits.
- Development of a facility of accelerated lawsuits against enterprises-borrowers who are not able to redeem extended bank credits, their bankruptcy and property transfer for provisional management by recommendation of the bank-creditors.
- Development and adoption of a facility of coercive sale of the controlling block of stock of those banks that regularly fail to observe prudential norms and jeopardize the safety of the entire banking system. That will allow speeding up the procedure of owner change in the inefficient banks without their bankruptcy and public commotion, to attract more

professional management, and to reduce a share of problem banks in the banking system.

- Creation of the Union of commercial banks is to be initiated. The Union will assume jointly and severally responsibility for the financial position of the member-banks, up to setting up a special non-public company insuring deposit risks of the depositors and creditors of the "union banks" on one side, and providing recommendations to the agency supervising the banks on coercive sale of the controlling block of shares of the banks suffering financial problems, on the other side. That should prevent unexpected bank bankruptcies.
- The service in charge of surveillance over the commercial banks should be removed from the National Bank. An independent agency is to be set up on its base. That will allow to split the functions of licensing, regulation and supervision of the banking system, and to increase its transparency.
- Calculation of all prudential regulations proceeding from own capital of the banks and not from their equity capital. That will allow to abandon artificial attraction of new shareholders and to enlarge capitalization of already issued shares and their market value.
- Branches of reliable foreign banks are to be attracted to the country; their participation in the capital of already operating Belarusian banks will be encouraged, for example, through issue of American and European depositary receipts. That will allow to attract additional resources to the banking system and to intensify competition between commercial banks.
- Transfer to the international standards of financial reporting of the Belarusian banks for the purpose of their prompt adaptation to the world financial markets and procuration of appropriate bank ratings.
- Development of necessary actions aimed at getting

credit rating for Belarus and appropriate bank rating for the commercial banks. The banks that do not possess commonly accepted international rating, will have limited foreign currency licenses. Furthermore, the banks that do not possess internal national rating, will have limited domestic license to service the households.

- Review of all current banking legislation of the country in the following directions:
  - Distinct differentiation of powers between monetary entities;
  - Competition between monetary entities;
  - Supremacy of law in regulation of monetary relations;
  - Consideration of disputable issues by courts;
  - Material, administrative and other responsibility of any entity, including state authorities, for the damage inflicted by wrongful actions;
  - Transparency in relations between entities;
  - Provision of information to the public on the National Bank policy and position of the monetary institutions.

The measures suggested are aimed at financial strengthening of the Belarusian banking system, making it dynamic, transparent, including entry to the world financial markets as a full member. Unlike the block of monetary policy, their implementation does not require comprehensive approaches and may be executed any time as economic and political conditions get ready.

PERFECTION OF BANKING LEGISLATION

Appraisal of the Situation

Analysis of the monetary policy pursued in 1995-2000 has displayed that within the frames of the present institutional arrangement of the monetary sphere no regulating efforts on the part of the monetary authorities are able to radically improve its position, and relative stabilization of the money market is of short-term character. The legislation administering banking activities in Belarus proceeded from market principles on some positions. In the second half of the 90-ies when backtrack from the economic reforms began, bank regulating acts appeared unprotected from the edicts and decrees, equated to laws, of the President. Legal field of activity of the National Bank and commercial crediting and financial institutions was considerably deformed.

Suffice to note, that by the Presidential Decree of March 21, 1998 the National Bank, contrary to the Constitution, was subordinated in operative terms to the Government and remained in this position till June of 2000. The only way out is to develop and to introduce promptly the legislative base needed to implement market reforms in the monetary and banking system, and coordinated with the legislation in the real sector of economy. Adopted in the fall of 2000 a variant of the Banking Code of the Republic of Belarus does not meet the given requirements since it has retained to a great extent the drawbacks of the preceding legislation and in some positions deterioration has taken place.

Major Directions Banking Legislation Perfection

- Market principles applied in the majority of dynamically developing countries will be laid down in the basis of legislation regulating the banking activity.
- Transition to the monetary system of open type and market-based determination of the national currency official exchange rate should be sounded by legislation.
- Introduce historic name of the national currency - taler. That will emphasize final selection of the country development as a sovereign state.
- To establish the object of money regulation - amount and structure of money base, and total money mass in circulation as well.
- To determine main instruments and methods of

money regulation, principles of arranging money turnover, and order of cash money circulation.
- To set a rigid ban on using monetary emission to finance budget deficit and any public or other projects as well as banks for a period of over one year..
- To introduce limitations for participation of the emission bank in economic activity including participation in the capital of commercial banks.
- To secure exclusive responsibility of the National Bank for the development and execution of the monetary policy in the Republic of Belarus.
- Maximum transparency and openness of the National Bank should be established by legislation.
- The norms connected with central bank status should be significantly changed.

The most important legislative provision ensuring independence of the National Bank should be its accountability before the Parliament. Principle objectives and tasks of the National Bank are suggested to be defined in a legislative way: maintenance of price stability, securance of steady purchasing power of the national currency and its exchange rate with foreign currencies.

Independence of the National Bank of the executive power should be based on three chief principles: institutional, financial, and personal. Institutional independence means that no agency of state power and management as well as the highest state officials cannot give instructions to the National Bank in terms of its activity. Financial independence presumes own budget of the National Bank. That includes also establishment of the level and forms of labour compensation of its employees.

Personal independence of the National Bank management is arranged by strictly regulated order of appointment and dismission of its highest officials by the Parliament. The provision that stipulates the status of the Chairman of the Board of Directors of the National Bank as member of the Government should be cancelled. By virtue of the suggested autonomy of the National Bank the norms should be provided for regulation of interrelations between different levels of its management - Board and Council of Directors, by removing them from the internal statute of the central bank.

The law should legally arrange relations of the central bank with the government (prohibition of direct centralized crediting of budget deficit, commitments to secure liquidity of public short-term liabilities), mutual responsibility for pursued common monetary policy, and division of surveillance functions over crediting and financial institutions. An important part of the law is legal arrangement of the limits of licensing and surveillance powers of the National Bank, rules of their application, as well as the order of presentation of surveillance information on the activity of the banks and non-bank crediting and financial institutions to other agencies of state management and mass media. A new approach is needed to perform surveillance of the commercial banks and non-bank crediting and financial institutions.

State registration, licensing and cancellation of licenses of the commercial banks, establishment of main norms associated with regulation of the money market in the country should be left with the National Bank. Surveillance of the banks and non-bank institutions should be passed over to a special committee on surveillance of the activity of the crediting and financial institutions, rights and obligations of which will be defined in a special law. Licensing and regulation of the activity of the non-bank crediting and financial institutions should be entrusted with the Ministry of Finance.

Furthermore, all prudential supervision (control of liquidity, solvency, large risks, etc.) of the activity of all crediting and financial institutions will be given to a special supervising committee. Practice of the recent years has shown inefficiency of concentration of all functions in the National Bank. To temporary suspension of any license issued by the National Bank or Ministry of Finance. The supreme governing body of the committee is to be set up on a parity basis out of the representatives of the National Bank, Ministry of Finance, and members of the committee itself.

The following provisions should be specified in the law on the non-bank crediting and financial institutions:

- Non-bank institutions must not perform exclusively banking functions - attraction of deposits, extension of credits on their own behalf, and account keeping;
- Non-bank institutions must not have correspondent accounts in the single payment system;
- Specialization of the non-bank institutions should be maintained by issuing a limited number of licenses (not more than three);
- Relatively low start-up equity capital;
- Licensing of the non-bank crediting and financial institutions by the Ministry of Finance that suggests participation of the latter in pursuing of the financial policy coordinated with the National Bank.

New Banking Code will be structurally composed of a package of independent laws - on monetary system, on central bank, on banking universal and specialized crediting and financial institutions, on active, passive and intermediary banking operations, on non-bank crediting and financial institutions, on banking trust, on foreign currency operations and foreign exchange control, on mutual crediting of small business entities, on surveillance of the activity of the crediting and financial institutions (banking supervision) and some other legislative acts.

Each of them regulates in a legislative manner a separate sphere of monetary activities and defines responsibilities of separate legal entities and corresponding public authorities. Advantages of the suggested structure consist in the following: some component parts of the general code may be adopted and refined not as a whole but successively as corresponding economic conditions change, and as public authorities are ready to guarantee their observation and economic entities - their implementation.

BANKING REFORM IN INDIA

Measured by share of deposits, 83 per cent of the banking business in India is in the hands of state or nationalized banks, which are banks that are owned by the government, in some, increasingly less clear-cut way. Moreover, even the non-nationalized banks are subject to extensive regulations on who they can lend to, in addition to the more standard prudential regulations.

Government control over banks has always had its fans, ranging from Lenin to Gerschenkron. While there are those who have emphasized the political importance of public control over banking, most arguments for nationalizing banks are based on the premise that profit maximizing lenders do not necessarily deliver credit where the social returns are the highest. The Indian government, when nationalizing all the larger Indian banks in 1969, argued that banking was "inspired by a larger social purpose" and must "sub serve national priorities and objectives such as rapid growth in agriculture, small industry and exports." There is now a body of direct and indirect evidence showing that credit markets in developing countries often fail to deliver credit where its social product might be the highest, and both

- We thank the Reserve Bank of India, in particular Y.V. Reddy, R.B. Barman, and Abhiman Das, for generous assistance with technical and substantative issues. We also thank Abhiman Das for performing calculations which involved proprietary RBI data, as well as Saibal Ghosh and Petia Topalova for helpful comments. We are grateful to the staff of the public sector bank we study for allowing us access to their data. We gratefully acknowledge financial support from the Alfred P. Sloan Foundation.
- If nationalization succeeds in pushing credit into these sectors, as the Indian government claimed it would, it could indeed raise both equity and efficiency. The cross-country evidence on the impact of bank nationalization is not very encouraging. For example, find in a cross-country setting that government ownership of banks is negatively correlated with both financial development and economic growth.

- They interpret this as support for their view, which holds that the potential benefits of public ownership of banks, and public control over banks more generally, are swamped by the costs that come from the agency problems it creates: cronyism, leading to the deliberate misallocation of capital, bureaucratic lethargy, leading to less deliberate, but perhaps equally costly errors in the allocation of capital, as well as inefficiency in the process of mobilizing savings and transforming them into credit. Unfortunately the interpretation of this type of cross-country analysis is never easy, and never more so than the case of something like bank nationalization, which typically occurs as part of a package of other policies. For example, Bertrand et. al. study a 1985 banking deregulation in France, which gave banks much greater freedom to compete for clients.
- They find that deregulated banks respond more to profitability when making lending decisions. After the reform, firms that suffer a negative shock are much more likely to undertake restructuring measures, and there is more entry and exit in bank-dependent industries. Micro studies of the effect of bank nationalization are rare: an important exception is Mian who examines the privatization of a large public bank in Pakistan in 1991.
- He finds that the privatized bank does a better job both at choosing profitable clients and monitoring existing clients, than the commercial banks that remained public. Micro data from a nationalized bank to evaluate the effectiveness of the Indian banking system in delivering credit.
- The Indian financial system is characterized by under-lending in the sense that there are many firms that could earn large profits if they were given access to credit at the current market prices.

The work with the aim of using that evidence and evidence from other research by ourselves and others, to come to an assessment of the appropriate role of the Indian government vis a vis the banking sector. We first provide a very brief history of banking in India.

We begin by presenting evidence that there is substantial under-lending in India. To understand what role public ownership of banks may play in underlending, we identify differences between public and private banks in the sectoral allocation of credit between public and private banks. In particular, we focus on the question of whether being nationalized has made these banks more responsive to what the Indian government wants them to do. We report results, based on work by Cole showing that on many of the declared objectives of "social banking," the private banks were no less responsive than the comparable nationalized banks, with the exception of agricultural lending.

Finally, the last sub-section compares the performance of public and private banks as financial intermediaries and concludes that the public banks have been less aggressive than private banks both in lending, in attracting deposits and in setting up branches, at least since 1990. We find that official lending policy is very rigid. Moreover, loan officers do not appear to use what little flexibility they have. We argue that the evidence suggests that bankers in the public sector have a preference for what we may call passive lending.

To understand why this is the case, we examine the incentives and constraints faced by public loan officers. We focus on whether vigilance activity impedes lending, and whether public sector banks prefer to lend to the government, rather than private firms. The penultimate part compares the performance of public and private banking in two other areas. First, we examine how nationalization of banks has affected the availability of bank branches in rural areas, and find that, if anything, nationalization appears to have inhibited the growth of rural branches. Second, we try to say something about the sensitive issue of NPAs and bailouts.

While the dataset we have now is rather sparse, it appears that the bailouts of the public banks have proved more expensive for the government, but once we control for differences in size between the public and private banks, it is less clear-cut. We conclude in a short discussion of the implications of these results for the future of banking reform. Background India has a long history of both public and private banking. Modern banking in India began in the 18th century, with the founding of the English Agency House in Calcutta and Bombay. In the first half of the 19th century, three Presidency banks were founded. After the 1860 introduction of limited liability, private banks began to appear, and foreign banks entered the market. The beginning of the 20th century saw the introduction of joint stock banks. In 1935, the presidency banks were merged together to form the Imperial Bank of India, which was subsequently renamed the State Bank of India. Also that year, India's central bank, the Reserve Bank of India (RBI), began operation. Following independence, the RBI was given broad regulatory authority over commercial banks in India. In 1959, the State Bank of India acquired the state-owned banks of eight former princely states.

Thus, by July 1969, approximately 31 per cent of scheduled bank branches throughout India were government controlled, as part of the State Bank of India. The post-war development strategy was in many ways a socialist one, and the Indian government felt that banks in private hands did not lend enough to those who needed it most. In July 1969, the government nationalized all banks whose nationwide deposits were greater than Rs.500 million, resulting in the nationalization of 54 per cent more of the branches in India, and bringing the total number of branches under government control to 84 per cent.

Prakesh Tandon, a former chairman of the Punjab National Bank (nationalized in 1969) describes the rationale for nationalization as follows: Many bank failures and crises over two centuries, and the damage they did under 'laissez faire' conditions; the needs of planned growth and equitable distribution of credit, which in privately owned banks was concentrated mainly on the controlling industrial houses and influential borrowers; the needs of growing small scale industry and farming regarding finance, equipment and inputs; from all these there emerged an inexorable demand for banking legislation, some government control and a central banking authority, adding up, in the final analysis, to social control and nationalization.

After nationalization, the breadth and scope of the Indian banking sector expanded at a rate perhaps unmatched by any other country. Indian banking has been remarkably successful at achieving mass participation. Between the time of the 1969 nationalizations and the present, over 58,000 bank branches were opened in India; these new branches, as of March 2003, had mobilized over 9 trillion Rupees in deposits, which represent the overwhelming majority of deposits in Indian banks. This rapid expansion is attributable to a policy which required banks to open four branches in unbanked locations for every branch opened in banked locations. Between 1969 and 1980, the number of private branches grew more quickly than public banks, and on April 1, 1980, they accounted for approximately 17.5 per cent of bank branches in India.

In April of 1980, the government undertook a second round of nationalization, placing under government control the six private banks whose nationwide deposits were above Rs. 2 billion, or a further 8 per cent of bank branches, leaving approximately 10 per cent of bank branches in private hands. The share of private bank branches stayed fairly constant between 1980 to 2000. Nationalized banks remained corporate entities, retaining most of their staff, with the exception of the board of directors, who were replaced by appointees of the central government.

The political appointments included representatives from the government, industry, agriculture, as well as the public. (Equity holders in the national bank were reimbursed at approximately par). Since 1980, has been no further nationalization, and indeed the trend appears to be reversing itself, as nationalized banks are issuing shares to the public, in what amounts to a step towards privatization. The considerable accomplishments of the Indian banking sector notwithstanding, advocates for privatization argue that privatization will lead to several substantial improvements.

Recently, the Indian banking sector has witnessed the introduction of several "new private banks," either newly founded, or created by previously extant financial institutions. The new private banks have grown quickly in the past few years, and one has grown to be the second largest bank in India. India has also seen the entry of over two dozen foreign banks since the commencement of financial reforms. While we believe both of these types of banks deserve study, our focus here is on the older private sector, and nationalized banks, since they represent the overwhelming majority of banking activity in India.

The Indian banking sector has historically suffered from high intermediation costs, due in no small part to the staffing at public sector banks: as of March 2002, there were 1.17 crores of deposits per employee in nationalized banks, compared to 2.05 crores per employee in private sector banks. As with other government-run enterprises, corruption is a problem for public sector banks: in 1999, there were 1,916 cases which attracted attention from the Central Vigilance Commission.

While not all of these represent crimes, the investigations themselves may have a harmful effect, if bank officers fear that approving any risky loan will inevitably lead to scrutiny. Advocates for privatization also criticize public sector banking as unresponsive to credit needs. We use recent evidence on banking in India to shed light on the relative costs and benefits of nationalized banks. Throughout this exercise, it is important to bear in mind that the Indian banking sector is going through something like a transformation. Thus, it is potentially a dangerous time to evaluate its performance using historical data.

Under-lending therefore is a characteristic of the entire financial system: the firm has not been able to raise enough capital from the market as a whole. In other words, while as suggested, focus on the clients of a public sector bank, if these firms are getting too little credit from that bank, they should in theory have the option of going elsewhere for more credit. If they do not or cannot exercise this option, the market cannot be doing what, in its idealized form, we would have expected it to do. However, we know that the Indian financial system does not function as the ideal credit market might. Most small or medium firms have a relationship with one bank, which they have built up over some time–they cannot expect to walk into another bank and get as much credit as they want. For that reason, their ability to finance investments they need to make does depend on the willingness of that one bank to finance them. In this sense the results we report might very well reflect the specificities of the public sector banks, or even the one bank that was kind enough to share its data with us, though given that it is seen as one of the best public sector banks, it seems unlikely that we would find much better results in other banks in its category.

On the other hand we do not have comparable data from any private bank and therefore cannot tell whether under-lending is as much of a problem for private banks. As suggested,, however, later report some results on the relative performance of public and private banks in terms of overall credit delivery Our identification of credit constrained firms is based on the following simple observation: if a firm that is not credit constrained is offered some extra credit at a rate below what it is paying on the market, then the best way to make use of the new loan must be to pay down the firm's current market borrowing, rather than to invest more.

This is because, by the definition of not being credit constrained, any additional investment will drive the marginal product of capital below what the firm is paying on its market borrowing. It follows that a firm that is not facing any credit constraint will expand its investment in response to additional subsidized credit becoming available, only if it has no more market borrowing. By contrast, a firm that is credit constrained will always expand its investment to some extent.

A corollary to this prediction is that for unconstrained firms, growth in revenue should be slower than the growth in subsidized credit. This is a direct consequence of the fact that firms are substituting subsidized credit for market borrowing. Therefore, if we do not see a gap in these growth rates, the firm must be credit constrained. Of course, revenue could increase slower than credit even for non-constrained firms, if the technology has declining marginal return to capital. These predictions are more robust than the traditional way of measuring credit constraints as the excess sensitivity of investment to cash flow.

Our approach inscribes itself in a literature that tries to identify specific shocks to wealth in order to identify credit constraints. In Banerjee and Duflo we test these predictions by taking advantage of a recent change in the so-called "priority sector" rules in India: all banks in India are required to lend at least 40 per cent of their net credit to the priority sector, which includes small scale industry (SSI), at an interest rate that is required to be no more than 4 percentage points their prime lending rate.

If banks do not satisfy the priority sector target, they are required to lend money to specific government agencies at low rates of interest. In January, 1998, the limit on total investment in plants and machinery for a firm to be eligible for inclusion in the small scale industry category was raised from Rs. 6.5 million to Rs. 30 million. Our empirical strategy focuses on the firms that became newly eligible for credit in this period, and uses firms that were always eligible for priority sector credit as a control. The results from our analysis are reported briefly in the next sub-section.

The evidence for under-lending Data: The data we use were obtained from one of the better-performing Indian public sector banks. We use data from the loan folders maintained by the bank on profit, sales, credit lines and utilization, and interest rates. The loan folders also report all numbers that the banker was required to calculate (e.g. his projection of the bank's future turnover, his calculation of the bank's credit needs, etc.) in order to determine the amount to be lent.

We have data on 253 firms (including 93 newly eligible firms). The data is available for the entire 1997 to 1999 period for 175 of these firms. We are in effect comparing how the outcomes change for the big firms after 1998, with how they change for the small firms. Since y is always a growth rate, this is, in effect, a triple difference–we can allow small firms and big firms to have different rates of growth, and the rate of growth to differ from year to year, but we assume that there would have been no differential changes in the rate of growth of small and large firms in 1998, absent the change in the priority sector regulation.

Using, respectively, the log of the credit limit and the log of next year's sales (or profit) in place of y in equation 1, we obtain the first stage and the reduced form of a regression of sales on credit, using the interaction BIG POST as an instrument for credit. As suggested, present the corresponding instrumental variable regressions. Results: The change in the regulation certainly had an impact on who got priority sector credit. The credit limit granted to firms below Rs. 6.5 million in plant and machinery (henceforth, small firms) grew by 11.1 per cent during 1997, while that granted to firms between Rs.6.5 million and Rs. 30 million (henceforth, big firms), grew by 5.4 per cent.

In 1998, after the change in rules, small firms had 7.6 per cent growth while the big firms had 11.3 per cent growth. In 1999, both big and small firms had about the same growth, suggesting they had reached the new status quo. This is confirmed when we estimate equation 1 using bank credit as the outcome. The coefficient of the interaction term BIG POST is 0.95, with a standard error of 0.033. Estimates the probability that a firm's credit limit was changed: the coefficient on BIG POST is close to zero and insignificant, suggesting that the reform did not affect which firm's limits was changed. This corresponds to the general observations that whether or not a firm's file is brought out for a change in limit has nothing to do with the needs of the firm, but respond to internal dynamics of the bank.

As suggested, make use of this fact to partition the sample into two groups on the basis of whether there was a change in the credit limit or not: the sample where there was no change in limit can be used as a "placebo" group, where we can test our identification assumption. Finally, gives the estimated impact of the reform on loan size for firms whose limit was changed: the coefficient of the interaction BIG POST is 0.27, with a standard error of 0.10. This increase in credit was not accompanied by a change in the rate of interest. It did not lead to reduction in the rate of utilization of the limits by the ratio of total turnover to credit limit is not associated with the interaction BIG POST.

The additional credit limit thus resulted in an increase in bank credit utilization by the firms. The coefficient of the interaction BIG"POST in the sales equation, in the sample where the limit was increased, is 0.19, with a standard error of 0.11.

By contrast, in the sample where there was no increase in limit, the interaction BIG POST is close to zero (0.007) and insignificant, which suggests that the sales result is not driven by a failure of the identification assumption. The coefficient of the interaction BIG POST is 0.27 in the credit regression, and 0.19 in the sales regression: thus, sales increased almost as fast as loans in response to the reform. This is an indication that there was little or no substitution of bank credit for non-bank credit as a result of the reform, and that firms are credit constrained.

We restrict the sample to firms which have a positive amount of borrowing from the market both before and after the reform, and thus have not completely substituted bank borrowing for market borrowing. In this sample as well, we obtain a positive and significant effect of the interaction BIG POST, indicating that these firms must be credit constrained. we present the effect of the reform on profit. Because our dependent variable is the logarithm of profit, we can only estimate the impact on firms whose profits were positive. The effect is even bigger than that of sales: 0.54, with a standard error of 0.28.

Here again, we see no effect of the interaction BIG POST in the sample without a change in limit, which lends support to our identification assumption. The large effect on profit is not sufficient to establish the presence of credit constraints: even unconstrained firms should see profits increase when they gain access to subsidized credit, because they would substitute cheaper capital for more expensive capital. However, if firms were not expanding, we should not expect to see sales or costs (not reported) expand as well. Note that the coefficient is a lower bound of the effect of working capital on sales, because the reform should have led to some substitution of bank credit for market credit.

The coefficient is 0.75, with a standard error of 0.37. The effect of working capital on sales is very close to 1, a result which would imply that there cannot be equilibrium without credit constraint. The estimate of the impact of bank credit on profit is 1.79, though again the sample is limited to firms with positive profits. This is substantially greater than, which suggests that the technology has a strong fixed cost component. However, these coefficients also allow us to estimate the effect of credit expansion on profits. We can use this estimate to get a sense of the average increase in profit caused by every rupee in loan.

The average loan is Rs 8, 6800. Therefore, and increase of Rs. 1,000 in the loan corresponds to a 1.15% increase in loans. Taking 1.79 as the estimate of the effect of the log increase in loan on log increase in profit, an increase of Rs. 1,000 in lending causes a 2% increase in profit.

At the mean profit (which is Rs. 36,700, this would correspond to an increase in profit of Rs. 756.13 A last piece of important evidence is whether big firms become more likely to default than small firms after the reform: the increase in profits (and sales) may otherwise reflect more risky strategies pursued by the large firms. In order to answer this question, we collected additional data on the firms based in the Mumbai region (138 firms, a bit over half the sample). In particular, we collected data on whether any of these firm's loan had become non-performing assets (NPA) in 1999, 2000 or 2001, or were NPA before 1999.

The number of NPAs is disturbingly large (consistent with the high rate of NPAs in Indian banks), but large and small firms are equally likely to have a non-performing loan: 7.7% of the big firms and 7.29% of the small firms (who were not already NPA), default on their loan in 2000 or 2001. Among the firms in Mumbai, 2.5% of the large firms, and 5.96% of the small firms had defaulted between 1996 and 1998. The fraction of firms that had defaulted thus increased a little bit more for large firms, but the difference is small, and not significant. The increase in credit did not cause an unusually large number of big firms to default. Default rate, and the higher cost of lending to the firms in the priority sector, is not sufficient to narrow significantly the gap between our estimate of the rate of returns to capital and the interest rate.

Using these estimates and our previous estimates of the cost of lending to small firms, we compute that the interest rate banks should charge to these firms is close to 22% (rather than the 16% they are charging on average). This means that the gap between the social marginal product of capital is at least 66%. These results provide clear evidence of very substantial under-lending: some firms clearly can absorb much more capital at high rates of return.

Moreover the firms in our sample are by Indian standards quite substantial: these are not the very small firms at the margins of the economy, where, even if the marginal product is high, the scope for expansion may be quite limited. These data do not tell us anything directly about the efficiency of allocation of capital across firms. However, the IV estimate of the effect of loans on profit is strongly positive, while the OLS estimate is not different from zero. In other words, firms that have higher growth in loans do not generate faster growth in profits, suggesting that normally banks do not target loans enhancements to the most profitable firms.

This is consistent with evidence reported in Dasgupta15, that the interest rate paid by firms and by implication the marginal product of capital varies enormously within the same sub-economy. It is also consistent with the more direct evidence in Banerjee and Munshi showing that there is very substantial variation in the productivity of capital in the knitted garment industry in Tirupur.

Furthermore, while we have no direct data on this point, banker's lore suggests that the firms that have relatively easy access to credit tend to be the bigger and longer established firms. The underprovision of credit to small-scale industry was one of the key reasons cited for nationalization in 1969: thus, it might in fact be the case that while the public sector banks provide relatively little credit to SSI firms, private banks are even worse. In the next sub-section we examine the effect of bank ownership on bank allocation of credit.

Bank Ownership and Sectoral Allocation of Credit An important rationale for the Indian bank nationalizations was to direct credit towards sectors the government thought were underserved, including small scale industry, as well as agriculture and backward areas. Ownership was not the only means of directing credit: the Reserve Bank of India issued guidelines in 1974, indicating that both public and private sector banks must provide at least one-third of their aggregate advances to the priority sector by March 1979.

In 1980, it was announced that this quota would be increased to 40 per cent by March 1985. Sub-targets were also specified for lending to agriculture and weaker sectors within the priority sector. Since public and private banks faced the same regulation, in this part we focus on how ownership affected credit allocation. The comparison of nationalized and private banks is never easy: banks that fail are often merged with healthy nationalized banks, which makes the comparison of nationalized banks and non-nationalized banks close to meaningless.

The Indian nationalization experience of 1980 represents a unique chance to learn about the relationship between bank ownership and bank lending behaviour. The 1980 nationalization took place according to a strict policy rule: all private banks whose deposits were a certain cutoff were nationalized. After 1980, the nationalized banks remained corporate entities, retaining most of their staff, though the board of directors was replaced by nominees of the Government of India.

Both the banks that got nationalized under this rule and the banks that missed being nationalized, continued to operate in the same environment, and face the same regulations and therefore ought to be directly comparable. Even this comparison between banks just nationalized and just not nationalized may be invalid, because policy rule means that banks nationalized in 1980 are larger than the banks that remained private. If size influences bank behaviour, it would be incorrect to attribute all differences between nationalized and private sector banks to nationalization. In this part, based on Cole, we adopt an approach in the spirit of regression discontinuity design, and compare banks that were just above the 1980 cutoff to those that were just below the 1980 cutoff, while control- ling for bank size in 1980. The idea behind this comparison is that the relationship between size and behaviour should not change dramatically around the cutoff, unless nationalization itself causes changes in bank behaviour.

This will allow for credible causal inference on the role of bank ownership on bank behaviour. In order to get a sense of the magnitude of lending differences among bank types, we first divide the banks into five groups, based on their size in 1980: State Bank of India and its affiliates, large nationalized banks (nationalized in 1969), "marginal" nationalized banks (nationalized in 1980), "marginal" private banks (relatively large, but just too small to be nationalized in 1980), and small private banks. Because the geographic districts in which banks are located vary (soil quality, rural population, etc.), and face different economic shocks, we focus here on comparing differential bank behaviour within each district. Our outcomes of interest include average loan size, residual interest rate, 20 and share of bank lending to the following areas: agriculture, rural credit, small scale industry, government credit, and "trade, transport and finance."

To estimate bank-group effects, we regress credit outcome variables for each bank group g in district d on D district dummy variables, and BG1..., BGG bank group dummy variables. The estimated bank group effects, BG1..., BGG give the average share each bank gives to each sector, after controlling for differences across districts. For example, the estimated BG for the average loan size from banks in the State Bank of India group is Rs. 56,190. Compared to the average loan size of the State Bank of India, nationalized banks gave slightly smaller loans (an average of 6,430 Rs. lower), while marginal nationalized banks gave slightly larger loans (the average was 8,350 Rs. greater), marginal private banks gave much larger loans (35,310 Rs. more), and small private banks gave loans much larger on average (58,500 Rs. more).

These results appear to confirm conventional wisdom that nationalized and public banks give smaller loans than private banks. The most informative comparison is between what we called the "marginal" nationalized and the "marginal" private bank, which were similar in size, but the former were nationalized while the latter weren't. Many of the differences between the marginal nationalized and the marginal private banks are large: the marginal private banks gave 5 percentage points less credit to agriculture than the marginal nationalized banks: given that the all-India share of credit to agriculture is 11 per cent, this difference is substantial.

The results also suggest that nationalization led to more credit to small scale industry (an increase of 2 percentage points relative to the private banks; India-wide small scale industry receives 9 per cent of total credit), four percentage points more credit to rural areas (compared to a national average of 12 per cent), and slightly more to government enterprises. These increases come at the expense of credit trade, transport, and finance (nationalized banks gave 6 per cent points less, compared to the national average share of 21 per cent). The rural and government lending differences are significant at the 5 per cent level, while all others are significant at the one per cent level. While this is suggestive that private and public banks behave differently, the values in the table vary not only between marginal private and marginal nationalized banks, but across other bank groups as well. Thus, from this data alone, we cannot rule out the possibility that the difference in lending behaviour is attributable to bank size, rather than ownership.

To obtain an accurate measure of the impact of nationalization, we examine lending behaviour at the individual bank level, adopting a full-fledged regression-discontinuity approach. We first estimate bank effects analogous to the group effects estimated in equation (2), by replacing the Bank Group dummy indicators with individual bank dummy indicators, to obtain coefficients β 1... β B. These coefficients tell us to what extent bank b behaves differently from other banks, after controlling for the characteristics of the districts in which each bank operates. We then regress the individual indicators bâ b on log deposits of the bank in 1980 (sizeb), an indicator variable (Natb),which takes the value of one when the size was larger than the cutoff and the bank therefore nationalized, and an interaction term.

Banks are ordered by the size of their deposits in 1980, so that banks below the cutoff of 14.5 are private, while banks above were nationalized in 1980.21 Contrary to the results obtained by simple comparison of means, there does not appear to be any significant difference in lending to small-scale industry between public and private banks that are of similar size. That is, we cannot reject the hypothesis that nationalization had no effect on credit to small-scale industry. On the other hand, nationalization appears to have had the effect of lowering the amount of credit banks provide to trade, transport, and finance. Nationalization appears to have had a large effect on credit to agriculture.

There is a relationship between size in 1980 and lending to agriculture in 1992: larger banks lend more to agriculture. However, there is a visible break in the relationship at the nationalization cut-off: banks just above the cutoff lend substantially more to agriculture than banks, even after accounting for the effect of size. For example, for agriculture in 1992, the estimated break is.084, with a standard error of.029: the difference between nationalized and private banks is quite significant, both economically and statistically. The point estimates of the structural break confirm some of the differences, but suggest that others are merely functions of bank size. In particular, as measured by credit in 1992, nationalization had a causal effect on agricultural credit and rural credit, increasing each by about 8 percentage points.

These numbers are large, given that the set of all banks lent only 11 per cent of credit to agriculture and 12 per cent to rural areas. These results are significant at the 1 per cent level.

Nationalization appears to have had no effect on the amount of credit banks lend to small scale industry, but caused a nine percentage point decrease in the credit banks issued to trade, transport and finance. Not surprisingly, we see that nationalized banks lend more to government-owned enterprises; the two-percentage point difference is particularly large in light of the fact credit to government borrowers represents only two per cent of bank credit. Public sector banks appear to lend at slightly lower interest rates, though the point estimate, seventy basis points, is not statistically significant. We also attempted to measure whether public sector banks gave more credit to industries that had been identified for support in various five-year plans after 1980, but found no evidence that these industries were favoured.

The differences between the nationalized and private banks seem to have decreased over time: in the 2000 data, the point estimate on agricultural lending drops from 8 to 5 points, on rural lending from 7 to 3 points, and on trade and transport and finance from -11 to -6 percentage points. In sum, bank ownership does seem to have had a limited impact on the government's ability to direct credit to specific sectors. Through the early 1990s, the credit environment in India was very tightly regulated.

The government set interest rates, required both public and private banks to issue 40 per cent of credit to the priority sector, and to meet specific sub-targets within the priority sector. Nevertheless, banks controlled by the government provided substantially more credit to agriculture, rural areas, and the government, at the expense of credit to trade, transport, and finance. Though, surprisingly, there was no effect on credit to small scale industry. Lending differences shrunk over the 1990s, and in 2000 were about half of what they were in the early 1990s.

This might reflect the increasing dynamism of the private sector banks in the liberalized environment of the 1990s or the loosening grip of the government on the nationalized banks. To determine whether public ownership of banks inhibits financial intermediation, we again compare banks just above and just below the 1980 nationalization cut-off, using data from the Reserve Bank of India, for the period 1969 to 2000. We include the six, which were nationalized, which were not.

Since we have data from both the pre and post period, we adopt a difference-in-differences approach. Specifically, we regress the annual change in bank deposits, credit, and number of bank branches on a dummy for post nationalization, and a dummy for post-nationalization in a liberalized environment. We break the post-nationalization analysis up into two periods because the former period was characterized by continued financial repression, while substantial liberalization measures were implemented in the beginning of the 1990s. Public and private banks could well behave differently before and after liberalization. Because larger banks may grow at different rates than small banks, we include bank fixed effects (βi).

The parameters of interest are $\gamma 1$ and $\gamma 2$, which capture the differential behaviour of nationalized banks after the nationalization. Standard errors are adjusted for auto-correlation within each bank. The results suggest that while the overall rate of growth in deposits and credit slowed substantially in the period 1980-1990 relative to the 1969-1979 period, there was no differential effect for nationalized and private banks. In the nineties, deposit and credit growth slowed further still. In this liberalized environment, deposits and credit of the nationalized banks slowed down more than the private banks: deposits grew 7.3 per cent slower, while credit grew 8.8 per cent less quickly. These results are significant at the ten and five per cent level, respectively.

The growth rate in bank branches generally tracked credit and deposits, though the decline after 1980 was more severe. While the growth rates for nationalized banks were slightly lower in both periods, the differences are not statistically significant. To answer the question of whether there was a significant difference between public and private banks prior to nationalization, were estimate equation, replacing the bank fixed effects with a nationalization dummy, and a control function (Kb, 80) = π1Kb,80 + π2K2 b,80, which controls for the effect of 1980 log deposits of each bank in 1980 (denoted

Kb,80). (These results are not reported, but are available from the authors). The control function allows bank growth to depend on bank size, while the nationalization dummy will pick up any differences between the nationalized and non-nationalized banks that are not related to size. The estimates suggests that credit, deposit and number of branches grew at the same speed between 1969 and 1979 for banks that were going to be nationalized in 1980 and those that were not. The coefficients on the interaction terms remain negative, and are virtually unchanged from the specification. Thus, it is only after the 1980 nationalization that banks nationalized in 1980 started to grow more slowly.

These results provide some evidence that nationalization hindered the spread of intermediation in the 1990s, but not earlier. We look for features of public banks, examining both official lending policies, and other incentives faced by employees of public sector banks. Official Lending Policies While public sector banks in India are nominally independent entities, they are subject to intense regulation by the Reserve Bank of India (RBI). This includes rules about how much a bank should lend to individual borrowers–the so-called "maximum permissible bank finance."

Until 1997, the rule was based on the working capital gap, defined as the difference between the current assets of the firm and its total current liabilities excluding bank finance (other current liabilities). The presumption is that the current assets are illiquid in the very short run and therefore the firm needs to finance them. Trade credit is one source of finance, and what the firm cannot finance in this way constitutes the working capital gap. Firms were supposed to cover a part of this financing need, corresponding to no less than 25 per cent of the current assets, from equity.

The sum of all loans from the banking system was supposed not to exceed this amount. This definition of the maximum permissible bank finance applied to loans above Rs. 20 million. For loans below Rs.20 million, banks were supposed to calculate the limit based on the projected turnover of the firm. Projected turnover was to be determined by a loan officer in consultation with the client. The firm's financing need was estimated to be 25 per cent of the projected turnover and the bank was allowed to finance up to 80 per cent of what the firm needs, *i.e.* up to 20 per cent of the firm's projected turnover. The rest, amounting to at least 5 per cent of the projected turnover has again to be financed by long term resources available to the firm. In the middle of 1997, following the recommendation of the committee on financing of the small scale industries (the Nayak committee), the RBI decided to give each bank the flexibility to evolve its own lending policy, under the condition that it be made explicit.

Moreover the Nayak committee recommended that the turnover rule be used to calculate the lending limit for all loans under Rs. 40 millions. Given the freedom to choose the rule, different banks went for slightly different strategies. The bank we studied adopted a policy which was, in effect, a mix between the now recommended turnover-based rule and the older rule based on the firm's asset position. First the limit on turnover basis was calculated as: min (0.20 Projected turnover, 0.25 Projected turnover “ available margin). The available margin here is the financing available to the firm from long term sources (such as equity), and is calculated as Current Assets “ Current Liabilities from the current balance sheet. In other words the presumption is that the firm has somehow managed to finance this gap in the current period and therefore should be able to do so in the future.

Therefore the bank only needs to finance the remaining amount. Note that if the firm had previously managed to get the bank to follow the turnover based rule exactly, its available margin would be precisely 5 per cent of turnover and the two amounts in 6 would be equal. The rule did not stop here. For all loans below Rs.40 million, the loan officer was supposed to use both equation 6 and the older rule represented by 5. The largest permissible limit on the loan was the maximum of these two numbers. Two comments about the nature of this rule are in order. First, this turnover based approach to working capital finance is relatively standard even in the USA. However the view in the USA is that working capital finance is essentially financing inventories and is therefore backed by the value of the inventories. In India, the inventories do not seem to provide adequate security, as evidenced by the high rates of default. In such cases it may be much more important to pay attention to profitability, since profitable companies are less likely default. Second, in the USA the role of finding promising firms and promoting them is carried out, to a significant extent, by venture capitalists. In India the venture capital industry is still nascent and it will be a while before it can play the role that we expect of its US equivalent.

Therefore banks may have to be more pro-active in promoting promising firms. Following a rule that does not put any weight on profits may not be the way to favour the most promising firms: while the projected turnover calculation does favour faster growing firms, the loan officer is not allowed to project a growth rate greater than 15 per cent. This may be enough to meet the needs of a mature firm, but a small firm that is growing fast clearly needs much more than 15 per cent. It is important that the rules encourage the loan officers to lend more to companies on the basis of promise.

Actual Lending Policy

The lending policy statements give us the outside limits on what the banks can lend. There is nothing in the policies that stops them from lending less, though bankers are always enjoined to lend as much as possible in official documents. It is also possible, given that it is not clear how these rules are enforced, that the banks sometimes exceed the limits–it is, for example, often alleged that loan officers in public sector banks give out irresponsibly large loans to their friends and business associates. It is not even clear how one would necessarily know that banker had lent too much given that he is given the task of estimating expected turnover. In this sub-section, based on work by Banerjee and Duflo, we therefore look at the actual practice of lending in our sample of loans. We use the same data source that was used in previous work by Banerjee and Duflo to look at what bankers actually do. Since we have data on current assets and other current liabilities, it is trivial to calculate the limit according to the traditional, working capital gap-based method of lending (henceforth LWC). We can also calculate the limit on turnover basis (henceforth LTB). The maximum of LTB and LWC is, according to the rules, the real limit on how much the banker can lend to the firm. Inertia and the fear of prosecution Since public sector banks are owned by the government, employees of the bank are treated by law as public servants, and thus subject to government anti-corruption legislation.

There is an impression among bankers that it is very easy to be charged with corruption, and that the law states that if any government functionary takes a decision which results in direct financial gain to a third party, the individual is prima facie guilty of corruption, and must prove her or his innocence. The executive director of a large public sector bank was quoted saying "Fear of prosecution for corruption hangs over every loan officer's head like the sword of Damocles."

The Economic Times of India has attributed slowdowns in lending directly to vigilance activity. A working group on banking policy set up by the Reserve Bank of India, and chaired by M.S. Verma, noted: The [working group] observed that it has received representations from the managements and the unions of the banks complaining about the diffidence in taking credit decisions with which the banks are beset at present. This is due to investigations by outside agencies on the accountability of staff in respect of some of the Non Performing Assets. The group also noticed a marked reluctance at various level to take any credit decision."

In response to criticism from bankers, economists, and others, the Central Vigilance Commission (henceforth CVC), which is the body entrusted to investigate potential cases of fraud in the public sector, introduced in 1999 a special chapter of the vigilance manual, on vigilance in public sector banks. The language would probably not reassure anyone with experience working in a western bank. The manual reads, for example, that "every loss caused to the organization, either in pecuniary or non-pecuniary terms, need not necessarily become the subject matter of a vigilance inquiry... once a vigilance angle is evident, it becomes necessary to determine through an impartial investigation as to what went wrong and who is accountable for the same." Interviews with public sector bankers revealed widespread concern: the legal proceedings surrounding charges of corruption can drag on for years, leaving individuals charged with corruption in an uncertain state. Even if an individual is exonerated, she may have been relieved of her duties, transferred, or passed over for promotion during the time of investigation. In theory (as well as practice), even one loan gone bad may be sufficient to start vigilance proceedings.

The possible penalties stand in stark contrast to rewards. While banks are constantly urged by the Reserve Bank of India to lend as much as possible, there are no explicit incentives for making good loans, or ways to penalize officers who make conservative decisions. In effect, bankers are accountable to more than one authority –the loan officer's boss is one of them but central vigilance may be another, and the press may be yet another. In such circumstances, it may be very difficult to provide effective incentives.

If this were the case, loan officers would prefer not to take new decisions. Simply renewing the loan without changing the amount is one easy way to avoid responsibility, especially if the original decision was someone else's (loan officers are frequently transferred). And when they do take a decision, making sure that they did not deviate enormously from the precedent, is a way of covering themselves against charges of wrong-doing or worse.

Not surprisingly, the Central Vigilance Commission disputes the claim that there is a "fear psychosis," and, to bolster their position, released in 2000 a "critical analysis" of vigilance activity in public sector banks in 1999. The analysis reveals that in 1999, the Central Vigilance Commission received 1916 references, 72 per cent of which were credit-related, recommending punishment in the majority of cases. Their 2000 report states "out of every 100 cases coming before it, the Commission would advice major penalty proceedings in 28 cases, minor penalty proceedings in 32 cases, and administrative warning/exoneration in 40 cases." The author of the report, a CVC official, argued that this level of activity should not be enough to cause "fear psychoses": "These figures reveal that a person is not damned the moment his case is referred to the Commission... These statistics appear to indicate a very fair and objective approach on the part of the Commission to the cases that were referred to it."

The rest of this sub-section, based on work by Cole looks at whether there is any evidence for the so-called fear psychosis. The basic idea is simple: we ask whether bankers who are "close to" bankers who have been subject to CVC action, slow down lending in the aftermath of that particular CVC action. Monthly credit data, by bank, were provided by the RBI. Data on frauds are naturally very difficult to come by. It is also the policy of the government of India to keep the data on vigilance activity confidential: while some aggregated statistics are published, they are too aggregated to be useful for econometric analysis.

However, in 1998, in an effort increase the penalty for fraud through stigma, the government authorized the CVC to publish the name, position, employing bank, and punishment of individual officers of government agencies charged with major frauds. This list consists of eighty-seven officials in public sector banks between the years 1992 and 2001. While nature of the fraud with which they are charged is not known, we do know that approximately 72 per cent of frauds relate to illegal extension of credit, while the balance is classified as kite-flying or "other." Since our hypothesis is that vigilance results in a decrease in lending activity, the inclusion of spurious non-credit related vigilance activity should bias coefficients towards zero.

The first approach is to use bank level monthly lending data to estimate the effect of vigilance activity on lending, using the following equation, where yit is log credit extended by bank i in month t, ái is a bank fixed-effect, ât is a month fixed effect, and Di,t"k is an indicator variable for whether vigilance activity was reported by the CVC for bank i in month t-k. Standard errors reported are adjusted for serial correlation and heteroscedasticity. The basic idea is to compare the bank that was affected by the vigilance activity with other public sector banks, before and after the vigilance event. Which event window to use is not immediately clear: the appropriate start date would most likely be the month in which it became known that vigilance proceedings were under way, or perhaps the date bankers learned of the judgment.

The data published by the CVC give only the date at which the CVC provided advice on the case, and the date on which action was taken. Nor is it clear how long it should take before an effect appears, or for how long one would accept this effect to last. We therefore let the data decide, by estimating models which allow effects ranging from one month to four years.

9

Importance and Growth

To motivate farmers and food processors, and to provide an interactive coupling between technology, economy, environment and society for speedy development of food processing industries to build up a substantial base for production of value added agro food products for domestic and export markets with a strong emphasis on food safety and quality enabling the farmers especially to realise direct benefits of new technology and marketing network and to ensure adequate availability of quality food products for the consumer at economic prices.

To fulfill the VISION so as to contribute to all round economic and social development of India through generation of employment opportunities especially in rural areas. Food Processing Industry is of enormous significance for India's development because of the vital linkages and synergies that it promotes between the two pillars of the economy, namely Industry and Agriculture. India is world's second largest producer of food and has the potential to become number one in due course of time with sustained efforts.

The growth potential of this sector is enormous and it is expected that the food production will double in the next 10 years and the consumption of value added food products will grow at a fast pace. This growth of the Food Processing Industry will bring immense benefits to the economy, raising agricultural yields, meeting productivity, creating employment and raising the standard of very large number of people through out the country, specially, in the rural areas. Economic liberalization and rising consumer prosperity is opening up new opportunities for diversification in Food Processing Sector. Liberalization of world trade will open up new vistas for growth.

The Food Processing Industry has been identified as a thrust area for development. This industry is included in the priority lending sector. Most of the Food processing Industries have been exempted from the provisions of industrial licensing under Industries (Development and Regulation) Act, 1951 with the exception of beer and alcoholic drinks and items reserved for Small Scale Sector, like vinegar, bread, bakery. As far as foreign investment is concerned automatic approval for even 100% equity is available for majority of the processed food items.

Food processing involves any type of value addition to the agricultural produce starting at the post harvest level. It includes even primary processing like grading, sorting, cutting, seeding, shelling packaging etc.

The sector comprises of the following major areas:

- *Fruit and Vegetable*
  - Major Products

    Beverages, Juices, Concentrates, Pulps, Slices, Frozen and Dehydrated products, Wine Potato Wafers/Chips etc.
- *Fisheries*
  - Major Products:

    Frozen and Canned products mainly in fresh form.
- *Meat and Poultry*
  - Major Products

    Frozen and packed mainly in fresh form, Egg Powder (only a couple of units).
- *Milk and Dairy*
  - Major Products

    Whole Milk Powder, Skimmed milk powder, Condensed milk, Ice cream, Butter and Ghee
- *Grain and Cereals*
  - Major Products

    Flour, Bakeries, Biscuits, Starch Glucose,

Cornflakes, Malted Foods, Vermicelli, Pasta Foods, Beer and Malt extracts, Grain based Alcohol.

- *Consumer Industry*
  - Major Products

    Chocolates, Confectionery, Soft/Aerated Beverages/Drinks.

    Plantation

    Major Products:

    Tea, coffee, cashew, cocoa, coconut etc.

CHALLENGES, CONSTRAINTS AND CONCERNS

India is already a major producer of food (first in cereals, livestock population, milk and second in fruits and vegetables), producing over 600 million tons of food products, and in case the immense untapped potential of growth is achieved the country can emerge as the largest producer of major food items. Processing level presently being extremely low, the wastage levels are very high resulting in colossal wastage of national wealth running in thousands of crores.

Value addition to the raw produce in the country is only seven per cent, compared to as much as 23% in china, 45% in the Philippines and 188 in the U.K. The small scale and unorganized sectors today account for 75% of the total industry having only local presence without much access to knowledge, technology and marketing network. The differential between the farmer's realization and the final consumer price is very high in our country even in the fresh produce.

In processed food products the high price on account of cumulative effect of low productivity, high cost of raw material, spoilage due to poor infrastructure, inefficient and costly transportation, high cost of finance an high incidence of taxes and duties, leads to the vicious cycle of:

low demand → low capacity utilization → high per unit cost → low demand.

Despite the existence of a strong and wide network of R&D institutions (CSIR labs, ICAR institutions, ICMR Establishments, Universities and Private institutions), their linkage with the users like farmers and industry, is not well established resulting in lack of technology flow, pure and academic research rather than applied and commercial, lack of involvement of industry in research work, and resource crunch. The unattractive nature and the high risk profile of food processing industry has impeded required flow of credit from financial institutions who are yet to acquire the proper understanding of this sector to attain the requisite levels of appraising skills.

Low margins, seasonality and high perishability being the distinct features of this industry, the access to seed capital and working capital is not easy. Despite having been declared a priority-lending sector, there is hardly any growth in capital flow to this industry. Despite vast domestic market size, the present level of processed food marketability is very low but by doing massive awareness and educational campaigns this market could grow higher enough to consume substantial part of any quantum of our processed foods. Indian brands are yet to establish in the international markets calling for a concerted effort to capture world market share in tune with our standing in the production front. With the coming in of WTO regime the country has to prepare for meeting the requisite quality standards in order to compete with imported goods in the domestic market itself.

This calls for adoption of high tech machine and technologies as also development of entire chain of the infrastructure. Weak database and lack of market intelligence are the prevailing features of this sector. Poor infrastructure of not only processing but even transportation, ports, airports, storage and handling etc. The backward linkage between the farmer and the processor is yet to take proper shape to tide over the impediments which exist on account of fragmented and small land holdings, erratic production due to natural factors, non uniformity and inconsistent supply of raw material and longer chain of intermediaries.

Multiplicity of laws and regulatory authorities throttle the industry in its further growth calling for harmonization of laws, development and administration of standards in consonance with international standards like Codex through a single authority. Prevailing packaging system lacks requisite quality and presentability parameters creating handicap as compared to the imported products. Cooperative institutions and other parastatal organizations are weak and peoples participation, either through Panchayat Raj Institutions or NGOs or farmers organizations, industries association in food sector remains far from adequate.

THE POLICY

CREATING ENABLING ENVIRONMENT

The Policy will seek to create an appropriate environment for entrepreneurs to set up Food Processing Industries through:

- Fiscal initiatives/interventions like rationalization of tax structure on fresh foods as well as processed foods and machinery used for the production of processed foods.
- Harmonization and Simplification of food laws by an appropriate enactment to cover all provisions relating to food products so that the existing system of multiple laws is replaced and also covering issues concerning standards Nutrition, Merit goods, futures marketing, equalisation fund etc.
- A concerted promotion campaign to create market for processed foods by providing financial assistance to Industry Associations, NGOs/Cooperatives, Private Sector Units, State Government Organization for undertaking generic market promotion.
- Efforts to expand the availability of the right kind and quality of raw material round the year by increasing production, improving productivity.
- Strengthening of database and market intelligence system through studies and surveys to be conducted in various States to enable planned investment in the appropriate sector matching with the availability of raw material and marketability of processed products.

- Strengthening extension services and to the farmers and co-operatives in the areas of post harvest management of agro-produce to encourage creation of pre-processing facilities near the farms like washing, fumigation, packaging etc.
- Efforts to encourage setting up of agro-processing facilities as close to the area of production as possible to avoid wastage and reduce transportation cost.
- Promotion of investments, both foreign and domestic.
- Simplification of documentation and procedures under taxation laws to avoid unnecessary harassment arising out of mere technicalities.

INFRASTRUCTURAL DEVELOPMENT

The Policy will facilitate:

- Establishment of cold chain, low cost pre-cooling facilities near farms, cold stores and grading, sorting, packing facilities to reduce wastage, improve quality and shelf life of products.
- Application of biotechnology, remote sensing technology, energy saving technologies and technologies for environmental protection.
- Building up a strong infrastructural base for production of value added products with special emphasis on food safety and quality matching international standards.
- Development of Packaging Technologies for individual products, especially cut-fruits and vegetables, so as to increase their shelf life and improve consumer acceptance both in the domestic and international markets.
- Development of new technologies in Food Processing and Packaging and also to provide for the mechanism to facilitate quick transfer of technologies to field through a net work of R&D Institutions having a Central Institute at the national level with satellite institutions located strategically in various regions to cover up the whole Country and to make available

the required testing facilities. This could be done by establishing a new institution or strengthening an existing one.

- Development of area-specific Agro Food Parks dedicated to processing of the predominant produce of the area e.g., apple in J&K, pineapple in North East, Lichi in Bihar, Mango in Maharashtra and Andhra Pradesh etc.
- Development of Anchor Industrial Centre and/or linkage with Anchor Industrial Units having net work of small processing units.
- Development of Agro-industrial multi-products units capable of processing a cluster of trans-seasonal produces.

BACKWARD LINKAGE

The Policy will promote:

- Establishment of a sustained and lasting linkage between the farmers and the processors based on mutual trust and benefits by utilizing the existing infrastructure of cooperative, village panchayats and such other institutions.
- Development of Futures Market in the best interest of both the farmers and the processors ensuring a minimum price stability to the farmer and a sustained supply of raw material to the processor.
- Mechanism to reduce the gap between the farm gate price of agro-produce and the final price paid by the consumer.
- Setting up of an Equalisation Fund to ensure sustained supply of raw material at a particular price level and at the same time to plough back the savings occurring in the eventuality of lower price to make the Fund self-regenerative.

FORWARD LINKAGE

The policy will promote:

- Establishment of a strong linkage between the processor and the market to effect cost economies by elimination of avoidable intermediaries.

- Establishment of marketing network with an apex body to ensure proper marketing of processed products.
- Development of marketing capabilities both with regard to infrastructure and quality in order to promote competitive capabilities to face not only the WTO challenge but to undertake exports in a big way.

SPECIAL PROVISION

The following shall receive higher priority and special consideration in policy and plans:

- The North Eastern Region, the Hilly Areas, Islands and the ITDP areas in the country to be given not only special attention but also special consideration.
- The fiscal incentives like excise duty/sales tax concession and the tax holidays to be provided not only to those units which are set up in these areas but also to those units which though set up outside these areas near the market centre, are engaged in processing the produce coming from these areas.
- Tax holiday for food processing units, with the exception of liquor, cigarettes and aerated drinks and similar luxury items, for a period of 10 years.

India is one of the world's major food producers but accounts for less than 1.5 per cent of international food trade. This indicates vast scope for both investors and exporters. Food exports in 1998 stood at US $5.8 billion whereas the world total was US $438 billion. The Indian food industry's sales turnover is Rs 140,000 crore (1 crore = 10 million) annually as at the start of year 2000.

The industry requires about Rs 29,000 crore in investment over the next five years to 2005 to create necessary infrastructure, expand production facilities and state-of-the-art-technology to match the international quality and standards. The office of the Agricultural Affairs of the USDA/ Foreign Agricultural Services in New Delhi says that one of India's proudest accomplishments has been achieving a tenuous self-sufficiency in food production and that the country produces a wide variety of agricultural products at prices that are at or below world values in most cases. The Indian palate is accustomed to traditional foods, mostly wheat and rice-based, rather than potato and corn-based western palate. In marketing perspective, this is considered an important factor for foreign marketers. The USDA report says initially consumer-ready food products may have to be tailored to include Indian spices and traditional ingredients.

In addition to traditional tastes, there are other social factors which affect consumption in India. Hindus account for approximately 80 per cent of India's population, and while only 25 or 30 per cent are strict vegetarians, beef slaughter is prohibited in all but two states (Kerala and West Bengal) and consumption of other meats is limited.

Incidentally, India is the only country where the US-based MacDonalds sells its burgers without any beef content and even offers purely vegetarian burgers. India's middle class segment will hold the key to success or failure of the processed food market in India. Of the country's total population of one billion, the middle class segments account for about 350-370 million. Though a majority of families in this segment have non-working housewives or can afford hired domestic help and thus prepare foods of their taste in their own kitchens, the profile of the middle class is changing steadily and hired domestic help is becoming costlier.

This is conducive to an expansion in demand for ready-to-eat Indian-style foods. India's food processing sector covers fruit and vegetables; meat and poultry; milk and milk products, alcoholic beverages, fisheries, plantation, grain processing and other consumer product groups like confectionery, chocolates and cocoa products, Soya-based products, mineral water, high protein foods etc. Latest official statistics, India exported processed fruits and vegetables worth Rs 5240 million in 1997-98.

The horticulture production is around 102 million tonnes. Foreign investment since 1991, when economic liberalisation started, stood at Rs 8,800 crore. Products that have growing demand, especially in the Middle East countries include pickles, chutneys, fruit pulps, canned fruits, and vegetables, concentrated pulps and juices, dehydrated vegetables and frozen fruits and vegetables. Another potential processed food product is meat and poultry products. India ranks first in world cattle population, 50 per cent of buffalo population and one-sixth of total goat population of the world. Buffalo meat is surplus in India.

There is vast scope to set up modern slaughter facilities and cold store chains in meat and poultry processing sector. India's current level of meat and meat-based exports is around Rs 8,000 million. In last six years foreign investment in this segment stood at Rs 5,000 million which is more than 50 per cent of the total investment made in this sector. Compared with meat, poultry industry has registered significant growth. India ranks fifth in the world with annual egg production of 1.61 million tones. Both poultry and egg processing units have come in a very big way in the country. India is exporting egg powder, frozen egg yolk and albumin powder to Europe, Japan and other countries. Poultry exports are mostly to Maldives and Oman. Indian poultry meat products have good markets in Japan, Malaysia, Indonesia and Singapore. While meat products registered a growth of 10 per cent, eggs and broilers registered 16-20 per cent growth. There are about 15 pure line and grand parent franchise projects in India. There are 115 layer and 280 broiler hatcheries producing 1.3 million layer parents and 280 million broiler parents.

They in turn supply 95 million hybrid layer and 275 million broilers, day-old chick. Presently there are only five egg powder plants in India which is considered insufficient in view of growing export demand for different kind of powder - whole egg, yolk and albumen. The scope of foreign investment and state-of-the-art technology in this field is therefore tremendous. Milk and milk products is rated as one of the most promising sectors which deserves foreign investment in a big way. When the world milk production registered a negative growth of 2 per cent, India performed much better with 4 per cent growth.

The total milk production is around 72 million tonnes and the demand for milk is estimated at around 80 million tonnes. By 2005, the value of Indian dairy produce is expected to be Rs 1,000,000 million. In last six years foreign investment in this sector stood at Rs 3600 million which is about one-forth of total investment made in this sector. Manufacture of casein and lactose, largely being imported presently, has good scope. Exports of milk products have been decanalised. Grains could emerge as a major export earner for India in coming years. India's food grains production is now at around 225-230 million tones.

These include rice, jawar, bajra, maize, wheat, gram and pulses. Indian basmati rice enjoys command in the international market. Besides growing Middle east market for basmati rive, many other countries are showing interest for this food grain. In 1998-99 export of basmati and non-basmati rice stood at Rs62000 million. There is a total rice milling capacity of 186 million tones in the country. Among plantation, tea emerged as major foreign exchange earner. India is the largest producer and exporter of black tea.

However, the most worrying factor for Indian tea industry is that from early next year with the implementation of tea imports into the country, India tea may face a stiff competition within the country as well, specially threat of Sri Lanka's presence in the Indian market is looming large. The current year's tea export prospect is not that very good in terms of forex earnings because international prices has fallen significantly this year. India exports between 150-170 million kilogram's of tea per annum.

Of course, the scope of foreign investment in this sector is good and the multinational tea companies would either be trying for marketing joint ventures with the Indian producers or acquire stakes in Indian tea companies. There is strong possibilities of third country exports through such joint venture as quality wise still Indian teas are ruling the international market. Alcoholic beverages is another are where India witnessed substantial foreign investment. Foreign investment in this sector stood at Rs 7000 million which about

70 per cent of the total investment made so far. The IMFL (Indian Made Foreign Liquor) primarily comprises wine, vodka, gin, whisky, rum and brandy. Draught beer is a comparatively recent introduction in the Indian market. The Indian beer market is estimated at Rs7000 million a year. One of the major advantages for any investor eyeing the Indian liquor market is that India offers enough raw materials like molasses, barely, maize, potatoes, grapes, yeast and hops for the industry. Yet another catchy investment sector is fisheries. There is growing canned and processed fishes from India.

The marine fish include prawns, shrimps, tuna, cuttlefish, squids, octopus, red snappers, ribbon fish, mackerel, lobsters, cat fish etc. In last six years there was substantial investment in fisheries to the tune of Rs 30,000 million of which foreign investments were of the order of Rs 7000 million. The potential could be gauged by the fact that against fish production potential in the Exclusive Economic Zone of 3.9 million tones, actual catch is to the tune of 2.87 million tones.

Harvesting from inland sources is around 2.7 million tones. The biggest bottleneck in expanding the food processing sector, in terms of both investment and exports, is lack of adequate infrastructure. Without a strong and dependable cold chain vital sector like food processing industry which is based mostly on perishable products cannot survive and grow. Even at current level of production, farm produce valued at Rs 70,000 million is being wasted every year only because there is no adequate storage, transportation, cold chain facilities and other infrastructure supports.

Cold chain facilities are miserably inadequate to meet the increasing production of various perishable products like milk, fruits, vegetables, poultry, fisheries etc. Prevention of Food Adulteration laws is not only stringent one but time consuming also. It is considered as an archaic and no industry friendly food law. It substantial varies from Codex standard. Harmonization of multiple food laws is an urgent necessity. Top sector for foreign direct investment in India Food processing Industry poised for growth. The Food Processing Industry in India is one of the largest in terms of production, consumption, export and growth prospects. Important sub-sectors in food processing industries are: Fruit and Vegetable Processing, Fish Processing, Milk Processing, Meat and Poultry Processing, Packaged/Convenience Foods, Alcoholic Beverages and Soft drinks and Grain Processing, etc.

As a result of several policy initiatives undertaken since liberalization in July 1991, the industry has witnessed fast growth in most of the segments. As per a recent study on the food processing sector, the turnover of the total food market is approximately Rs.250, 000 crore out of which value-added food products comprise Rs.80, 000 crore.

Primary food processing is a major industry with lakhs of rice-mills/hullers, flour mills, pulse mills and oil-seed mills. There are several thousands of bakeries, traditional food units and fruit/veg./spice processing units in unorganized sector. In the organized sector, there are over 820 flour mills, 418 fish processing units, 5,198 fruit/vegetables processing units, 171 meat processing units. India is the world's second largest producer of fruits and vegetables, but hardly 2% of the produce is processed. India is the land of spices producing all varieties worth over Rs. 3,500 crore amounting to 25-30% of world production, which is processed for value-addition and export.

It grows 22 million tonnes of oilseeds covering most of the varieties. Other important plantation products include tea, coffee, cocoa and cashew. It has large marine product and processing potential with varied fish resources along the 8,041 km. long coastline, 28,000 km. of rivers and millions of hectares of reservoirs and brackish water. India's livestock population is largest in the world with 50% of world's buffaloes and 20% of cattles, but only about 1% of total meat production is converted to value added products.

India is the largest milk producer in the world and about 15% of the total milk production is processed through the organized sector. Size of the semi-processed and ready to eat packaged food industry is over Rs. 4,000 crore and is growing at over 20%. Providing a fillip to logistics and food retail, custom duty on refrigerated motor vehicles has been reduced from 10% to zero and the excise duty/countervailing duty from 16% to 8%. The market size of the ready to eat packaged food segment is around Rs.100 crore. Biscuits priced at less than Rs 100 per kg. will now be fully exempt from excise duty. Food habits, ready-to-cook and ready-to-eat and so life-style have given a new dimension to the food processing industry. This industry is in transformation mode. Presently this industry is nascent and highly fragmented, employing between 13 to 15 million people. The output from the sector is estimated at $65-70 billion. This sector has been growing at about 7% a year. It is expected to touch 10% as incomes are rising and demographic pressure is on the increase.

Major trends in the Indian food processing industries reveal an expanding product variety and improved packaging 100% foreign direct investment (FDI) is allowed in this industry. Investment opportunities are available not merely in food production, but also in infrastructure development, marketing inspection and testing services, technology development etc.

MARKET OPPORTUNITIES

India's humungous market size ravenous appetite for food, with growing incomes and changing life styles create incredible market opportunities for food producers, machinery makers, and food technology and service providers. Fruit and vegetables is an area of farming with great export and employment potential. The policies are investor-friendly and more importantly technological and human resources are available aplenty in the country.

Recent initiatives taken to give a special focus to this industry in a bid to provide logistics management and technology for increasing exports of fruits, vegetables and processed foods as the next areas of growth for exports. The proposed food parks would be equipped with facilities to sort and grade agriculture produce for export. The recent announcements of supplements to the Foreign Trade Policy have given a service of measures to boost exports of agro product. The scope of VKGUY (*Vishesh Krishi and Gram Udyog*

Yojana) has been expanded to include exports of valueadded variants of several agro and forest products, including coconut oil, soyabean oil, potato flakes, meals and flours, cardamom, food preparation like soup, and sauces and forest produce. To strengthen, cold chain infrastructure, a plan for incentivising agro processing has also been launched with stakeholders being rewarded with duty credit scrip equal to 10% of the value of agro exports. The Government is considering a Rs. 1,500 crore subsidy plan for the development of mega food parks in select cities of the country.

These food parks would be developed by a special purpose vehicle (SPV) on PPP (Private Public Partnership) model. The Indian food sector estimated to be worth over $200 billion is expected to grow to $310 billion by 2015. It also contributes to a major part of the retail basket. The $6.1- billion Indian food retail chain is also growing at a hefty 9% and has invited FDI to the tune of over $3 billion. Developing countries like India who are emerging as major players in global food trade not only need to develop their own technologies based on local conditions life styles but also need to assert its relevance in the global fora.

Export Scenario

Export of processed fruits and vegetables is another thrust area for encouraging export of value added products. A number of large national and multinational companies have now entered processed food industries with a thrust on exports. There has been significant increase in the export of fresh fruits and vegetables during the past few years. Exports increased from Rs. 433 crore in 1994-95 to Rs. 2,012.16 crore in 2005-06.

The major fruits exported are mangoes, grapes, citrus fruits pomegranates, *lychees*, dried nuts etc. To increase the volume and price competitiveness, APEDA (Agricultural Processed Food Export Development Authority) proposes to the reefer technology to transport mangoes to Europe. China has opened its market for Indian mango, grapes and bitter gourd. Efforts are on to secure market access for the fruits in

Japan, USA and Australia. The long awaited access to the Japanese market for Indian mangoes was achieved in June 2006. The first consignment of mangoes left the Indian shores for USA recently. The promotional programme for mangoes was organized in leading super markets in Dubai and Germany during the year. Wet sampling and free distribution of major varieties of mangoes was carried out during the promotion programmes. To boost exports of Indian horticultural products APEDA is providing support in the form of infrastructure, packaging, quality, commercializing research for purpose of export as well as providing transport subsidy.

As a result of the assistance extended by APEDA, integrated pack houses have come up in the major production areas of grapes, mango, pomegranate and gherkins. Products like vegetable *curries, dals*, sweets, etc., in improved packaging have been introduced for reaching the new markets. The growth in this group is contributed by pulses, processed fruits and juices and processed vegetables.

Role of Technology

Advancement in food technology can play an important role in not only harmonising quality norms, but also by developing good manufacturing practices, including conformity to traceability norms hazard analysis at critical control points (HACCP). The area where the technology can help is the fixation of the rational maximum residue limit (MRL) for pesticides and veterinary drugs in food, which can be acceptable for implementation by member countries of Codex.

Codex has also incorporated HACCP system for identifying risk and their control. HACCP also covers pathogenic bacteria also. In HACCP system critical points are identified for control through appropriate technologies. International bodies like Codex Alimentarius Commission and International Standards Organisation (ISO) set quality norms for food; Office International des Epizooties (OIE) addresses issues relating to animal health; International Plant Protection

Convention (IPPC) sets norms for plant quarantine. Though the quality norms of these global bodies are accepted as base for reference, countries are allowed to set more stringent norms. The developed countries, who are technologically advanced are in a more advantageous position to set stringent norms, which many feel, could performance as non-tariff barriers in trade.

In India, the contact point for Codex Alimantarius Commission is the Union Health Ministry, while that for OIE is the animal husbandry department and that for IPPC is the Union Agriculture Ministry. The Bureau of Indian Standards is the affiliate member of ISO. The Union Health Ministry has notified that from August 2007 onwards, all packaged food should carry labels stating nutritional value and trans-fat content. The ministry is also finalising the procedures for labelling of genetically modified (GM) food. Already, there are labelling norms for distinguishing packaged vegetarian and non-vegetarian food. These measures are necessary for giving the consumers an informed choice and to caution against any possible hazards. OIE has played a pioneering role during the past outbreaks of Avian Flu and foot and- mouth disease in cattle across the world.

"As a result of globalisation and climate change, we are currently facing an unprecedented impact of emerging and reemerging animal diseases and zoonoses (animal diseases transmissible to humans). Improving the governance of animal health system in both the public and private sector is the most effective response to this alarming situation," says the OIE director-general, Bernard Vallet. Vallet a fund has been set up to assist member countries in control of animal disease, promotion of animal welfare and animal production for food safety. OIE's crucial role in helping the veterinary services meets their new challenges, through the development and use of the performance, vision and strategy tool.

Eleventh Plan Proposals

Many of the plans under Tenth Plan are to be continued during the Eleventh Five Year Plan. Proposals submitted by the

Ministry of Food Processing Industries (MFPI) for the Eleventh Plan, however, are to be restructured with appropriate management/implementation arrangements in Public Private Partnership mode with strong project implementation capabilities.

The new integrated approach not only addresses issue of financial assistance but also issues such as skill development, entrepreneurship, institutional development, providing a policy environment which stimulates growth.

Core Elements of the Proposed Strategy are:

- Better project selection, development and implementation.
- Decentralized cluster based development, particularly for creation of infrastructure and fostering linkages to retail outlets.
- Industry-led capacity building and upgradation of standards.
- An integrated food law and science based food standards.
- Strategic intervention with redesigned plans and efficient implementation arrangements.
- Importantly, the Ministry has to be strengthened appropriately, to meet the challenges in implementing various new initiatives proposed for energizing the food processing sector in the country.

The Priority Areas identified for Intervention are:

- Infrastructure development
- The food park plan is proposed to be modified into a plan for a Mega Food Park
- Modernization of Abattoirs.
- Cold Chain, Value Addition and Preservation infrastructure (Cold storages, Reefer vans)
- Irradiation Centres
- Research and development – Products, Technology, Quality and Skills
- Capacity Building – Human Resource Development, Research and Development, Quality, Safety, Related Infrastructure

- Establishment of NIFTEM
- Upgradation of PPRC, Thanjavur into a National Crop Processing Centre
- Upgrading safety and quality of street food and establishing food streets in identified cities
- Setting up of National Meat Board.
- Wine Sector Development—establishment of Wine Board

Salient Features of Proposed Plans

Based on the review of Tenth Plan plans, it is proposed that all existing plans be continued under the Eleventh Plan with or without modifications. However, certain components under some of the plans are proposed to be merged or discontinued as follows:

- The components of Packaging Centre, Cold Chain Facilities, Value Added Centres and Irradiation Facilities under the Plan of Infrastructure Development may be merged into a single component.
- The component of Bar Coding under plan for Quality Assurance, Codex Standards and R&D not to be continued under the Eleventh Five Year Plan

The component of Strengthening of Codex Cell under Plan for Quality Assurance, Codex Standards and R&D to be merged with the plan for Setting up/Upgradation of Quality Control/ Food Testing Labouratory. Plan for Backward and Forward Integration not to be continued under the Eleventh Five Year Plan A new plan for upgrading the safety and quality of street foods is proposed under the Eleventh Plan. It will have two components of 'Safe Food Towns' and 'Food Corner/ Food Court'.

The food processing industry in India occupies a unique position in the Indian economy in terms of its potential for employment generation, increasing the farmers' income and export growth. With a view to provide for improvement of processing capabilities the plan for technology upgradation/ expansion/ modernization/ establishment being implemented by the MFPI is proposed to be decentralized during the

Eleventh Plan period by way of implementation through Banks and financial institutions to provide a thrust and wider coverage for food processing industries in the country and simultaneously decentralise the procedures for appraisal, grant of assistance and monitoring.

Though the nascent food processing sector may still be trying to find its feet, it constitutes 14% of manufacturing GDP amounting to estimated Rs 2,80,000 crore in terms of value. Its growth over the last decade has been at the rate of 7.1% per annum and is expected to rise to 7.3% per annum in the next five years. The 10 potential of the food processing industry remains untapped despite the huge quantities of processable food items that the country produces. And yet, India is unable to capitalise on surpluses like food, fruits and vegetables etc. with just a very small percentage of production being processed.

Processing levels are a mere 2% in fruits and vegetables, 4% in fish and 2% in meat and poultry. The encouragement that is needed for this sector like a 10-year tax holiday, the simplification of documentation, the setting up of an Equalisation Fund which will ensure the sustained supply of raw materials at a particular price, the development of a futures market, and improved infrastructure—cold storage facilities at present are minimal— will undoubtedly help nurture this sector.

The food-processing sector is crucial for the India's development in the era of globalisation, to not only do well on the international front but also to achieve self adequacy on the domestic front. It establishes a vital link between agriculture and the consumer, hence ensuring the manifold growth of the economy. India is the world's second largest producer of food next to China and holds the potential to acquire the numero uno status with sustained efforts. India ranks amongst the largest producers of milk, tea, fruits and vegetables in the world. But its share in the Rs 280 bn ($6.2 bn) global trade in processed foods is less than 1%. Processed food consumption in India has been estimated at Rs 4600 bn, however, processing still remains mostly at primary level.

The level of processing and value addition is significantly lower than developed countries and several developing countries. The quantity of processed food produced in the country is under 2.2% as compared to countries such as Thailand, Malaysia and Brazil where it is 65-75%. Similarly, the level of processing in India in the case of fruits and vegetables is at a dismal 2% while in advanced countries like France and the US it goes as high as 70-80%. There is tremendous amount of wastage and value loss in respect of agricultural products, especially perishable products (approx.$13 billion as per Dun and Bradstreet Study 2006) due to inadequate processing, transportation, storage and handling facilities.

The processed food industry is set to grow at more than 10% per annum driven by consumer demand, organised distribution and policy initiatives by the government. The segments with the largest growth potential for processing are dairy, fruits and vegetables, wine, confectionary and poultry. Products that have growing demand in the export market are pickles, chutneys, fruit pulp, canned fruits and vegetables, concentrated pulps and juices, dehydrated vegetables and frozen fruits and vegetables along with processed animal based products.

In recent times the government has rightly recognised that it is essential to promote investment in the food processing sector so as to ensure that it leads to increase in India's share in the global trade of agricultural products, generates employment for large number of people, increases the income of the farmers and contributes to the overall economy of the country. The government on its part has initiated certain reforms to remove legislative barriers and introduce facilitative measures to catalyse private sector activity in food and agri-business sector.

Some of the key measures undertaken by the government recently include: amendment of Essential Commodities Act to enable free trade and storage of commodities, amendment of the Agriculture Produce Marketing Commission Act, rationalisation of food laws, implementation of the National Horticulture Mission to increase horticulture production through increased investments along the supply chain, removal of restrictions on milk procurement and reduction in taxation of food products and all the formulation of Food Safety and Standards Act 2006. India's fast growing consumer market is slated to include 500 million consumers by 2010.

A report by Research and Consultancy Outsourcing Services (RNCOS), the food processing industry is expected to treble from 6% to 20% with its share in global agro-trade expected to rise to 3%. Considering the significance of the issues facing the processed food industry with the focus on the taxation and regulatory issues, the Federation of Indian Chambers of Commerce and Industry (FICCI)) recently conducted a survey to assess the existing state of affairs.

It has proposed a 12-point package of fiscal measures to ensure the overall development of food processing industry. The study clearly recommended without a strong and dependable cold chain, food processing couldn't survive and grow. The government should provide a 10-year tax holiday for cold chain infrastructure under *section 80-IA* of the Income-Tax Act for undertakings involved in complete supply chain. It is important to note that cold chain infrastructure is not inviting the much needed investment as the existing units engaged in the manufacturing sector prefer to focus on the core competencies instead of diversifying.

The investment in cold chain has become important particularly in the context that new players are entering in organised retail and existing players are on an expansion spree. The intention in the case of big players is to go for complete supply chain-from farm to fork.

This would need huge investments in infrastructure for storage facilities, transportation etc. The appropriate fiscal stimulus would encourage investment in cold chain infrastructure in the country.

RESEARCH AND DEVELOPMENT

The food-processing sector has viewed that the low research intensity is mainly owing to inadequate expenditure. While the expenditure figure on R&D is close to 3% in the case of Japan and US and between 2 and 2.5% in France and Germany respectively, it stands at less than 1% in India. The survey suggested following measures to encourage R&D in food processing sector.

- Weighted deduction of 150% with regard to R&D expenditure should be made available to food processing sector as well
- Customs Duty exemption should be given to manufacturing establishments who have R&D facilities and invest in R&D activities/infrastructure
- Government should set up a nodal agency to performance as a facilitator for setting up R&D activity, which may be required by existing/ prospective entrepreneurs. R&D activity may be considered as the priority sector lending.
- Government should make necessary efforts to bring renowned inventions related to agri-food sector developed by other countries to India and the concerned institutes should improvise on them.

ANOMALY IN VAT RATES ACROSS STATES

The Value Added Tax has been put in place from April 1, 2005. VAT avoids cost-cascading effect and this is the single most important factor that has found favour in India. The study recommended that uniform VAT rate should be introduced in the case of processed foods. The Empowered Committee of State Finance Ministers' should take up the cases where deviations are present, with respective states. Anomalous situation exists with regard to items such as instant mixes, tea, ketchups, sauces, coffee powder, ice, branded bread and processed and branded salt, meat products etc. For example, though a large number of food products are charged VAT @ 4%, the states of Bihar, Chattisgarh, Goa, Gujarat, Jharkhand, Karnataka, Madhya Pradesh, Maharashtra, Rajasthan and Uttar Pradesh, continue to charge VAT @ 12.5% on biscuits - an item of mass consumption. All the states should uniformly align the VAT on biscuits with the 4% rate generally fixed for food products.

The ultimate objective of bringing VAT is to facilitate seamless movement of goods without any hindrances making India as 'One Common market'.

Classification Problems in Excise Duty Structure

The FICCI report strongly suggested that there is an urgent need for a massive cut in commodity taxes, especially on demand elastic items to stimulate demand in the economy. Tax cuts would provide the much-needed boost to India's manufacturing sector. The study various classification problems with regard to excise duty structure in case of select processed food items.

Countervailing duty (CVD) of 4% has now been imposed on almost all imports. This has been made applicable to all inputs of the processed food industry like tomato paste, packaging materials and other raw materials. Since finished products are exempt, it is therefore necessary to include inputs imported for food processing industry in the exempted category. The study also recommended proper classification of items in the food products categories like ready-to-eat packaged foods, instant food mixes like dosa and idli, instant pre-mix used in tea, coffee vending machines, sauces, ketchup, tea, coffee, and skimmed milk powder. The study also that it is necessary to issue a clarification/ notification confirming that all intermediate excisable products arising during the manufacture of exempted final products will also be exempted

Other Major Fiscal Issues

- *Industry's view on Fringe Benefit Tax (FBT):* The study said that there is unanimity amongst food processing majors that FBT is a retrograde step and should be abolished altogether. However, if complete abolition is not possible at this juncture then at least it should be suitably modified so that compliance cost of the corporate can be reduced. The food processing majors strongly viewed that sales promotion including publicity expenses should be outside the ambit of deemed benefit list.

- *APMC Act:* The study strongly recommended that the government may consider abolishing APMC Act altogether. There is a need to abolish APMC Act (e.g. Bihar), as it has become an obstacle to industry for sourcing raw material directly from producers and primary processors. APMC requires industry to obtain licence, maintain specified records, submit monthly statements, pay cess and thus increase the cost of inputs. The act has some outdated provisions like inputs purchased by the industry must be consumed in one month only. The Act *per-se* as stated should be abolished, as this is more in the archaic nature. However, if the complete abolition of the same is not possible, then at least it should be modified to meet the emerging requirements.
- *Central Sales Tax:* The study said that Central Sales Tax (CST) should be abolished and roadmap should be laid down for Goods and Services Tax (GST).
- *Transport Subsidiary:* The study observed that transport subsidy should be available across India and not restricted to a few states (which is the current position). Moreover this should be available not only on exports of the final product but also on domestic sales. Domestic consumption of processed foods can be growth driver for the food processing industry.

It is recognised worldwide that a strong and dynamic food processing industry is important for diversification and commercialisation of agriculture. However, this is not possible unless and until we have conducive regulatory regime in place. Time is ripe now to review various outdated rules, regulations and laws so that the sector can grow in leaps and bounds. The study urged that there is a need to implement Food Safety and Standards Act 2006 at the earliest.

The most critical suggestion received was that it has been almost six months since the Food Safety and Standards Act 2006 has been passed. However, the industry has no idea when and how the act will be implemented. Concern has been expressed as to how the integration of various laws, orders, acts currently in place would happen. In the absence of implementation of the Food Safety and Standards Act 2006, the government should at least present a roadmap so that the industry can take necessary steps to meet the current and future requirements. Industry also expressed distress on the numerous amendments in the PFA Act and the manner in which these amendments are being done. FICCI strongly suggests in the report that there should be adequate representation from the food industry in the proposed Food Authority and Central Advisory Committee under the new Food Safety and Standards Act.

Indian food processing aims at consumer convenience; with push from government for private participation is coming of age. The food processing industry is coming of age it is ranked fifth among industries of India. Nearly, one third of the entire Indian food market share comprises of processed food. With policy measures from the government, the food processing Industry accounts for 13% of the country's exports. The industry's size is estimated at US $ 70 billion; including US $ 22 billion of value added products. Indians spend half of their household expenditure on food items at present.

The industry would create 9 million employment opportunities from the current 1.6 m and investment of Rs 1,50,000 crore in the coming 10 years. With over 1 billion population and 350 million strong urban middle class and changing food habits, the processed food market is promising a huge potential to be tapped. A joint study by CII and AC Nielsen (market research firm), to understand demand drivers for processed food brings forth the changing Indian meal patterns: Working lunch seems to be replacing conventional meals in the day, with a need for no fuss packaging. In addition to this, the study says, Indians are willing to spend on global cuisines. Multi-cuisine restaurants are mushrooming even in small cities and towns.

This reasons the array of foreign investors coming to India which is driving the growth of the industry. Like investments to offer Indians the real taste of Italian pasta; conglomerates from Emilla Romagina are looking at major Indian cities to set up Italian food processing plants. Most recent one was the proposal from West Midlands of UK to the Ministry of Food Processing Industries of India. Other foreign food companies like McDonald's, Pizza Hut, Cadbury's, Tropicana, Pepsi, Coke, HLL, Nestle, etc. are already earning huge returns by processing Indian food for domestic and global markets. Besides foreign Investors, food processing sector is a major attraction for Indian corporate houses to invest. Reliance, Godrej, Bharti, ITC, Hero, Ballarpur Industries, DSCL, Tata and Mahindra and Mahindra are prominent corporate houses are with end-to-end integrated operations in the food chain. India is the world's second largest food producer.

Yet contribution to GDP is only about 20%, despite 60% of Indians employed in agriculture related activities. This is owing to improper value-addition of the produced food. With as many as 20 agro-climatic zones and various soil types, a wide spectrum of food-types is produced like - fruit and vegetable, fisheries, meat and poultry, milk and dairy, grain and cereals, beverages and consumer foods. The wide variety and large scale production ensure India's food security and steady export revenues, topping the world's food production list in milk, sugarcane, tea, and cattle population. But the abundant food is marketed unprocessed due to inadequate infrastructure; it seems that the food processing industry is still in its nascent stage. Only 2% of fruits and vegetables and 15% of milk are processed at present, despite rising demand for processed food.

Further, out of total food produced in India, barely 7% is processed, compared to China's 23%, or 188% processing in the UK food sector. Such relatively low level of food processing is due to insufficient preserving techniques and supply chain infrastructure. The loss from inadequate cold storage is 37% of annual food production which is worth a colossal Rs.30, 000 to Rs. 40,000 crore. Besides infrastructure problems in fruit and vegetables processing, inadequate infrastructure for meat processing (seafood, poultry and cattle-meat processing) also exists. Also a huge a daunting challenge is to meet the world's basic quality standards of safety and hygiene standards like

Sanitary and Phyto-Sanitary (SPS) rules and Vapour Heat Treatment (VHT) especially to build the export potential. This needs organizing the meat processing industry to adhere to modern, scientific techniques. To overcome the infrastructure shortage the industry needs an investment of US$ 28 billion. Unfortunately, most of the Indian farmers are small holders; their average farm size is 1.6 hectares, and farmers are linked with exploitative intermediaries in the food chain who are unable to invest in food processing units either. There a severe need to integrate the farming with the food processing. Earning profits through food processing comes from an efficient backward and forward integration.

Even though value addition begins at the post harvest level it needs critical integrated efforts of both pre-harvest and post-harvest functions. In this context Prof. Sukhpal Singh, IIMA says -"The stakeholders are expected to face this challenge on a- priori level, because success of food processing industries depends on nature of the produce and the type of processing involved. Integration begins with procurement of such superior quality of seeds". That is because traditional Indian seed varieties do not yield enough pulp content vital to undergo processing. Since the farmers are short in financial and technical abilities: the quality of food produced doesn't meet the required processing standards. They find it hard to link their farming activity with food processing and are unable to reap rewards of value addition. If there must be a way out to the grim situation, then it is finding an end to end link in the food chain. The government has offered opportunities for FDI and private participation: a right direction for the industry's promotion.

The outcome of 100% equity from foreign investments, for a majority of processed food items can be seen from the 105 FDI proposals worth Rs. 640 crore approved by the government in last three years. Private companies can integrate the food chain with supplying quality seeds to farmers who get back their fair-share of returns, and the companies can process the food linked to hypermarkets with efficient supply chain infrastructure. Like the successful initiative taken by

PepsiCo, which was one of the first to initiate integrated food processing. Initially the tomatoes from the Punjab farms did not meet the standards for making ketchup; neither a logistically efficient nor any procurement model existed. Pepsi had to integrate the farming (supply of superior tomato) activities with the processing infrastructure and only then start the tomato-processing plant in that area. This and other successful experiences are evidences for the government to invite integrated efforts in the food chain by private hands. Food processing has been declared as a priority sector.

The National Food Processing Policy has been revised for an integrated approach in 2004-05, to facilitate speedy growth. The aim of the policy is to simplify procedures to comply with the need and growth of the sector. Under infrastructure development, Agro-Food Parks are identified in various Indian cities. Proposals to set up 20 Mega Parks and 50 Food Parks adopting the French Food Park as a model are undertaken by the Ministry of Food Processing Industry. Tapping the industry's export potential is one of the major concerns. Presently, current exports of Indian processed food are worth Rs. 2500 billion. Agri- Export Zones (AEZs) are earmarked with nearness to highways, airports and marketing centres from the areas of food processing.

The Policy urges private companies to grow processable varieties under contract farming. Under the AEZ plan, state governments and private firms are entitled privileges of Special Economic Zones, like tax holidays up to 10 years and duty free imports of capital-goods to set up processing units. To provide financial credit without any bottlenecks NABARD in the present plan is given with a corpus of Rs. 1100 million in single window clearing. This loan is for setting up new unit or to modernize an existing food processing units.

Further, the government will give 25% subsidies for greenfield projects up to the corpus of Rs 100 crore for Mega Food Parks and up to Rs.105 crore for Food Parks. For holistic approach, R&D initiatives to work on emerging challenges of the food processing technology and food engineering are underway. The industry's revenues can be increased if quality rules of SPS, VHT and the Codex international standards are approved. The Thanjavur paddy processing centre will be added to the nationalized list of research institutes. Likewise, Indian packaging Industry is working on low cost and competitive packaging solutions. Packaging costs, 20-70% of processed food.

Growth Potential

Over the past decade money spent by Indians on ready to eat food outside home, has more than doubled. While 5 billion USD is spend on ready to eat food this year research estimates it to double up in over five years. This year, the growth in sales (domestic and export) of processed food is more than 150%, most remarkable are the two sectors which showed remarkable growth in sales. Processed Poultry's sales grew by 64%, and spirits and beverages by 75%.

Food process outsourcing is presenting good prospects in multi cuisine hotels and restaurants abroad for processed or semi-processed Indian seafood, dairy and Indian curries. 'Made in India' brands like Amul Dairy, Cobra Beer, Bikanervala Foods, MTR Foods, ITC's Kitchen of India, Satnam Overseas' Basmati rice are finding prime global retail shelf-space. Convenience, variety and health issues are key drivers for quality of packaged food. With clear demand in the future if India can harness its production to the quality its dream to become the world's food basket is sure to come true. Food processing creates form, time and place utilities. Value addition through food processing and exports makes the farmer benefit through better returns to his produce due to larger demand- Prof Sukhpal Singh, IIMA.

They are expected to play, on a-priori grounds, an important role in promoting agricultural development at least in those areas from where the raw materials are drawn. The second facet of their role is to bring about a greater integration in agricultural marketing. This integration may be vertical or horizontal. Whereas the former refers to the linking together of successive functions or operations in the production or marketing of a product under unified control, the latter means linking of different business units in the same stage of production or marketing under unified control. Whatever may be the form of integration, processing generally leads to the tying up of different onfarm and offfarm functions such as production, storage, transportation, wholesaling and distribution. In fact, the modern processing plants not only create form utilities, but their integrated structure, combining processing and distribution, has led to the adding of place and time utilities as well. Value addition through food processing and exports helps the farmer benefit through better returns to his produce due to larger demand. The growth of food processing industries reduces post harvest (raw material) losses which ranged from 15 -31 per cent across fruits and vegetables in Gujarat.

A large part of it (50 per cent) was at farmer level and the remaining at the APMC (10 per cent), local trader (3 per cent), wholesaler (3 per cent), broker (7 per cent) and retailer (25 per cent) levels. In wheat and rice, it is estimated to be 10 per cent and 12 per cent at farm level respectively and 13 per cent and 10 per cent at trader and FCI level in paddy alone compared with only two per cent in the USA. The losses account for almost 20 per cent of total farm production and are valued at Rs. 50, 000 crore annually. In fruits and vegetables, the wastage is of the order of 40 per cent of total value of production and estimated at Rs. 23,000 crore annually. It is more than the value of annual fruit and vegetable consumption in the U.K.

Food processing like many other agro industries also generates offfarm employment as in India it is found to be more labour intensive and capital saving than many other industries. It also encourages agricultural production through assured market and remunerative prices and adds value to the primary product in various ways. The processed foods can be promising item in the exports from the developing countries and thus, may help in saving and earning foreign exchange. Still, the value addition to food production in India is only 7 per cent compared to over 22 per cent in China, 45 per cent in Philippines and 188 per cent in the UK. Further, only two per cent of the fruit and vegetable production is processed in India compared with 30 per cent in Thailand, 70 per cent in Brazil and the USA, 78 per cent in Philippines, and 83 per cent in Malaysia. Value addition in agro processing should also take into account, besides the value added to main product due to processing, the value addition due to byproduct processing. Would setting up of the Food Zones help in realizing the potential of Indian food processing industry? Yes, as it will help it will generate economies of agglomeration and help achieve quality production with the help of centralized product testing labs and mechanisms.

How are the State and Central government working on increasing this momentum? What are the thrust areas under the agro processing zones? Many states are providing incentives for such zones in terms of investment and export facilities especially in horticultural and related high value businesses. Interestingly, the focus of many of these project sand plans is domestic market which is a step in the right direction.

What are the challenges in setting up Agro-processing zones? Infrastructure, large investments required, and acquisition of land are major issues involved in such projects. Leasing out of land does not help unless it is very long term lease w3hic his possible only in case of govt. land, as investors want to make longer term fixed investment for which they need to own land. How will the existing lack of processing and storage infrastructure be tackled? Through public private partnerships which brings together the resources and strengths of the two sectors.

10

Utilisation and Structure of Working Capital

ANALYSE FINANCIAL STATEMENTS

Analysing financial statements help a firm to gain insight as to how their future looks. Since its creation, the PC has changed the way people work, play and communicate. Computers have eased the transition for businesses to adapt in the world of ever changing technology. PC's have continued to be a strong and growing industry.

However, some computer manufacturers have done a better job than others at becoming financially stable. In this analysis as suggested, gain insight about Dell's and Gateway's future by comparing the companies' historical date in five different aspects: liquidity, cash flows, operating performance, asset utilization and capital structure.

LIQUIDITY

Short-term liquidity analysis allows the analyst to discover if the company in question can repay their investors, including shareholders and corporate debt, in a timely manner. All commitments of a company must be considered when looking at a company's liquidity, both in the short and long-term. It is important to consider long-term and short-term analysis because they are still an essential part of a company's portfolio of commitments. In order to consider both Dell and Gateways' liquidity our group considered the following ratios: inventory turnover, number of days in inventory, accounts receivable turnover, days in accounts receivable, working capital, and accounts payable turnover. When examining Dell's inventory turnover and day in inventory we found a large improvement from 1994, when our analysis started, to 2002 the last year included in our analysis.

They increased their turnover by 8% to almost 76 times a year and reduced their days in inventory by almost 87% leaving inventory on the shelves for approximately four days. Gateway also was at a much lower turnover of 34.66 times year. Their turnover number was unstable during the analysis period. Their inventory also stayed in the company longer at 10.53 days. We believe that Dell's numbers are so favourable in large part to the fact that they practice just-in-time manufacturing. Dell builds their computers and products when ordered by the customer instead of the computer waiting on the customer. This means that they are more accurately predicting what inventory to have on hand.

The accounts receivable (A/R) and days in A/R ratios inform analyst how quickly the companies are able to collect their cash from credit sales. Dell's accounts receivable was turned over twelve times in a year and their average credit sale was outstanding for approximately thirty days before being realised as cash. Gateway collected their A/R almóst thirteen times in 2002 and their average credit sale was outstanding for around eighteen days before being realised as cash. Both companies have found ways to decrease the amount of time before collecting cash over the time analysed, however it appears that Dell is lowering their number more efficiently than Gateway. Working capital is critical ratio that determines if a company's assets are being utilized compared the amount of liabilities. Dell's working capital ratio has been on the decrease for the last four years but still remains above one at 1.24 in 2004.

Gateway's working capital ratio is also above one at 1.95 in 2002 with a 23% increase from the previous year. These working capital ratios indicate that neither company according to working capital will have short-term liquidity issues in the near future.n Accounts payable turnover demonstrates how often a company has to payoff their debts. Dell's turnover has steadily decreased since 1996, from 9.73 to 5.48 in 2002. The decrease of this ratio works favourably in Dell's liquidity, due to the fact, that the company is paying off their short-term debt fewer times per year. This leaves available cash to reinvest into the company. Gateway's turnover had been decreasing between 1994 and 1999, from 15.12 to 8.82. In 2000, however, the ratio began to increase until 2002 when it reached 11.63.

This increase is not favourable for Gateway because this means that they are not able to finance their short-term obligations for extended periods, this reflects on decreasing liquidity. After reflecting on all of the ratios that our group used to determine the liquidity of Dell and Gateway we have concluded that Dell has sound liquidity, while Gateway may be on the verge of not being able to meet some of their short-term obligations.

CASH FLOW ANALYSIS

Cash flow analysis can be broken into two parts. The first part consists of several ratios that comprise cash sufficiency. Cash sufficiency measures whether or not the company can adequately compensate investors and maintain its productive capacity. The second part of cash flow analysis is cash efficiency. Cash efficiency measures the extent to which the preferred cash flow results have been achieved. When analysing cash flow sufficiency, the cash flow adequacy ratio is the most important measure. Dell's cash flow adequacy ratio has been rising steady since 1992.

The only time it decreased was during 2001. Standard and Poor's Industry Surveys on the Computer industry, 2001 was the first time global shipments of personal computers had decreased in 16 years1. The substance attributed the decrease in global shipments to the economic slowdown that occurred during 2001. From 2001 to 2002, the ratio jumped upward four points. This could be attributed to economic recovery. Although Dell's ratio slipped a little during 2001. This indicates that the company is achieving positive cash flows from operations. Gateway has not been doing as well as Dell in achieving positive cash flow results. This is a bad sign because it indicates that Gateway is not generating enough cash flows from operations. Excluding the year 1995, Gateway was generating positive cash flows up until the year 2000, as shown by the cash flow adequacy ratio. "Another key reason for the slump in PC demand was that the 1997-2000 surge in investment in PCs made further growth of this base difficult." We believe that since Gateway did not capture a large share of the market during the growth period, it is even harder for the company to grab a share of the market when growth of the market has slowed.

Operating Performance

An operating performance analysis of a company can allow an analyst to determine whether or not the company has sufficient and/or sustainable earnings from operations. This analysis can also help determine a company's earnings quality. In our group's operating performance analysis of Dell, we concluded that Dell's earnings are both sufficient and sustainable with a high earnings quality. Conversely, Gateway's earnings are neither sufficient nor sustainable, with a low quality of earnings. Overall, Dell seems to be operating on a fairly smooth basis, with Dell's gross profit margin having been stable since 1995, with a decreasing trend beginning in 1999.Their margin decreased from 22.5% in 1999 to 17.7% in 2002.

This decrease resulted from an increase in cost of goods sold, and in 2002, the increase in cost of goods sold was accompanied by a decrease in sales revenue. The decrease can also be partly attributed to a global recession that plagued the economy in 2001. While Dell's sales revenue has been increasing over time until 2002, their cost of goods sold as a percentage of sales have also been steadily increasing. We do not feel that this is a tremendous cause for alarm, however, because of their performance in other areas, which seems to indicate that they are still doing well overall. While Dell's gross profit margin has been decreasing only slightly, both their operating and net profit margins have dropped by nearly half between 1999 and 2002. The operating profit margin decreased from 11.2% in 1999 to 5.7% in 2002, while the net profit margin fell from 8.0% in 1999 to 4.0% in 2002. These large decreases can be attributed to rising total operating expenses, as well as an unusually large amount of "special charges" (1.5% of sales revenue) in 2002. Despite Dell's decreasing profit margins, the company is still doing better than their competitors and is still showing positive profit margins. Because of this, our group feels that Dell is not doing poorly, but is in fact doing quite well. While Dell is doing well for itself and is earnings positive net income, Gateway's operating performance analysis is not so positive.

Based on the various ratios that our group took into consideration, Gateway's earnings are neither sufficient not sustainable. All three of Gateway's profit margins have been very unstable over time, resulting in data patterns that can neither be trended over time nor predicted in the future. Gateway's sales revenue and cost of goods sold have been fluctuating greatly between 1993 and 2002, creating a very random assortment of gross profit margins. Between 2000 and 2002, cost of goods sold for Gateway did begin to decrease, but their sales revenue began decreasing even quicker, resulting in decreasing gross profit margins for all three years. The 2001 global recession could also have some part in the decreasing sales. Meanwhile, larger amounts of selling, general, and administrative expenses have driven the operating profit margins of 2001 and 2002 to negative percentages. Between 2000 and 2001, Gateway's operating profit margin dropped from 5.3% to (19.5%), a drop of 24.8 percentage points. The margin was also negative in 2002 at (12.3%). As a result of the negative operating profit margins in 2001 and 2002, Gateway's net profit margins in those years were also negative. Gateway also decided to close their retail stores in 2002 as a result of their poor performance.

Asset Utilization

Asset utilization is assessing the relationship between wealth creation and resources used to create that wealth.

Return on assets, return on equity, profit margin, asset turnover, and the financial structure leverage ratio give analysts a way to establish how a company uses their assets. The first ratio considered in asset utilization was Return on Assets (ROA), which determines the performance of management. Dell has consistently surpassed Gateway's performance in this area. Dell's ROA was increasing from 1994-1999 and then has gone on a downward spiral.

Dell's profit margin has followed the same pattern ranging from (1.497%) in 1994 to 3.998% and is likely the cause for the declining ROA. Gateway on the other hand started out acceptable in 1994 at 3.517%, but has been unpredictable since, even falling into the negative numbers in 2001 and 2002. Gateways revenue had begun to decrease in these years while expenses were increasing causing a negative net income. The negative net income was the main reason for the poor ROA. Therefore, Dell has been getting a satisfactory return on their assets, while Gateway has not. Return on Equity (ROE) is another measure of asset utilization.

Dell is again outperforming Gateway. Dell has had an outstanding growth in their ROE over the past several years with the peak being at 80.80% in 1999, but was a more feasible 24.16% in the year 2002. The results come from Dell's growth in net income over the years along with an increase in common stockholders equity. Gateway's ROE on the other hand started out strong in 1994 at 28.92%, but has bounced around the charts landing into the negatives in the years 2001 and 2002. Again the negative net income is the main contributing factor to the negative ROE along with a significant increase in long-term debt over the years. We conclude that Dell has a good relationship between wealth creation and resources used to create that wealth while Gateway does not share that same relationship with their asset utilization.

Capital Structure

Capital structure analysis determines if a company has a healthy balance of debt to equity. Ideally a company's balance of debt to equity enables wealth creation without jeopardizing the company's long-term solvency or inhibiting their financial flexibility. When determining a company's capital structure things such as financial leverage index, debt to capital, debt to equity, and earnings coverage. An analyst almost must consider if a company has enough long-term debt and equity financing to compensate their creditors for their investments in the company.

It is also important for a company to maintain the appropriate level of return to their investors for the amount of risk they have taken. Having financial flexibility also means having the resources to be able to take advantage of unforeseen opportunities that further the wealth of shareholders. Our group considered the capital structure of both Dell and Gateway.

Our group first considered the company's debt to capital ratio. Ideally a company would like to have a ratio closer to 0 than 1. Dell's debt to capital ratio has been fairly stable over the last few years and was. 62 in 2002. Most of Dell's debt is short-term, or in the form of current liabilities, their long-term debt to capital was.10 in 2002. Gateway's debt to capital ratio was has been decreasing slowly since 1994, to.49 in 2002. Gateway also does not have much long-term debt.

Their long-term debt to capital was.108 in 2002. One other method of looking at a company's capital structure is to consider the likelihood of a company entering into bankruptcy. Gateway has consistently had their z-score above 3.00 with a high of 11.98 in 1999. Recently, however, their z-score has dropped and was at 2.52 in 2002. This puts Gateway into a gray category of whether or not they are a going concern entity or not. Dell's z-score has been increasing since 1994 as well but in the last four years has been decreasing but remains well above 3.0 at 8.07 in 2002.

The z-score Dell has very little likelihood of filing for bankruptcy. After looking over all of our research our group has concluded that both companies have a healthy position of their debt and equity. Dell seems to be doing well at financing their assets with the appropriate amount of debt. The only dark cloud over Gateway is their z-score. In terms of liquidity, it seems that Dell will be able to pay current obligations and still have enough to continue operations. Gateway, on the other hand, may be able to meet their obligations but struggle in continuing operations. As far as cash flows are concerned, Dell is generating ample cash flows from operations, while Gateway is unable to produce sufficient cash flows.

Dell's operating performance seems to show that they have high quality earnings that are sufficient and sustainable, while Gateway's operating performance shows just the opposite. In the asset utilization component, we believe Dell has a positive correlation between its wealth creation and its invested capital; however, Gateway does not have this same correlation.

The capital structure component finally shed some light over Gateway showing that they have a good balance of debt and equity, however, they it was also discovered that they have a high possibility of bankruptcy. Dell, also, portrayed a healthy balance of debt to equity, yet they show a very low possibility of bankruptcy. After analysing the five components that represent a company's financial position, our group has concluded that Dell is stable and Gateway is unstable.

Cost-effective Capital Management and Utilization

Performance consumes capital for costs, effectiveness, capacity, and uncertainty in producing results. Performance is the utilization of invested performance capital by the business to produce economic output in results. Performance is the actions, activities, processing, tasks, functions, work on jobs, or workflows that produce results. Performance incurs costs to create value in results. Every enterprise utilizes capital in performance to produce value in results.

Every enterprise has performance capital in the assets, people, reports, information from studies, knowledge or management directives created, and other capital developed and utilized. This performance capital is utilized through business performance solutions to create value in the business results produced. Many essential business attributes and data elements are not recorded or managed today, because capital items deployed to be utilized as performance solutions are not managed.

Performance solutions must be managed as one information set for effective 21st Century Management, since:

- Solutions provide the capital that must be utilized to produce economic output value in results
- Solutions are one of two entities that comprise a business
- Solutions must be managed to manage the business and performance expectations
- Solutions and performance must be managed to provide qualified solutions to produce specific results
- Solutions must be planned, developed, improved, and supported by human capital with the appropriate capabilities
- Solutions embody business capacity, costs, effectiveness, and uncertainty
- Solutions have common attributes like manager, category, class, type, capital group, component, support unit, vendor, etc. that form manageable solution sets
- Solutions must be defined and organized to be aligned, integrated, and utilized with other solutions to produce a result
- Solutions must be deployed to a result to apply costs to result value, to know effectiveness for result quality, to adjust capacity for result volumes, and to manage uncertainty to control result risk
- Solutions to be developed to produce new or improved results must be defined to know specific solutions to develop, and to capture development costs to be amortized to future results

If we do not manage the capital in performance solutions utilized to produce results as one complete set, we cannot know and manage all costs incurred to produce result value, the capacity needed and utilized to produce results, the worth of solutions and capital related to result value-added, the effectiveness of performance shown by the quality of results, actual performance against expectations to contribute to result goals, or the strategic solution investments needed to create strategic result value.

Capital must be defined as Performance Solutions to be managed. Performance capital should be broken down into specific business performance solutions in order to deploy capital to produce specific business results. Performance solutions include any capital utilized, such as:

- You, your capabilities, and the knowledge you use as human capital
- Your organization, the process and software systems, and the data that directly describe results and related entities, like customer, as business capital
- Your company infrastructure and computer and communication networks and financial and equipment assets, supply lines and working capital, and the records kept on results, as facility capital
- Your company strategy and plans for results, tactical policies and guidance, and customer and business intelligence that show the right results, as management capital.

Performance solutions are utilized at a level of performance. Performance can be planned and expectations can be set for each solution over time periods. Most Performance Solutions are not defined or managed today. Most companies do not know what performance solutions they have. Human personnel are administered as employees and facility equipment is administered as fixed assets, rather than managed as performance solutions.

Information is administered and reported as a routine. Knowledge solutions may be created, but are administered for availability rather than managed to produce results. Many solutions are developed, but are never identified or managed as capital.

Much business, information, and management capital is labeled as "intangible assets". Capital must be managed to provide Solutions that produce results. Performance solutions must be organized in a Performance Structure to provide the specific capabilities needed for capital management and support, and to integrate with other solutions utilized to produce a specific result.

The Performance Structure applies the specific capability to develop, improve, and support the capital in four categories: business, capital specific to produce a particular result; human, people who produce the result; facility, tangible assets and documentation; and management, the capital that plans and controls results.

The Performance Structure organizes solutions to be utilized in three classes: readiness, to be able to produce a set of results; production, to produce a specific result; and information, to provide and capture information. The Performance Structure organizes four capital categories by three capital classes to give twelve solution types:

- *Business capital*: Business organization, business process, and business data
- *Human capital:* Human personnel, human capability, and human knowledge
- *Facility capital:* Facility equipment, facility supply, and facility records
- *Management capital*: Management strategy, management tactics, and management intelligence

Every performance solution developed and utilized is defined in one of the solution types and to the detail that it can be deployed to specific results. The Performance Structure manages all performance solutions available as a set.

Performance Solutions Embody Cost, Capacity, and Effectiveness

Every well-managed enterprise wants to control costs. Performance solutions consume capital and generate costs. Unknown solutions produce unknown costs. Performance costs charged to activity, centre, or other entity not produced by the performance, provide limited meaning. Performance costs must be charged against the result value created. We must know costs for all solutions utilized, in order to determine the value added to a result. There is no such thing as performance quality. But, every solution must be effective to produce a quality result. One ineffective solution can produce a defective result.

The volume of results is limited by the lowest-capacity solution utilized. All other solutions have excess capacity. Performance uncertainty such as sick personnel, poor application of capability, equipment breakdown, etc. creates risk that a result may not be produced as planned. Specific Performance Solutions must be managed for capital development. It is important to define and manage performance solutions for business change and capital development.

The costs of change and investment arise from developing and implementing specific performance solutions to increase the value of specific results. Solutions must be defined to know all solutions that need to be developed, all costs from solution development, and then continuing cost of solution operation, in order to know the costs to charge to results. Each solution needed must be developed as a managed result in the development project. Development costs can be systematically charged to results to know the value-added return on investments.

RURAL EMPLOYMENT AND WORKING CAPITAL INVESTMENTS

There is an obvious need to utilize the resources of the absentee landowners more effectively. There is also a need to provide stable employment in rural areas to prevent the mass migration that transformed the rural poor into the urban poor. An agro based property management service for absentee landlords can address both of these problems.

A company offering such a service can ensure a higher income for the landowners while increasing employment and incomes for the landless poor. The concept of a property management service is not new to urban areas in developed countries. However in Bangladesh, the concept has not yet developed.

While rural land have tenancy, lease and sharecropping arrangements, this proposal for a management company takes the further step of partnering with the landowner and investing in the land for the purpose of providing more employment and generating more income. Land use and ownership patterns in Bangladesh are also different from developed countries.

Most of the agricultural land is owned by non-farmers and non-residents *i.e.* absentee land owners. Thus there is a disconnect between the farm owners and the farmers. If landowners can be given the right incentives to invest in their land, they can get better returns and generate more employment.

However as most absentee landowners hold on to their lands as savings instruments, they lack the manpower resources needed to run a more complex operation.

The business will have a number of goals:

- Provide employment for landless poor and rural women
- Provide essential skills training for workers
- Utilize land more efficiently
- Bring investment to rural communities
- Provide higher incomes for landowners

Absentee landholdings vary widely in the size of holdings, the quality of the property as well as the availability of capital for further investment. Thus each project will have to be evaluated as an independent operation.

A typical step by step outline for implementing a project is as follows:

- Evaluate the potential of the land for alternative use.
- Evaluate the level of infrastructure investment the landowner is willing to undertake
- Evaluate the risk profile of the land owner.
- Prepare a business proposal for the land owner.
- If the landowner agrees to make the investments to upgrade his property the management company will execute the plan and manage the property on agreed upon terms.

- The management company will initially staff the farm with a trained who will work towards training local staff.

Each of these farms will be a semi-independent unit operating as a standalone profit centre. However all independent units will be managed by the umbrella organization who will be responsible for setting up the unit, training new staff, insuring staff wages during negative business cycles.

In addition the parent organization will coordinate the activities of multiple farms and exploit economies of scale in marketing, procurement and other areas. While the focus of the independent farming units will be on production the parent organization will also manage other value added services such as further processing and storage. A few social goals will also have to be emphasized.

Firstly the object is to provide local employment, thus the emphasis on training local staff. A second goal is to provide employment for women. Women in villages are used to farm work, though it is usually in their own farms and not as cash-based employees. A third goal is to focus on the landless farmer. Another social goal is to provide training for alternative crops and methods to farmers with small holdings.

The Need for Such an Enterprise

The main goal of this enterprise will be to extract more utilization from already available resources. The primary resource that is underutilized in rural Bangladesh is land and manpower. The most obvious beneficiaries are the landowner, who will see increased productivity and profits from his land and the rural poor and landless, who will be able to avail cash-based employment.

Large agro processors will also benefit from the plan by being able to outsource some of their production to smaller farmers and maintain a relationship with one company that will manage the smaller relationships. In addition the local communities will benefit from the trained alumnus that will emerge from this enterprise.

Employment

Employment in the rural areas has been traditionally tied to land ownership. Most of the employment was being generated by land owners either farming their own land or employing others to do so. Sharecropping is still a major form of employment in rural Bangladesh. Cash based employment includes traders and craftsmen as well as a small number of unskilled labour.

The opportunities for cash based employment are severely limited. Fragmentation due to inheritance is also reducing the size of landholdings of farm owners. The average landholding in rural Bangladesh has dropped to below 1 hectare. Only owners of land who have purchased land for investment purposes and who have other sources of income have increased their land holdings.

Many small farm owners try to supplement their income from their own holdings by sharecropping or working for larger landowners on a cash basis. However, very often the amount of available land is not sufficient for a farmer to rise above the subsistence level. Thus for most farmers saving and investing for the future is unthinkable. The current types of employment available in rural areas are subject to risks from weather or disease outbreaks. A single outbreak can push workers into unemployment and debt with a very long recovery period.

Utilization of Resources

Most rural agricultural land is owned by absentee landlords. A survey showed that 50.6% of land is owned by absentee landlords. We conducted a survey of 4 districts in 2006 which showed that of plots over an acre in area almost 82% are owned by absentee landowners.

Absentee landlordism has also limited the kind of farming that can be conducted on their lands. As they have no management manpower, they usually lease their land for cash or share of the output. And since the sharecropping/tenant farmer is making the investments in the land he normally chooses the least capital intensive, low cost, low return model.

Any crop cycle that is longer than 3-6 months or at most a year are also automatically eliminated, reducing the options for livestock or fisheries. Any system with infrastructure costs is also not considered. Most land owned by smaller farmers has been fragmented into even smaller holdings over several generations.

In many cases these holdings are insufficient for even subsistence farming. Because of the fragmentation of land into small holdings and the lack of capital and education, a very labour intensive and inefficient style of agriculture has developed. A plan to manage the larger holdings of absentee landlords will generate more revenue per acre of land than is possible under current methods.

Active management will allow better utilization of resources and generate more employment and income for both the landowner and the workers. We have found that most landowners hold land in their native villages and are thus predisposed to ideas that can generate employment in those areas. However it is the lack of manpower and expertise that have been the primary reason they have not invested to further that social goal.

Economies of Scale

The management company will control a large number of farms giving it certain economies of scale it can exploit to its advantage. More effective training can be conducted at a lower cost than a single standalone farm. In many cases a small landowner/farmer is unable to avail any training at all, increasing his risk when he attempts any promising new venture.

In addition there are marketing advantages as well that can be availed when dealing with a large volume of product. Because there are multiple farms with different outputs, byproducts for one facility can also be used as an input for other products. For example, organic fertilizer from poultry and cattle can be used for plant crops or to promote plankton growth in fish farms. Moreover, excess litter can be consolidated, packaged and sold in the market. A larger and more organized company will also have better access to markets and be able to bypass middlemen and retain more profits for itself which will allow it to provide better paying jobs.

Small farmers have almost no direct access to markets. Further processing and post harvest technologies can increase the value addition of agricultural products. However for a small farmer such technologies are cost prohibitive. Thus agricultural products are usually sold with very little value addition to further processors and middlemen.

Risk Reduction

Because of geographically diverse farms, as well as a diverse product mix, the risk for the overall enterprise and its employees can be minimized. Thus a disease outbreak, flooding, or bad crop and other negative externalities in one region will have no effect on the employees.

The company can cushion the losses in one region and retain employees and make investments to improve the situation. While each individual farm may face uncertainties, the jobs created will be secure.

Migration

Because of the seasonal nature and the risk profile of agricultural employment we see a significant amount of migration of the rural population. On the one hand there has been mass migration to urban areas on a permanent basis. On the other hand there is seasonal and employment based temporary migration within rural areas.

Migration to cities has put tremendous pressure on urban centres. Moreover, it has been demonstrated in other studies that such migration have not improved the lives of the migrants. Migration of labour within rural areas also has had an adverse social effect as the families are often split up for long periods of local seasonal unemployment. An enterprise that can provide year round employment in a local area can therefore reduce migration and negate its impact on families and on the urban poor.

Women's Employment

Women, especially married ones, are generally more reluctant to migrate to urban areas seeking employment. However because of the lack of available cash-based employment locally women are forced to either remain underemployed or migrate to the cities.

Providing local employment will create opportunities for women and allow for dual income families who are able to better provide for their dependents.

Training

Training is an important component of farming. New methods and skills are being developed regularly. However it is impossible for a small farmer to keep abreast of these new developments.

Access to information and access to training are a limiting factor that prevents the rural farmer from introducing new methods, products or technologies. Our plan aims to provide continuous training to its employees, many of whom will have small farms of their own. This vocational training will enable the employees to improve the outputs of their own farms as well.

Industry Restructuring

Most agro processors in Bangladesh, do not operate at the production level. In fact most of the raw material production is outsourced to small farms and middlemen are used to procure them. Agro processors are operating in the input stage (breeding, seeds, fertilizer, feed) and in the consumer space (packaged branded products).

The middle belt is produced by small farmers and their products make their way to the processors through middlemen.

A new player in this field will benefit the industry by being able to sell directly from the farms to the agro processors. In addition because of its presence in the local community it can also play the part of the middleman for other farmers.

Structure of the Enterprise

A company will be formed to manage the resources and coordinate the interests of the stakeholders. This company will initially operate fully owned facilities which will be used as training centres and manpower development. The management company will train and place trained employees at each farm.

The company will enter into agreements with individual landowners regarding the use and infrastructure development of the land. The landowner will be expected to provide the land and infrastructure and permanent establishment investments.

The working capital investments will be negotiated on a case by case basis as will the profit sharing structure. Manpower will be employed and trained by the management company.

Index